More praise for
STAR TEAMS, KEY PLAYERS

"The book reveals the qualities that get rewarded in the workplace and fashions a strategy to meet them in a way that accepts and allows individual differences."

—*Business Digest*

"We've seen that following the Lone Ranger's path leads nowhere; now creative collaboration with others, not competition, is the winning way for the nineties. STAR TEAMS, KEY PLAYERS tells us why—and *how*—in a book that's interesting, powerful, and fun."

—ELAINA ZUKER
President
Success Strategies Inc., and
Author of *The Seven Secrets of Influence*

STAR TEAMS, KEY PLAYERS

Successful Career Strategies for Women
in the 1990s

Michele Jackman
with Susan Waggoner

FAWCETT CREST • NEW YORK

A Fawcett Crest Book
Published by Ballantine Books
Copyright © 1991 by Michele Jackman, Susan Waggoner, and New Chapter Press

Library of Congress Catalog Card Number: 91-10875

ISBN 0-449-22226-8

This edition published by arrangement with Henry Holt and Company, Inc.

Manufactured in the United States of America

First Ballantine Books Edition: July 1993

THIS BOOK IS DEDICATED TO ALL
STAR TEAMS OF THE FUTURE:

to Jarrell C. Jackman, a "world-class player," to future Key Player Renee "Rain" Jackman, and to my first coach, Connie Marmo, who taught me how to get into the game.

Contents

Acknowledgments

I feel that the subject of this book, teamwork, necessitates identifying the extraordinary team roster that participated in its completion. But first I must acknowledge the "hard to identify" efforts of assistants who suggested Key Players, secretaries who made sure their bosses had time to participate, and many team leaders who shared their insights. Neither can I forget to mention the faithful twenty-four-hour crew at Kinko's Copies, Santa Barbara, who relay faxes, copy chapters, and work round the clock for those of us who work odd hours. Thanks also for great diligence to Jean Hotchkiss of Eight to Five Answering service; to DOS services, for the transcription of tapes; and finally, to both Federal Express and Airborne Express, our bicoastal, "next day" messengers.

First in the lineup for individual acknowledgment is Wendy Reid Crisp, national director of the National Association for Female Executives (NAFE). Wendy is the magician "coach-player" who put this project together, in collaboration with our very patient and supportive editor, Cynthia Vartan, and the expert Holt team. But best of all, Wendy found writer Susan Waggoner. This project certainly would have been more difficult without the insights, research, scanning, sorting of materials, and weaving of details Susan brought to the tapestry of diverse stories and important findings. Her coaching, extraordinary skills, and loving care with the material are greatly appreciated.

A great deal of credit for the completion of this book and

the quality of the interviews goes to my Star Player/colleague Andrea Daniel, who conducted many of the interviews for me and manages the normal chaos of events at PSI Santa Barbara. She remained cool, focused, and a "pinch-hitter" for me throughout the entire project, and came through in all the difficult moments. I am deeply indebted to her for her level of personal support and commitment, even though her own writing projects had to be interrupted. Special appreciation goes to Kate Armstrong for research, feedback, and excellent clipping services.

Incredible was the support I received from many women and men who were interested in the book and provided their ideas and insights. While these people are not cited directly in the book, their contributions were significant. We, the team, acknowledge Susan Rose, executive director of the Los Angeles Commission on the Status of Women; CFO Sue Andrews; Ann Douglas; Marty Glenn; Susie Lewis; Kim Kellogg; Mary Wickstrom; Connie Cotillier; Tom Sugi; Darcy Campbell; Charlott Hill; Jan Zimmerman; Georgia Tobey; Betty Smith; Diane Piper; Leah Ireland; Nancy Brown; Kim Hopper; Christine Craft; Doe Melrose; Connie Williams; Rita Werden; Sandy Panchak, Kaarin Simpson, and Louise Chamis; Marina Margetts; Crystal Tramel; Gwen Evans; Rose DiSomma; and mentor A. J. Noble. Added to this list are the thousands of clients and participants who have attended my seminars and classes over the years and shared their horror stories of problem teams, misplaced ambition, and difficult players enabling me to develop practical team strategies to overcome them.

Several presidents and top-level executives provided their points of view on teamwork issues. I have also played alongside a wonderful group of players who have helped me pursue my own vision. A partial list of our "great guy" network includes managers and team leaders from many companies, large and small, who support women playing on their teams, including Charles Miles, John Wigle, Dr. Mike Kaufmann, Scott Steele, George Hansell, Karl Kucen, Robert Adkins, Bud Enright, Ron Boehm, Larry Borels, and many executives of The Prudential who helped brainstorm information for the exercises.

An acknowledgment goes to my personal support team: cheerleader, visionary, and best friend Cheri Jasinski; career counselor Margi Mainquist; and colleague/consultant Terry Walker. Without their encouragement when I was feeling overwhelmed or less confident, I might have lost momentum. My wish for readers is that they find a similar group for global vision, support, fun, and an occasional "kick in the gears."

On the theoretical side of things, I can't possibly name all the pioneer authors/scholars who have influenced my work, but they include Betty Lehan Harragan, Adele Scheele, Betty Friedan, Peter Vaill, Tom Peters, Frank Burns, Roger Harrison, Harrison Owen, Leo Buscaglia, John Naisbitt, Peter Drucker, Gordon Lippitt, Edward De Bono, Rosabeth Kanter, and the research of John Greer and William Marston on behavioral styles, which provided the foundation for the development of my own systems. I greatly appreciate the coaching of publisher/author Mindy Bingham, a talented and tireless advocate who writes exciting career development workbooks for Key Players of the future and shares my vision.

A final and predictable acknowledgment goes to the home team: husband Jarrell, with his loving pushes and shoves when I was weary, and for his fine editorial eye; and daughter Renee, with available hugs of encouragement and pride. With my travel schedule and the intense pace generated by the book and my work, the moments together were rarer, but filled with loving support and understanding (most of the time). Sometimes they think I'm nuts.

Michele Jackman
Santa Barbara, California

Key Players Interviewed for This Book

ANNE ADAMS: *president*, Adams & Allgood

DEBORAH SLANER ANDERSON: *executive director*, Women's Sports Foundation

KERRY ANDRADE: *human resources manager*, ABC Clio Publishers

ELLEN BOUGHN: *manager*, After Image/Tony Stone Worldwide

LAURAINE BREKKE: *assistant city manager*, Ventura, California

HELEN GURLEY BROWN: *editor-in-chief*, *Cosmopolitan*

EMILY CARD: *attorney*, independent financial consultant

GERRY CUNNINGHAM: *plant manager*, Jostens

WENDY REID CRISP: *national director*, NAFE

DANYA DARRINGTON: *associate editor*, *Cosmopolitan*

TERRI DIAL: *executive vice-president*, Wells Fargo Bank

CANDICE DUNN: *lighting director*, ABC network

LAURA FELBERG: *director of human resources*, The Prudential Insurance Corporation

VIRGINIA FLEMING: *manager of personnel relations*, The Prudential Insurance Corporation

SALLY GEIS: *sociology administrator*, Iliff School of Theology, Denver

NANCY GLASER: *director of public relations*, Avon Products

MARY HADDENHAM: *manager*, plans and analysis, for a government engineering laboratory

ANN HARTMAN: *vice-president/publisher*, ABC Clio Publishers

CATHY HEMMING: *associate publisher and general manager*, Atlantic Monthly Press

JANICE WITMER HOWELL: *manager of human resources*, Wavefront Technologies

MIYA IWATAKI: *women's liaison and liaison to the Asian-Pacific community*, Los Angeles County

SHARON RICHARDSON JONES: *director of outreach activities*, Oakland A's baseball team

CRAIG KARDON: *coach to Martina Navratilova*

SUSAN KARONES: *former senior editor, Cosmopolitan*

RON KELLER: *store manager*, Sears Roebuck & Co., Santa Barbara

PERI LEVIN: *ESL instructor*, Los Angeles Community Adult School; partner, Language Express (on-site ESL instruction for businesses)

LAURA LOPEZ: *director of Hispanic marketing*, Avon Products

SHARON MAEDA: *president*, Spectra Communications

GWEN McCANE: *director of member services*, Oakland Athletic Club

CATHERINE MORRISON: *chief of staff to California State Assemblywoman Cathie Wright*

ANN PICCIUTO: *cost accounting manager*, electronics manufacturer

LOIS RICE: *executive vice-president*, Wells Fargo Bank

MARGARET RUSH: *district superintendent*, United Methodist Church, Denver

SEYRIL SEIGAL: *resident representative*, United Nations development programs; *resident coordinator*, United Nations System for Economic and Social Cooperation to Venezuela

CHERYL STERN: *president*, The Game Keeper (twenty-four-store retail chain)

MARGARET TUTWILER: *spokesperson*, U.S. State Department

BARBARA UEHLING: *chancellor*, University of California at Santa Barbara

CINDY WEBSTER: *former fire captain*, Santa Barbara, California

KAREN WEGMANN: *executive vice-president*, Wells Fargo Bank

MARILYN WEIXEL: *director of human resources*, Association Group Insurance Administrators

LYNN WILLIAMS: *senior broker*, Cushman Realty

Foreword

The two metaphors of business language—the military and organized sports—have been in constant use over the past century to explain, motivate, inspire, and exclude. For much of this time we women willingly accepted the proffered mythology: If we hadn't fought in a war or played on a football team, we didn't possess or understand the essential characteristics of a successful business person.

In the 1980s, as the editor of a women's business magazine, I saw hundreds of proposals for articles that began with the assumption that women were somehow inept at "playing on a team"—the corporate team, that is—and proceeded to quote various psychologists as to why this was true. Corporate types piped in with suggestions on how to overcome this career-paralyzing handicap. And successful women were quoted as saying that they were "team players," but they recognized that this was because they had brothers who let them join the pickup basketball game, therefore giving them incalculable executive potential.

And while I was reading these proposals and pondering their validity, I was managing a staff of fifteen people (fourteen of whom were women) who cheerfully and creatively invented and produced a new magazine every month. Since we were (nearly) all women, we didn't think of ourselves as a team; instead, we used female-directed euphemisms for team play: consensus management, participatory democracies, shared power, and that now thankfully forgotten management fad, the quality circle.

Thank heavens Michele Jackman has come along and spoken out at last, defining what a team is (a heresy to some, it can be a group of people who do *nothing* with a ball), showing us that we not only have been team players all of our lives but that we play on a number of teams simultaneously. Michele's theory—that no career is an island—is a welcome one, one that promises success not in terms of personal achievement and private rewards, but one that guarantees success defined by friendships, shared accomplishments, high-quality workmanship, and joy.

Wendy Reid Crisp
National Director,
National Association for Female Executives
New York, April 1991

PART I ☆

1 ☆

A New Way of Winning

"It's no coincidence that in business schools now they have you work in teams. You're given projects and you work on them in teams." The speaker, Deborah Slaner Anderson, pauses momentarily. "This is what works in real life."

Anderson is the executive director of the Women's Sports Foundation, and for her, blending the metaphors of sports with the realities of business is part of a day's work. Her board of directors glitters with top-seeded names like Billie Jean King (who established the organization in 1974), Donna de Varona, Chris Evert, Martina Navratilova, and other well-known athletes. When Anderson and the WSF leadership meet, sports is the common ground, sports metaphors the common language.

"I don't think it's a mistake that we use sports terminology when we're talking about business terms," Anderson continues. "In sports and business you work with different people. You may not know the people, but that doesn't matter. You have to learn how to work together. You have to learn to play on each other's strengths because that will make the team stronger. You have to learn to pick up the ball when someone makes a mistake or someone flounders."

Anderson's business-as-team-sports approach is representative of a small, vanguard-level of women I began to notice a few years ago while I was conducting training programs for large corporations and the military through my work as a business consultant.

These women, whom I've since come to define as *Key Players*, paid little attention to the conventional wisdom of the times. They didn't read Robert J. Ringer's *Looking Out for Number 1* or buy into his philosophy. They didn't have cast-iron goals and game plans. They didn't insist on personal recognition. They didn't feel victimized when they hit the glass ceiling. In fact, these women often seemed to do many of the "wrong" things: they took on jobs they felt unprepared for; they failed to file sex discrimination suits when sex discrimination was clearly the issue; they expected work to be fun. Yet over the years I saw these women surpass their colleagues who followed the "looking out for number one" advice of the times.

At first with mere interest, then with growing excitement, I realized that these women were defining a new way of operating and achieving. I began to examine their career paths in detail, searching for the organizing principle beneath. The whole cloth that emerged from the weaving together of these individual lives is what I have come to call the *Key Players strategy*.

Deborah Anderson is representative of the new way of doing business because she has an innate grasp of what it means to play on a team. Not all of us have this understanding. For many working women, the very words *team player* are tainted, and with good reason. In the past, being a team player often meant keeping your mouth shut, working like a dog, and stepping back while one of the guys took the credit.

That's not the kind of player this book is about. Being a Key Player is about playing and winning, not playing and hoping you get to stay with the team. As Anderson says, "It's the difference between playing football and cheerleading."

Like other women in Key Player positions, Anderson sees herself as an active, accountable member of the team at all times. She knows that her skills will raise or lower the team's level of play and that her personal performance, good or bad, will contribute to the team's record of wins and losses.

But Anderson also knows that team play is a two-way street. Sometimes you give up your chance for a basket and pass the ball to a teammate in a better scoring position, even though it means giving up your own chance for capturing the limelight. But just as often, if your team is strong, you benefit from the network of people around you.

When you're a Key Player you reap the benefits of your position every day. Anderson, who worked in advertising before moving into the executive director slot at WSF, recalls a time when her team captain bailed her out.

''We were giving a presentation. It was the biggest thing I had done in my advertising career, and I had a big role in it. I was right in the middle of it and all of a sudden—bingo!—I forgot what I was supposed to say next.''

Anderson glanced around the conference room and waited for her memory to reconnect. It didn't. For all of us, this is the stuff career nightmares are made of: it's the chance you've worked for, and you find yourself blowing it. Anderson was going down in flames, but before she hit the ground, her team took over for her.

''Someone picked up after me. He was able to pick up for me, and then I recovered. Everything went on. And you know what? No one remembered that I had stumbled because we all picked up after each other. That's how it works. No one's perfect, but you pick up. That's what men learn: picking up is teamwork.''

Anderson's colleague never mentioned her mistake because, in his eyes, it wasn't a mistake: it was just one play of the game. Anderson didn't feel guilty or apologetic or diminished when her co-workers bailed her out because, as a Key Player for her team, she'd earned the consideration. In the past she'd done the same for her teammates. The presentation went on, Anderson recovered, the client was pitched, and the account was captured. The team won. And how Anderson performed on one play wasn't important because she had performed well on other plays in the game. She was a Key Player.

KEY PLAYER

A Key Player is a peak performer plus. She can be found in any job at any level of the organization. She does her job with consistent excellence, but she's also acquired a second set of skills—team skills—that make her an indispensable member of her team. Because her unique combination of skills can't be easily replaced, she has more leverage, is presented with more opportunities and choices, and has greater latitude in shaping her own career than her peers in the workplace.

If this team sounds different from teams you've played on in the past, it is. It's a winning team, the kind of team I call a *Star Team*, poised for the new business world of the nineties and beyond. Just as a Key Player does more than perform her job, a Star Team does more than fulfill the corporate tasks assigned it.

You can be a Key Player without a Star Team to back you up, or you can be an ordinary player on a Star Team. But becoming a Key Player on a Star Team is your mission for the nineties, a move that will put you in total control of your career. In a climate of change and challenge, becoming a Key Player on a Star Team is the best method—and so far the only method—I've discovered for getting what you want from your career.

Getting what you want is what the Key Player strategy is all about. I've written this book to help you maximize your choices and opportunities, but not to make choices for you. If you want to be a corporate CEO, the Key Player blueprint will get you there. But if you want something quite different—part-time flexibility while you raise your family or a profitable business you can run from your home in the country—the Key Player strategy is just as effective.

Whatever your personal or quality-of-life goals, becoming a Key Player is the way to achieve them. And that's the essence of this book: your success on your terms.

STAR TEAM

A Star Team accomplishes its tasks with a high degree of energy, harmony, and enthusiasm. It repays the effort of individual members by protecting and nurturing their careers and providing them with challenge, responsibility, opportunity, and—above all—recognition for their labors.

THE NINETIES ARE GOING TO BE DIFFERENT

• Husband-and-wife television journalists Paul Miller and Kristie Wilde seemed to have it made in Los Angeles. But they swapped their jobs in the nation's second-largest media market for a shot at 111th-ranked Salinas, California. The lure wasn't money, job security, or a chance to leapfrog back to Los Angeles bigger and better than before. Miller and Wilde moved because KCBA, a small station undergoing a major revamp, told them they could build their own new department from the ground up. This meant hand-picking their thirty-two-person staff and creating a more egalitarian atmosphere. Among other things, Miller and Wilde jettisoned the anchor-as-star approach and aimed instead for "a lot of representation from reporters on the set, because they sound and feel good when they get to be out there.''

- Between 1984 and 1990, AT&T cut its work force by one-third. Most of the 92,000 eliminated employees were involved in management: progress report readers, permission givers, supervisors, supervisors who supervised supervisors. A new policy of employee ''empowerment'' replaced the bureaucracy, giving lower-level workers and managers greater leeway to act on their own initiative. Jeffrey McCollum, education director for the company's consumer products unit, says of his smaller work force: ''They've learned to work in teams, and I've learned to stop making them waste time on progress reports.'' To help along the empowerment process, McCollum's department developed an Outward Bound–type training program that ''gives individuals confidence that they can do things without layers of supervisors telling them how.''

- Robin Wolaner had a good idea, gumption, and tenacity, but no money. She needed a partner who would back her without stifling her entrepreneurial style, so she pitched her idea to media giant Time Warner, Inc. Warner was so impressed it scrapped development of a similar magazine and took Wolaner onto the team on her own terms. Acting as an ''intrapreneur'' (an entrepreneur functioning within a larger corporation), Wolaner created *Parenting*, a magazine for upscale young parents.

- In 1988 thirty-two public schools in Dade County, Florida, opted against the bureaucracy and for shared decision making. Using an experimental model called *school-based autonomy*, the schools are managed by teams of teachers and parents, not administrators.

- In the workplace, ''the power of the nineties will be people power,'' the speaker asserted. He went on to add that ''the successful business leaders of the eighties—those who imposed competitive rigor, produced the best results, and achieved the highest standing on the hierarchy—will not necessarily be the big winners in the nineties." The speaker wasn't telling workers what they wanted to hear. Frank Doyle, senior vice president for corporate relations at General Electric, was telling fellow managers at the 1989 World Management Conference that they'd better get ready for the future.

The scenarios above are bound by a common theme. Did you notice the recurrence of themes like team, innovation, and initiative? These are the important trends of the 1990s, trends that have come about in response to far-reaching changes throughout the world.

The challenges we're now facing began to surface early in the 1980s. Like an aging athlete, American business was becoming sluggish, bloated, and indifferent. As the world moved ever closer to a global economy, we found ourselves increasingly pressured to compete in new ways. Each time the playing field expanded to accommodate another participant, our old way of doing business became less tenable. Books like *In Search of Excellence* and *The One Minute Manager* did a good job of identifying solutions to the problems, but business was skeptical and slow to respond. Now, as we learn to work with a unified European Economic Community, as the Pacific rim grows in economic power, and as the Eastern bloc enters the arena of world trade, global competition has grown even more intense. If American business is to thrive in the next century, we must become more efficient, more innovative, more cost and quality conscious.

How to do it? In less demanding, less competitive times, the large corporation was a viable unit. So was the individual who chose to go it alone in the business world. Today, neither the corporation nor the individual is viable enough. The traditional corporation, with tier upon tier of management, is cumbersome, difficult to steer, and slow to respond to change. It has a stultifying effect on individual creativity, and its structure relies on a hierarchy that almost invariably undermines esprit de corps. But if the large corporation is handicapped, so is the lone individual: society is too specialized and too technologically complex for one person to cover all the bases.

Rather than choose either of these alternatives, corporations and individuals alike are more often opting for a third path: the team.

Teams, as we'll see, are ideally suited to the trends and changes shaping the future. I believe that as we move through the nineties, teams will become the dominant unit in the workplace, transforming both the traditional corporation and rarefied world of the entrepreneur.

What does this shift mean for us?

The woman who masters the team concept, joins a winning franchise, and becomes an all-star contributor is going to have more options, earn more recognition, and receive more rewards than the woman who plays the game by the old rules.

Like athletic teams you've played on in the past, the team you work on in the future will have players, a personality, and a communal goal: winning. In this, teams won't be equally successful. There will be average teams, scrub teams, workhorse teams, good teams, and unknown teams. And there will be a few Star Teams.

Star Teams in business, like star athletic teams, win more often than they lose. Moreover, they win real games, not exhibitions. In the workplace this means focusing time, talent, and energy getting things done together. Without exception, Star Teams focus on results, not just processes, rules, and personalities.

To succeed as a Star Team, players must share a common vision and a winning spirit. Their skills and personal attributes must complement each other, and their weaknesses must be compensated for by other members of the team. Achieving this balance isn't easy, and tampering with it once it's been achieved is risky business.

STAR TEAMS AND KEY PLAYERS IN A NUTSHELL: THE "TODAY" SHOW DEBACLE

An example of how tampering dropped a Star Team into the cellar can be seen in the "Today" show debacle of 1989. Until August of that year, the show—which had been number one in its time slot for four years—had a stable, four-person on-air team: Jane Pauley and Bryant Gumbel as coanchors, John Palmer on the news desk, and Willard Scott as weatherman. The show was also number one in its time slot, a position it had held since 1985.

The first crack in the wall came in February 1989, when a four-month-old memo written by Gumbel was leaked to the public. In the memo Gumbel heaped criticism on the show and many of his colleagues. A particularly harsh line attacking weatherman Scott for "holding the show hostage to his assortment of whims, wishes, birthdays, and bad taste" quickly became infamous. Despite the fact that the critique had been solicited by the show's then executive producer, Marty Ryan, and never intended for release, public blame went to Gumbel, who was seen as a back stabber eager to cast himself in a quasi-producer role.

Soon after Gumbel's memo, Ryan was replaced by NBC senior VP Dick Ebersol. Ignoring the "if it ain't broke, don't fix it" dictum, and in an effort to attract younger viewers to the show, the NBC executive hierarchy decided to replace newsman Palmer with Deborah Norville, then anchoring "NBC News at Sunrise." On paper the trade made sense: executives were certain the young, attractive Norville would appeal to viewers in the sagging eighteen- to forty-nine-year-old demographic bracket. To reinforce her presence, they gave her a role larger than Palmer's had been, bringing her out from behind the news desk and onto the sofa with Pauley and Gumbel.

The only problem with the strategy was that it backfired. The decision makers failed to take into account one crucial but nonquantifiable attribute: team synergy. The original cast had been a Star Team, producing a whole greater than the sum of its parts, a harmonious working together called synergy.

What had looked like a good move destroyed the synergy of the "Today" show team. Palmer's no-nonsense approach had acted as counterpoint for Scott's over-the-top entertainment style. The unfortunate pairing of Pauley and Norville looked like a competition. Female viewers in the very age group the show was trying to appeal to perceived the move as a campaign to edge Pauley out and protested the fact that the popular, intelligent anchorwoman was being retired at age thirty-nine. In newspaper columns TV critics compared Norville with the predatory Eve Harrington in the movie *All About Eve*. On radio call-in shows, the public was suddenly analyzing the "tension" and "negative body language" among Pauley, Norville, and Gumbel. Within a few weeks Pauley announced her departure from the show.

When a team goes down, its players go with it. Those who made up the posttrade team suffered unfair criticism and a loss of career prestige. Instead of showcasing individual talents and compensating for individual deficits, the new no-synergy team exaggerated each player's faults and obscured his or her talents.

Within three months the show relinquished its top spot in the ratings to ABC's "Good Morning America." By June 1990 Ebersol was gone and his successors were trying frantically to fix the new-and-improved team. Norville's role was pared down, two new newswomen were added to the cast, and Joe Garagiola was brought in to warm up what had become a stiff and sterile atmosphere. By autumn of 1990 executives were telling off-camera personnel they would no longer receive overtime pay (a substantial portion of crew members' salaries) because of the increased costs incurred in front of the camera. And by January 1991 the show had lost an estimated one million viewers.

As an example of how teams and players operate, the

"Today" show story has a lot to teach us. When the on-air cast was a Star Team, everyone on the team was perceived as a personal winner. Gumbel's memo was catastrophic because it went outside the team to criticize both fellow players and the product the team produced.

But the real unraveling came when NBC executives failed to perceive the Gumbel-Pauley-Scott-Palmer team as a winner or to understand what made it a Star Team. What began with one alteration, the swap of Palmer for Norville, started a chain reaction. When the new-and-improved lost, so did everyone on it. Norville's "dream job" turned into a sour plum, Gumbel became a villain, and Scott drifted to the show's periphery.

Ironically, it was the ousted Pauley who fared best, sustaining both personal prestige and professional credibility. As the minidrama played itself out, it became increasingly evident that the show needed Pauley more than she needed the show.

Pauley was more than a player on the "Today" show team—she was a Key Player. Her presence lent a unity to the show that wasn't easy to replace. Like all key players, she excelled at the job assigned her. Beyond this, she had highly developed team skills. She was reliable. She had the ability to reach upward to her bosses, sideways to her teammates, and outward to her audience: she was the connecting point that drew these disparate groups together. And while she did it, she made it look easy. Notice that Pauley achieved all this without positioning herself as the show's "star." In fact, her ability to hold her own with Gumbel without trying to overpower him was one of her most sorely missed talents.

Because Pauley was a Key Player on a Star Team, she was able to survive the fuzzy-brained fix-it strategies of the show's producers. While Pauley's former bosses looked for a way to mop the egg off their faces and resuscitate the new-and-improved team, other teams within the NBC news department drafted Pauley for their own rosters. A summer 1990 issue of *The New York Times Magazine* put Gumbel on its cover, along with the headline FORECAST FOR "TODAY": CLOUDY. A few weeks later *New York* magazine did the same for Pauley: Her blurb, however, read THE LOVED ONE.

THE PITFALLS OF CHANGE

When I was a youngster, one of my favorite stories was "Lazy Jack," and it went something like this:

On his first day at work Jack is paid with a penny but loses it because he doesn't understand the value of money. His mother tells him he should have put it in his pocket, and he agrees to follow her advice next time he receives any wages. The next day when Jack is paid with a jar of milk, he puts the jar in his pocket and spills it during the walk home. The jar of milk, his mother tells him, should have been carried home on his head. So on Wednesday Jack carries a cheese home on his head; on Thursday he tries to carry a tomcat home in his hands; on Friday he drags a piece of mutton home on a leash, and on the following Monday he carries a donkey home on his back.

Clearly, Jack can't adjust to changing business conditions.

Because this is a fairy tale, his less-than-zero capacity for innovation has a happy ending: a sad princess sees him struggling along with the donkey, laughs, and marries him on the spot. I loved this story not only for its humor, but for the larger-than-life size of Jack's stupidity. How could anyone be so thick?

Easily. Over the years I've seen many intelligent, hard-working women fall into the same stale-advice pitfall Jack did. Accepting yesterday's counsel as gospel is likely to leave you struggling along with a donkey on your back. Consider what happened to myriad women during the last decade in the arena of career planning. Beginning in the late 1970s, the MBA was held up as a magic ticket into the boardroom. Established as *the* formula to follow, the MBA and its spinoffs—endless seminars on management—dominated the 1980s' fast-track mystique.

And mystique it was. In 1990 some seventy thousand MBAs were conferred—ten times the number earned in 1960. Yet just as universities were awarding more MBAs than ever, companies began to slice out whole layers of middle management and scale back their hiring. Between 1980 and 1990 an estimated three million Fortune 500 jobs were eliminated, most of them at the middle-management level. By the end of the eighties the manager glut was already being felt. As if to underscore the degree's new nonmarketability, a 1990 brochure for the New School in New York offered an adult education course entitled ''Landing a Job with Your New MBA.'' There is no evidence to suggest the trend will reverse itself, either: one executive placement firm predicts that by 1995 there will be an estimated thirty-five managers for every available opening.

By following the must-get-an-MBA formula of the past, many well-educated women have landed magic tickets to nowhere.

As working women we need to know what changes are shaping our immediate future. But even more, we need to find a way to work with change itself: change that will be continual throughout our lifetime, change that will be swift, change that will not always be possible to predict.

When I say ''work with change,'' I don't mean survive it or cope with it. I mean thrive on it. This book came about because, too often, I've seen women given the wrong career-planning formulas. These formulas, based on a specific set of circumstances, fail because they aren't flexible enough to accommodate change.

The Key Players strategy is flexible. It will show you how to take advantage of the globally booming nineties. But more than that, it's a strategy you can take into the future because it's designed to accommodate change. This unique approach to career planning can be used

- by anyone in any field, inside the corporate structure or outside it, no matter what the position.
- any time, at any point in your career.

- throughout your entire career, to achieve a broad range of goals.
- to assess your current situation.
- to achieve short-term goals.
- for long-term career planning.
- to avoid career crashes and setbacks.
- to recover from mistakes and disasters.

THE POSITIVES OF CHANGE—NOT FUTURE SHOCK, FUTURE FANTASTIC

How can I say with such certainty that teams will dominate the workplace of the future? Because the transition is already under way. In the past few years a shift away from corporate bureaucracy toward corporate flexibility has begun. America can no longer afford the lethargic, resource-wasting, ego-driven bureaucracies of the past. Within the coming years the working world will change in three major ways. The workplace will change, the work force will change, and the way we work will change; and the meshing of these shifts will produce a working world different from any we've known before.

Shift #1: The Workplace

Sometime in the late eighties we began hearing references to a new, global economy, scheduled to arrive in the nineties. A few of the events shaping this trend are

- the economic unification of Great Britain, Ireland, France, West Germany, Italy, Spain, Portugal, Greece, Denmark, the Netherlands, Belgium, and Luxembourg.
- the rise of the Pacific rim as a producer of goods and services and, increasingly, as a source of new consumer markets.
- the entrance of Eastern Europe into the world economic playing field.

- the boom in overlooked exports—information, services, and culture—in which America leads the pack.
- the predominance of newly forged, peace-promoting economic alliances over the strife-promoting political alliances of the past.
- the newly implemented process of worldwide tax reform, which has stimulated productivity at almost all levels.

Shift #2: The Work Force

The work force of the 1990s will be markedly different from any in recent memory. Women who began their careers in the crowded work force of the sixties, seventies, and eighties will find an unexpected shift: a thinning of the work force and a move away from the buyer's market of the past decade. Between 1946 and 1955, 38.1 million Americans were born. Another 41.6 million were born between 1956 and 1965. But between 1966 and 1975, only 34.2 million Americans were born, and this dearth is creating a new shortage of laborers. No longer awash in a surplus of workers, employers will have to compete for talent and develop new attitudes toward their employees.

Another change in the work force is going to occur right at the top. As the old guard retires, a new, more diverse crop of senior executives is standing by to take the reins. Some of these new leaders are baby boomers, an experimental generation that values risk, innovation, and life balance. And many of these new leaders are women, moving at last into positions of influence and authority.

Instead of stepping into ready-made systems and shaping themselves to the old standards of success, the new leaders are offering new definitions of success and alternative ways of getting there. Kristie Wilde and Paul Miller, the couple who swapped their jobs in Los Angeles for a chance to build their own news team, are representatives of their generation. While acknowledging the importance of success and financial stability, they're also quick to acknowledge the importance of personal fulfillment and a chance to leave their unique stamp on industry.

Shift #3: Work Style

The rapid and inexpensive transfer of data, improved access to once remote parts of the world, and the shifts to an economy based on "portable" ideas and information rather than cumbersome manufactured goods are making the corporate beehive a thing of the past. Some companies are undertaking studies to evaluate how cost-effective it is to maintain large office buildings that are used only eight out of every twenty-four hours, and other companies are initiating experimental programs in which employees divide their work time between home and office. In the workplace of the past, maintaining employees away from corporate headquarters was seen as an extra expense. In the workplace of the future, it's more likely to be seen as a cost-cutting, productivity-building necessity. In the crowded, car-packed San Francisco Bay area, the 1989 earthquake and the collapse of the Nimitz Freeway caused a spate of articles trumpeting not only the efficiency but also the safety of telecommuting.

THE 1990s: A STAGE SET FOR KEY PLAYERS ON STAR TEAMS

What do the shift to a global economy, radical changes in the work force, and improved technology mean for us in the 1990s? Here are some likely outcomes:

• *In a global economy, there are more people with whom to compete.* Businesses that thrive will have to become highly efficient, free of middle-management fat, and devoid of wasteful corporate infighting. We'll have to find simpler, less costly ways to do things, which means shifting emphasis away from process and toward product. A 1989 MIT report, "Made in America: Regaining the Productive Edge," criticized businesses for the lack of teamwork "between individuals and groups within firms." To remedy the situation, MIT called for the elimination of power echelons and barriers between departments.

- *In a global economy, there are more potential customers.* To appeal to new foreign markets, we're going to have to understand the world these new customers live in as well as their needs, views, and desires. This means we Americans are going to have to become more mobile than ever before. We'll have to spend more time in our customer's environment, and establishing "outpost offices" that allow Americans to interface with employees in the foreign market will be more common than it is today. In the global economy of the future, the workplace is likely to be anywhere. Working for Sleek Software of Summerton, South Carolina, won't guarantee that you spend your entire work life in South Carolina. You may be asked to do a tour of duty in Sleek's London branch, or you may be moved to Denmark when Sleek launches a joint venture project with Carlson Creations of Copenhagen.

- *In a global economy, nations—and businesses within nations—are free to specialize.* In the interdependent world economy of the future, nations will concentrate on what they do most efficiently. Right now there's lament over America's loss of manufacturing jobs to overseas markets. But this doesn't mean our overall pool of jobs is shrinking. Information, technology, and a flair for public relations are some of the fields Americans excel at, and as unskilled factory jobs vanish, thousands of jobs in a new, service-oriented economy are being created. Before you picture yourself flipping hamburgers for minimum wage, remember that doctors, technicians, public relations consultants, and investment bankers are part of the "service" economy, too. America won't become the land of few jobs and high unemployment some predict it will. Just the opposite. For those who keep abreast of the wave, the repositioning now under way will offer a choice of new jobs in high-paying fields.

- *In a technological society individuals are free to specialize.* If knowledge is power—and it is—then information sharing, made possible by the telecommunications boom, has vastly increased the power of each individual employee. No longer is information available to top management only. In the contemporary corporation, current and detailed information on all aspects of the company's business—from research and development to marketing forecasts—is unrestricted. As employees, we can specialize efficiently and effectively because the "big picture" is available to us, freeing us from dependence on management guidelines and directives. One of the most succinct comments on the telecommunications boom was made by business consultant Steven Schlosstein, writing in *The New York Times*: "The information revolution has rendered centralized, inflexible bureaucracies—public or private—obsolete and inoperative. Decentralization, individual autonomy, and choice have become the watchwords of this new era, and America—not Japan, not Germany—has emerged as the clear leader."

- *The shrinking of the skilled labor pool will shift the balance of power from employer to employee.* The era of tough-guy management came to an official end, perhaps, when Frank Lorenzo was ousted from his own airline empire. Lorenzo's view of employees as interchangeable, highly expendable pawns was outdated and unacceptable. His was a dramatic example, but it was by no means an isolated one. Rather, it's a cautionary tale for managers who are operating under outdated precepts.

    No longer able to negotiate from a take-it-or-leave-it position, today's employers will have to search for ways to make jobs more appealing to employees—

particularly women, who will fill an estimated 66 percent of the new jobs of the nineties.

All of these changes, converging at this point in time, call for a move away from large, slow, centralized corporations and set the stage for a more flexible and streamlined work unit: the team.

If the corporation of the past was a pyramid with many interchangeable bricks at the bottom supporting a few key bricks at the top, the team of today is an arch: a compact structure that cannot stand if any brick is lost.

Like the pyramid, the corporation of yesterday was massive and cumbersome. Extravagant amounts of labor were required to build it. Bricks buried in the middle of the structure never saw the light of day. Time and weather could erode whole layers without affecting the overall structure. It was a masterpiece of gigantism, designed to awe the masses. Its actual purpose was to serve as a showy final resting place for an elite few.

Unlike the pyramid, the arch always has a practical function. Gothic arches can support cathedral walls. Arches in a series support aqueducts and bridges. Before the age of steel, Roman arches in the doorways bore the load of the wall above them. Unlike the pyramid, the arch is mobile. It can be disassembled and reassembled elsewhere. It can be endlessly redesigned to suit a multiplicity of roles. The genius of the arch lies in its absolute lack of redundancy: each brick is weight bearing, no two bricks are alike, and each is shaped to occupy a specific space in the arch.

So it is with the team of the nineties. Streamlined, mobile, and highly functional, today's team is composed of a small number of interdependent specialists. Each person on the team has a unique function, and how well or poorly each player performs affects the entire team. To make the most of these opportunities and responsibilites, we need to develop a new system for perceiving, planning, and acting. That system is the Key Player strategy.

2 ☆

Key Players:
The Five Star Qualities

In today's complex world, no one works alone. We're all part of a team, and many of us play simultaneously on more than one team. Whether you work within the corporate world or as an entrepreneur, your ability to perform efficiently depends on the people who co-labor with you. Even if you could produce a product totally unaided, who would help you package and sell it? Who would transport it to your customers? Who would help you keep the books? Would you be able to file your tax forms alone? Where would you get the materials you need to make more product?

Although everyone who works on a team is a player, not all players are of equal value. Some are peak performers and some are not; and among the select pool of peak performers, some are Key Players and some are not.

What must you be to qualify as a Key Player?

First of all, you do have to be a peak performer. You need to do your job better than anyone else can do it or you'll be traded off the team. Yet peak performance alone won't make you a Key Player. As I was working on this book, discussing it with friends and colleagues, I found it interesting to note how often people mistakenly assumed that Key Player meant heavy hitter, mover, shaker, or something similar. I have met a good many secretaries and administrative assistants who were Key Players on their teams, and I have met many so-called stars whose careers stalled when they failed to become Key Players.

Few people are so talented or irreplaceable that they become Key Players simply because they perform well. This is the hard truth that women fail to grasp. Instead, we try to get ahead by outperforming everyone else. We stay at our desks until eight every night, we accept assignments in Siberia, we turn in our reports ahead of deadline in leather-bound triplicate, and we wait for our rewards. There's only one problem: the strategy doesn't work. Despite a decade of hard work, our progress has been incremental. In 1990 a study by corporate placement firm Korn-Ferry and the UCLA Graduate School of Management showed that 95 percent of the top management jobs in the nation's largest corporations were held by white males—a figure virtually unchanged from a similar study completed in 1979. When the rewards are passed around, women and other minorities are still left empty-handed.

By the time the eighties ended, smart women began to notice that lone-star/peak-performance strategy hadn't worked very well for its practitioners. At the uppermost levels of success, Donald Trump floundered to rescue what had once seemed an unshakable empire. Down on earth, where you and I play the game, offices were strewn with burned-out women who'd discovered that "having it all" really meant "doing it all."

"What I saw in the workplace ten years ago was individual striving," says Cindy Webster, who's worked both as a nurse's aide and as a fire fighter. "There was intense competition to be the star performer. What I see now is 'human-ness.' People are supporting each other, and we're becoming a far stronger unit as a result. People are admitting their vulnerabilities and working together instead of trying to meet an impossible personal ideal. It's a big change."

"If you'd told me about this trend five years ago," says Karen Wegmann, an executive vice-president with Wells Fargo Bank, "I would have laughed hysterically. Everybody was out buying a Beemer [BMW]. That's what they cared about. But I see something different occurring now. It's amazing. We're going back to community concerns—affordable housing and the environment. Everybody is looking at quality-of-life issues. It's happening in business, too.''

The change can even be seen in real estate, the go-go, shark-eat-shark game of the eighties. ''Isn't being happy what life is all about?'' asks Lynn Williams, one of Cushman Realty's top brokers. ''Personal satisfaction is a lot higher on the Richter scale than it used to be.''

Sally Geis, an administrator at the Iliff School of Theology, is a career counselor for women of all ages. She, too, has seen a shift in priorities.

''The women I counsel are all different,'' Geis says, ''but there's a common thread running through them. They're concerned about balancing their professional lives and their families. They are talented and they are professionally ambitious, but they have deep concerns about preserving their marriages and taking care of their children. And, in some cases, taking care of elderly parents.''

For many of us, the goals and values of the nineties are very different from the ''glittering prizes'' goals and values of past decades. Learning to ''look out for number one'' and ''swim with the sharks'' will send you swimming—alone—in the wrong direction, and the pursuit of excellence by itself won't assure you of getting what you want. To succeed on our own terms, we have to stop embracing the unproductive strategies of the past. We have to discover what qualities *do* get rewarded in the workplace and fashion a strategy that will bring us the success we deserve.

THE FIVE STAR QUALITIES

I began this book with three certainties. First, that Key Players already existed within the workplace. Second, that I would be able to identify them with reasonable accuracy. And third, that interviewing them would yield information from which I could create a verbal map for other women, a blueprint that would show us all how to become Key Players.

I was correct in all three assumptions. There were other assumptions I was wrong about, and many of the findings that emerged from this field study were discoveries, not confirmations of preexisting theories. In a global era, for example, I'd expected to find Key Players ready to relocate at a moment's notice. This wasn't the case. Instead, the women I interviewed said they used their leverage as Key Players to live where they chose.

Because I was interviewing many women in high-powered executive positions or on male-dominated teams, I'd also anticipated writing about the magical "split" in their personalities. I expected these women to tell me they'd learned to cultivate a male-oriented work personality while finding a way to blossom as women in their private lives. Instead their stories showed me a way of achieving that was uniquely female, and this has been the exceptionally exciting revelation of this research.

As I listened I realized that what these women were telling me in words represented one type of information. What they told me without telling me, the information concealed between the lines, was perhaps even more important. Many of their own strengths were unacknowledged by them. Many of the grand themes that emerged were hidden from them by the exigencies of day-to-day living.

Just as Sally Geis finds a common thread among the women she counsels, I too found a common thread among the Key Players I interviewed. I discovered that these women shared five distinct qualities. They possessed these qualities regardless of age, education, ethnic background, job title, or the number of setbacks they'd encountered—and they possessed them, for the most part, without realizing they possessed them. These qualities laid an invisible foundation for achievement, and the choices and actions that flowed from them resulted in long-term success.

If you recognize some of these qualities within yourself, terrific. But if you don't, I can only tell you that the Key Players I interviewed didn't either. No one in any interview said to me, "I've succeeded because I have a sense of mission," or "I have so much faith in myself I cannot be deterred." Rather, they candidly shared their insecurities and their low moments with me. In all cases I looked to their behavior, not their feelings, for information.

THE FIVE STAR QUALITIES

1. A sense of mission
2. A need to be challenged by new experiences
3. An ability to stay focused on goals and results
4. An awareness that consensus is strength
5. An underlying faith in the game and in oneself
   as a player

Nor did the Key Players I interviewed begin with all these qualities intact. Many had one or two strongly developed traits, a few in the seedling stage, and perhaps one or two missing altogether. As they grew and gained in wisdom and experience, they developed their weaker qualities and came into possession of those that had been missing.

STAR QUALITY #1: A SENSE OF MISSION

There was a little of a missionary role in starting my own business.

> Anne Adams
> Owner, Adams & Allgood

* * *

I really am passionate about education, and I think that makes a long-term difference. I believe I'm able to do what's necessary because I deeply believe in it.

> Barbara Uehling
> Chancellor, University of
> California at Santa Barbara

When I hire, I look for people who are passion driven and who want to labor with love. If you work out of love, you'll be successful.

> Sharon Richardson Jones
> Director of Outreach Activities
> Oakland A's Baseball Team

Love, passion, and missionary zeal in the workplace? You won't often hear these words from men, but for many women they form the fundamental language of success.

Work is difficult, it's sometimes unrewarding, and it often takes us away from other places we'd rather be: home, with our friends, with our children, in environments altogether freer and less pressured. Why work? It's a good question, one we women ask ourselves more frequently and more searchingly than men do.

By and large, men start life on the premise that they have to work. There's no choice and, hence, little to be gained from questioning the whys and wherefores. Today, most women may have to work, too, but we still don't necessarily see it that way. We were raised with the illusion—if not the guarantee—that we might choose not to work, an idea that encourages us to wonder if we chose correctly. Would we be better off somewhere else doing something else? If we aren't convinced, the underlying doubt can affect our performance more than we know. An office manager friend of mine recently had to hire a number of people to enter numerical data on the company's computers. He told me that although he wasn't sexist, he preferred to hire men because "the work pays well, but it's very boring and women rebel against it. Men just plod along and get it done.''

Players persist in jobs that are just jobs. Key Players keep experimenting until they find jobs that infuse them with passion and inspire them to a sense of mission.

To some of the women I interviewed, this means seeing themselves in helping or nurturing roles. Sharon Richardson Jones, who directs Outreach Activities for the Oakland A's professional baseball team, has found a job that blends business and social work. "I have to make sure that the Oakland A's are seen as a contributing part of the community. People support the team by coming here, by buying tickets. Some of these people are disabled, some of them are non-English speaking, some are elderly, some are children. Some are boys who have dreams of playing baseball. We want to give back to the community by meeting their needs. It takes a certain sensitivity from me to be on target, to identify the needs and develop programs that meet those needs.''

Jones has a personal as well as a professional sense of mission. "I feel an obligation to give back,'' she tells me in the first ten seconds of our interview.

This perspective didn't come from a business manual. Her sense of purpose came from watching other black women who, she points out, "had to work two and three jobs before other women were actually working. I saw these women put children through college by having bake sales and fried chicken sales and working through the church. I've seen women do extraordinary things to make a better world.''

The desire to make a better world—or at least a better corner of it—is a strong motivating factor for many women. Barbara Uehling, chancellor of the University of California at Santa Barbara, says the trait that's allowed her to persist over the long haul is the "conviction that things worth attaining take time. You can't make a difference in just one day.'' Uehling looks past the work at hand and draws energy from the belief that she's able to make that difference.

Social work, nursing, the ministry, teaching—it's easy to see why women in these fields have a sense of helping. They don't have a monopoly on it, though. I've discovered that Key Players share this feeling no matter what industry they work in.

Anne Adams gave up corporate security to start her own company, Adams & Allgood, an executive search firm that specializes in high-level temporary placements in the computer industry. "It's a wonderful feeling to be able to generate income for people," she says. "To be able to place them in a position and know I've solved a problem for them. I love payroll days when we make out checks. I look at the stack of checks and think, Gee, all these people are earning money because of what we're doing. That's really satisfying to me."

Adams also finds excitement in the fact that she's a pioneer in a relatively new field. "In the computer industry," she explains, "people move in and out of jobs, often not of their own choice, and at any given moment there are lots of good people available, people who are a resource that could be tapped. On the other hand, companies are trying to keep head counts down. There's tremendous pressure to keep the permanent staff as small as possible." Adams, who worked for several computer companies before turning entrepreneur, says, "The idea for my company grew out of my own experience. There'd been several times when I'd needed somebody on a short-term basis, but I needed a high level of skills, somebody who could take responsibility for a project. One day it clicked that the mechanism for doing this was temporary employment, using the established procedures of a clerical firm, but focusing on a particular level of skills."

Though Adams had left her previous job, burned out, she tapped a fresh supply of energy when she saw a way of making her own contribution. "From the applicant side, there was an immediate sense that this was a good idea," she says. "From the client side, it took longer to get recognition. People would say the concept was a great idea, but they couldn't imagine how it could really work.

I had to show them. Over time it's become much easier. We have a very high repeat rate with companies who've tried us, something over 70 percent at this point.''

All of us work better if we believe we're engaged in something important, but for women, having a sense of mission is an especially strong stimulus. Key Players allow this zeal to guide their career choices and lead them toward success.

STAR QUALITY #2: A NEED TO BE CHALLENGED BY NEW EXPERIENCES

''Life is daring risk or it's nothing at all.'' To me it's no accident that these words belong to a woman, Helen Keller. Although it's a commonly accepted notion that we spend the first part of our career digging a cozy trench and the second part burrowing in, I continually see women leaving the trench the minute it starts to feel too cozy.

''You know what I think it is?'' asks Miya Iwataki, women's liaison and liaison to the Asian-Pacific community for Los Angeles County. ''It's the legacy of the 1960s. Those of us who were active then became the risk takers. Our minds were freed to consider new possibilities. Civil rights, the women's movement, the antiwar movement—those were our first experiences with empowerment. It wasn't just political empowerment, it was career empowerment, too. It showed us what women could do.''

Iwataki is both right and wrong. The sixties did yield an exceptional crop of women, women who are today coming on line as executives. However, seeking risk and challenge is much more than a trait of the Woodstock generation: it's also a trait of the Key Player of any generation.

Time and time again I've been struck by the consistency with which Key Players choose their jobs. If two positions are offered, one may have an enviable salary, offer an impressive title, and call for exactly the skills and experience level the Key Player already has. The other may be a bit out of reach in terms of skills and experience. It may require some quick cramming to land the position and plenty of on-the-job scrambling to keep it. It may be so fraught with risk and challenge that it's downright scary—and this is almost always the job the Key Player chooses.

"I didn't grow up knowing what our policy was in Angola," says Margaret Tutwiler, spokeswoman for the State Department in the Bush administration. "I didn't know at the top of my fingertips what our policy concerning the Middle East was in 1934. But I want to know. I want to understand it. I want to get it right." That desire to learn and understand, to "get it right," helped lift Tutwiler to Key Player position.

Before joining Cushman Realty, Lynn Williams wasn't exactly starved for diversity. As a lawyer with a large firm, she had an interesting and demanding caseload. Real estate offered something more. "I knew that commercial real estate was not without its challenges," Williams says wryly. "It's cynical and it's very cutthroat, and 85 percent of the people who go into commercial brokerage are out of the business in three years. But I thought, I want to see if I can do this. I have to do this, it's so exciting."

Williams joined the firm as John Cushman's chief assistant. After three years she became a senior broker. "One of the reasons I've been provided with opportunity," she says, "is that I accept challenge. Too many people are unwilling to accept major challenges. They aren't willing to put themselves on the line one little bit. As part of a team, you have to be willing to take the challenge."

Cheryl Stern, president of The Game Keeper, a chain of stores featuring intellectually challenging games for adults, echoes Williams's words. "You want to talk about advice for your soon-to-be or want-to-be Key Players? Take the risk! You are never going to be big if you don't risk. Period. I don't care if there are fifty people over you in the chain. Whatever environment you're in—corporate, entrepreneur, whatever—you must take the risk.''

A Key Player will stay with her company if it offers sufficient challenge. Terri Dial, an executive vice-president at Wells Fargo, has been with the bank since 1973. ''I've stayed because it's a big company with diverse interests. I've always been able to do something new and different, and it's always been intellectually challenging.''

If change doesn't flow naturally from the corporation, a Key Player will demand it.

''You have to take every opportunity you can possibly take,'' says Mary Lingua, a plans and analysis manager at a government engineering laboratory. ''Grab every opportunity that's offered, and if they're not offered, demand them. Lots of times opportunities aren't offered. You've got to take them anyway.''

Ann Picciuto was working with a Fortune 500 electronics manufacturer when she was hit by the urge to test her wings. ''I was the audit manager for two years, and I realized, Okay, enough of this. So I walked into my boss's office and said, 'I need a change now. I need to do something else.' ''

Like Williams, Picciuto's willingness to accept challenge provided her with opportunity.

''The company said, 'Well, there's a new organization that we want to set up. We don't know how it's going to work and we need someone to make it happen. Go do it.'

''Basically, that's what I did. All of a sudden, I had the responsibility of starting up a new organization, making it work, automating our proposal functions, negotiating multimillion-dollar contracts with major suppliers, and managing people. I went from supervising four people to having about twenty employees. It was a big challenge, but it was fun.''

If Picciuto hadn't received the challenge she'd asked for, she would probably have left the company—most Key Players do when faced with that choice. At one point in her career, Mary Haddenham was one of three candidates competing for the chance to head a new department. "I made an agreement with myself that if I didn't get the position, I'd leave," she says. Key Players don't enjoy unemployment any more than the rest of us do. One thing they dislike more than being unemployed, however, is being in a job devoid of challenge. Catherine Morrison, who currently serves as chief of staff to a California State assemblywoman, says, "I seem to have ten-year phases, after which I feel I've exhausted every possibility in the arena. Then I look for something different to do."

Anne Adams has switched positions for similar reasons. "I started out as a teacher," she says. "After about five years, I felt that I wasn't challenged enough." From the relatively secure world of teaching, Adams moved to the less secure world of the computer industry and then to the even less secure world of the entrepreneur. "A career isn't a straight line," she reasons, "it's a series of stepping-stones. You need to be open to the possibility of taking a different direction. That's where the opportunity is."

Key Players don't thrive on challenge simply because they like walking the razor's edge between success and failure. What they're after is the knowledge that comes from putting oneself in new situations.

Ann Picciuto had originally been a secretary who joined the audit staff "because the audit position was the best way to learn the most in the least amount of time."

Sharon Richardson Jones, who feels an "obligation to give back," says in the next breath, "I also feel an obligation to learn."

Karen Wegmann interviewed with several financial houses—including Bank of America, Crocker (later acquired by Wells Fargo), American Express, and Fireman's Fund—before making her choice. "The job at Wells Fargo was a check-processing job. I'd relocated from the East to San Francisco because of my husband's job. In the East, check processing is a small part of the business, small enough that I hadn't done it. When I looked at the Wells Fargo job I thought, This is something I haven't done, I'll learn something new.''

Anne Adams says, ''I switched from IBM to Qume and from Qume to Alp Electric purely because of opportunities I didn't have in the previous job. I went from IBM to Qume because I wanted to move out of sales and into marketing. Then Alp offered me an opportunity to start a new division. Now that was really opportunity, to go in and do something I hadn't done before, and it made it very attractive.''

Instinctively, the Key Player realizes that we learn *because of* our inadequacies. Thrust into an unfamiliar environment, most of us don't give up. Instead we set about collecting whatever skills and information are needed to survive. Challenge is the first stage of learning, risk the catalyst that stirs us to action, knowledge and experience the trophies we win from the struggle.

Because a Key Player sees challenge as a pathway to learning and success rather than a slope to failure and defeat, she perceives it as enjoyable rather than stressful. While men are likely to describe their jobs as ''stimulating'' or ''satisfying,'' women—even at the highest levels of power—are more likely to use the word *fun*, as Ann Picciuto did in describing the challenge of setting up a new department.

In trying to meet the personnel needs of clients in the volatile computer industry, Anne Adams must continually fine-tune her product. ''You think, This kind of person is in heavy demand right now, we'll go out and do some special advertising for those people and get our reserves built up,'' she says. ''Then, all of a sudden we don't get any more assignments for that kind of person.'' Yet Adams doesn't feel frustrated. ''It's fun,'' she insists. ''It's a lot of fun.''

When Ardis Krainik became general manager of the Lyric Opera of Chicago in the early 1980s, the organization was deeply in debt. During the first year she cut her projected operating budget by $500,000, then managed to come in $600,000 under her own projection—enough to give the opera company a positive cash flow. "The secret to good business management," she said in an interview with *Savvy* magazine, is to find "creative ways of cutting, as if it were a sort of game, making it a challenge to come in under budget."

Cindy Webster is another Key Player who can put a frustrating situation—getting on to an all-male team as a fire fighter—into the frame of positive gamesmanship. Trying to figure out how to get accepted, she says, "became fun."

Marilyn Weixel became human resources vice-president of a seventy-employee company at age thirty-five. "It was a very challenging position because I was carving it out as we went along," she says. "It was exciting. It was exhilarating. It was fun. It was hard."

Even Key Players who don't use the word *fun* convey a clear sense of it. Listen to the way Gerry Cunningham describes a job she once held in social services:

"There was a turnover in personnel and I became clinic coordinator, so I got to administer the birth control clinic. That was a wonderful opportunity because I got to do the purchasing and I got to do the training of the volunteers and I got to hire some people and I got to do a little bit of budgeting. I got to do a little bit of everything."

Notice how often the words *got to* recur? A player, as opposed to a Key Player, would perceive these tasks as demands: I had to do this, I had to do that. Cunningham perceives them as her turns at bat. The fact that she earned little money for her efforts mattered less than the fact that she was storing up skills for her next job. From this experience, she says, "I found out what I liked and what I didn't like, and then I decided if I had these skills and I wasn't making any money, I could take them into the private sector. I could sell the fact that I had management experience and that I'd done a little bit of everything. I could bring these to a new job and tell the people who were hiring me, 'Just train me on the specifics.' '' Cunningham did exactly that and stepped from the public sector to a plant managership with Jostens, the company from which most of us purchased our high school and college class rings.

Key Players place emphasis on fun because fun gets the hard job done. Deborah Slaner Anderson observes that, when Martina Navratilova lost her number one ranking to Steffi Graf, ''she said that tennis wasn't fun anymore. Martina attributes much to Billie Jean King for finding a way to make tennis fun again. It freed her to start working on the skills and attitudes she needed to win. Business works the same way. If someone does not think her job is fun anymore, she's not going to perform well.''

A Key Player experiences challenge as fun and, like Navratilova, is freed to do what she has to do to win.

STAR QUALITY #3: AN ABILITY TO STAY FOCUSED ON GOALS AND RESULTS

One of the things that struck me about the Key Players I interviewed was their ability to be objective about the strengths and weaknesses of both sexes in the workplace. While they didn't feel inadequate as women, neither did they romanticize women's capabilities. When men were better at something, they were quick to say so. One of the qualities they consistently pointed to as a ''male strength'' was men's tendency to be very goal-oriented.

Sharon Richardson Jones, who works within the predominantly male world of professional sports, says, ''Men often have a clearer idea of the goal than women do. They realize that sometimes they have to take a few steps forward and a few steps back, like a dance, to get to the goal. They're very goal-oriented. A woman may concentrate more on someone's personality.''

''Women,'' says Deborah Slaner Anderson, ''are often more relationship-oriented and less goal-oriented than men are. This is dangerous. Once you get away from what the big goal is, or even the minigoals that get you to the big goal, you lose.''

Men indeed may have a natural advantage here. Socially they're exposed to years and years of competitive play and mottoes like football coach Vince Lombardi's famous ''Winning isn't everything, it's the *only* thing.'' By the time they're adults, these priorities have become ingrained and are carried into the workplace with them.

Of course, the message can become distorted and result in total failure—as it did for Michael Milken, Ivan Boesky, and countless others. When tempered with a little reason, however, being goal-oriented is a plus. Anderson's right in her assessment: unless you stay focused on the goal, you won't win. In conducting a study for the insurance industry to identify traits that separated winners from losers, Albert Gray found that time spent working wasn't the chief denominator. Rather, he found that successful salesmen did what was necessary to achieve pleasing results (goals), while unsuccessful salesmen pursued pleasing methods and accepted whatever results those methods yielded.

Many of the women I interviewed had a natural sense of goal orientation. Other women, those who didn't learn this early in life, had to develop it before they became Key Players.

Miya Iwataki was part of the team whose goal was to get reparations from the government for the Japanese-Americans who were detained in camps during World War II. In a project of this duration and complexity, the opportunities for getting sidetracked, taking detours, and falling into disharmony were myriad. What Iwataki learned, she says, is that ''you have to stick to your goal and your principle to have a clean success.''

On a day-to-day basis, ''sticking to your goals'' means getting the job done and keeping the big picture in mind. When trouble comes up, it means stepping back and deciding which battles are worth fighting and which will only rob you of energy and resources without producing noticeable results.

Cindy Webster says her ability to keep the big picture in mind is directly responsible for her success as a fire fighter. "I asked myself during my first year, What's the fire service going to need in five years? In ten years? What kinds of skills? And then I set up one-year, two-year, five-year, and ten-year goals and pursued them.

"There was a new series of courses certified through the state, and that was one way I could get part of the knowledge I needed. I thought, I'd better start the courses at year two because at year seven I'm going to be competing for captain. When I started the courses, I was the only fire fighter. The others were all captains, sent by their departments. 'What the hell are you doing here?' they asked me. But by the time I took the captain's exam, I did well. I placed number one on the civil service list, thirty points ahead of the next guy, and this is a competition process where positions are usually measured by fractions of points. One of the reasons I was promoted ahead of several of my peers was that I had this long-term, 'big picture' perspective. Over a period of time, more and more fire fighters started to do what I'd done."

Keeping the big picture in mind also means getting the job done without being sidetracked by the need for personal praise or the accoutrements of glamour. "You need to be able to handle the fact that you're your own rewarder," says Barbara Uehling. "When I hire, I look for people who don't have a sense of turf, who have an ability to get the job done without worrying too much about who gets the credit." It isn't that Uehling believes women should toil in silence and be happy just to play the game. Like most Key Players, she realizes that when the team wins, every individual on the team becomes a winner. If the team doesn't win, if the job doesn't get done, personal recognition isn't worth much.

When Ardis Krainik took over the financially beleaguered Lyric Opera of Chicago, she instituted budget cuts from the top down. She flew economy class when she had to travel and booked single rooms—not suites—for herself. But when it came to the opera company's productions, she was far more generous. Krainik never lost sight of the fact that the goal of the company was producing opera. Her philosophy: "I don't believe in skimping on anything that's shown on stage. When it's on stage, it's got to be opulent and elegant and glorious."

Sometimes, to get the job done, a rule or two has to be broken. A Key Player knows this and isn't afraid to do it, but before she does, she evaluates the situation carefully. If she sees that a rule is keeping her team from getting the desired result, then the rule has to go. As long as she's convinced her rationale is correct, the Key Player even finds excitement in doing an end run around the rules. "When I was working as a product manager at Qume," says Anne Adams, "I would get these task force–type groups together to make things happen. It was interesting because I didn't have the authority to do it."

Key Players also break rules by doing battle with the status quo. They aren't afraid to enter the fray, they aren't even afraid to lose. What matters to the Key Player is that she pick her battles wisely.

As a civilian working with the government, Mary Haddenham found she had to file a sex discrimination complaint with the Office of Equal Opportunity to keep her career on track.

"I was an assistant program manager. I held that position for two years, and in that time frame I grew the program from being around a $300,000 operation to about a $5 million one."

Just as the government has an official hierarchy of rank for military personnel, it has a hierarchy for the general service workers (civilians) it employs. Haddenham's performance was impressive, but she didn't get a GS-13, the high official ranking that would automatically have gone to almost any male in the same position.

"We were in a freeze when I took the job, and there was an understanding that I was supposed to get the next thirteen that went out. I waited two years, and every time thirteens went out, they went to males. I got frustrated.

I said to myself, I'm doing the same work as my co-workers who already have their thirteens.''

Before she decided to fight, Haddenham explored the usual channels. ''I asked why there had been six white males promoted in the organization over the last five years while I'd been sitting on a thirteen, and I was told 'You're just not doing the work.' I got out my performance ratings for the last two years and a slew of wondrous recommendations from a slew of customers and said, 'This is ridiculous.' So I filed a complaint.''

Haddenham didn't take the step lightly. ''Filing that complaint was one of the hardest things I ever did,'' she says. ''Before you fight a battle, you have to make sure there will be some ultimate end product, some goal, some positive benefit. The benefit doesn't necessarily have to be to me. It can be, but it doesn't necessarily have to be.''

As you can see, Haddenham went into the battle with a strong sense of mission. This helped her endure the difficult process of fighting the bureaucracy. To win her case, she agreed to waive the back pay that would have been hers had she been awarded her rank earlier. What she refused to waive was ''time in grade,'' the months she would have had to her credit in a GS-13 position. Refusing to waive status was important because personnel are required to put in a certain amount of time at each level before receiving the next promotion.

''My goal was to be a GS-14 by the time I was thirty years old,'' Haddenham says. Because she was able to let the less important matter of money slide, she won her case and eventually achieved her goal.

Besides knowing when to fight, a Key Player also knows when not to fight. When she went to work with the Oakland A's, Sharon Richardson Jones found herself facing the nonsensical rules of a long-established hierarchy. ''There's a team bus,'' she says, ''and I eventually discovered the bus seating arrangement constituted the set order of who sits where at all times. The bus driver sits in front, even for long-distance trips on a plane. The manager will sit behind the bus driver, the coaches will sit behind the manager, and so on all the way back to the bat boy. When I got on, I took a seat behind the driver. I was asked to move. And then I sat behind the manager. I was asked to move. Finally I was taken by the elbow off the entire bus and asked to ride with the wives, even though my male colleagues rode on the bus.''

A battle worth fighting? Not to Jones. "Men just operate more on a hierarchical level," she says with a shrug. "I went ahead and rode with the women. You have to pick your battle. If I challenged everything, I would be taken out of here by men in white coats. They'd have to call 911 to come get me. You have to know when to accept a situation and move forward.''

Midway in her career, Margaret Rush, a Methodist pastor, found herself in a position to help players new to the game distinguish unimportant battles from important ones. "Women who had completed their education were coming to me saying, 'We're not getting through the Board of Ordained Ministry. They're turning us down.' So I met with Pat Curtain, a friend of mine who'd already been ordained, and we took it upon ourselves to have training sessions. This was the 1970s, the day of blue jeans and Indian-cloth shirts. I said to these women, 'If you don't have a navy blue skirt and a white blouse, go out and buy one. You can't go to an interview in jeans. You have to wear a dress. If you want your battle to be over what you wear, that can be the battle line you draw. But if you think the battle needs to be over whether or not you get past the board, draw the line there.' Clothing is no longer the issue it was in the seventies. Today, women dress more traditionally. One piece of advice I still give them, though, is to choose their battle.''

Key Players don't always come to the game with a special ability to focus on results, but in the course of play they invariably learn to identify the important goals and make them a priority.

STAR QUALITY #4: AN AWARENESS THAT
CONSENSUS IS STRENGTH

The pioneer is one of the dominant images of American lore. In today's world, if you try to go it alone, you may well lose your way. As Cindy Webster says, "You can't be a Lone Ranger. You need a team." Miya Iwataki puts it differently. "Smart people," she says, "know this is an era of coalition building."

As I've worked with women in business over the years, I've been struck by how many of us cling to the image of ourselves as pioneers and resist the benefits team play might bring. We fear teams, either because we've had little experience on them or because the experiences we have had have been exploitative.

Ellen Boughn became an intrapreneur when she sold her stock photo company, After Image, to Tony Stone Worldwide and stayed on as manager. Like many women, Boughn never felt she was a team player at heart. "Teams were always a problem for me," she explains. "I was an only child, and I didn't like being part of a group. I quit the Brownies. I quit my sorority. It seemed that any time I got involved in any kind of group, I didn't like it."

When After Image, the stock photo company she began on her kitchen table, proved successful and grew in size, Boughn found that entrepreneurial spirit wasn't enough. She enrolled in a business program at the John Anderson Graduate School of Management at UCLA.

"On the first day," she says, "we were divided into twelve-person groups and given an assignment. It had to do with figuring out a plan for surviving in the desert. You were given choices of what supplies you would need and what you would do, and the object was to make more right decisions than wrong ones. We had twenty minutes to put together a plan.

"Because it was the first day, I had no idea who my teammates were. It turned out that many of them were senior vice-presidents of Fortune 500 companies. If I'd known this, I wouldn't have opened my mouth. But not knowing, and being an entrepreneur, I immediately took charge. I said, 'Okay, here's what we're going to do. We've got twenty minutes. So let's use fifteen minutes for general discussion. Divide by twelve—that means everybody's got two minutes. Just state how you feel.' And then I told them how I felt. 'We should walk,' I said. 'I'm a biologist, so I can tell you I've got experience with desert survival, and these are the things we need.' And I went on, blah, blah, blah.

"The first person who spoke after I did said, 'I've got to go along with her. I'm not even going to use my two minutes because it sounds like she knows what she's talking about.' I found out later this man was the head of the Star Wars program at TRW. We went on around the table and everything was fine until we got to a guy who worked in the alumni office at UCLA. He said, 'I'm sorry, but I think she's wrong.' A lot of people said, 'No, no, she's right,' but he got the leadership away from me.

"Part of the assignment was that we had to arrive at the decision unanimously and not split up. Well, I was ready to mutiny. I was ready to say, 'Okay, fine. I'm not going to vote with you guys. Go ahead. Die. I don't care.' This was my first reaction because I'd never had to be on a team before. I'd never had to make a group decision. Somebody came around and told us we only had three minutes left, and I told myself, Don't walk out yet. You don't even know these people. You just got here and you're going to have to be with them a whole year. So I said, 'All right, I concede. I'll give up. But you're wrong. You're dead wrong.'

"The scoring came out that we had more right decisions and more dissension than any other group.

"It turned out that I was completely wrong. I had said, 'No, there's no way you would need a gun. That's really stupid.' But it turned out the gun was a way of signaling search crews. And the raincoat, which I also insisted you wouldn't need, would shield you from the sun. I was wrong at nearly every turn, even though I'd turned some of the brightest minds to my side as leader. If my group had listened to me, they would have died. And we would have come in last among all the groups.

"That was my first lesson in teamwork. It showed me that I didn't have to fear teams. It also showed me how stupid you can be if you can't work on a team. In the end, team knowledge far exceeds any one individual's knowledge or any one individual's decision-making ability. That's the best lesson I learned in the course. On my desk I have a piece of Plexiglas. It has a patch of sand in it and it says, 'We survived the desert. Executive Program 1987–88.' It's always sitting there, telling me about teamwork."

Learning to trust the group, as Boughn discovered, takes a lot of stress and strain off the individual. "In the last few years," says Lynn Williams, "we all discovered that you cannot work alone and keep up. It sounded good. It does not work. I've learned that. I feel extraordinarily comfortable handing off responsibility to other professionals in my office."

In my experience I've found that women have a harder time learning this lesson than men. Once we learn, however, we quite often build stronger, broader-based coalitions than men do. While many men support the team concept, most tend to look for teams made up of players exactly like themselves. Once women grasp the idea that different experiences and different points of view are desirable, they go out of their way to bring everybody into the game.

Ellen Boughn delights in the fact that her present team is a diverse one. "In my office I have people who were born in China, in the Philippines, in Mexico, and in Korea as well as people who were born in the United States. I like the mix. These are people who want to work. They're young, they're creative, and they're champing at the bit. They're not going to get a BMW by birthright, so they're ambitious to see what they can accomplish for themselves."

Ann Picciuto, who created a new organization within her company, feels she succeeded because of the teams she put together. "Developing my team was key. I inherited about a half dozen people, and I hired the rest: men, women, short, tall, fat, skinny, black, white, Hispanic, old, young. On a team, everybody doesn't look alike. A team is a blend. The more diverse the blend, the better the team."

The importance of having a broad-based team is something Key Players are likely to be passionate about. "I love diversity," says Catherine Morrison, chief of staff to California State Assemblywoman Cathie Wright. "It's stimulating to meet people from different backgrounds. This is the great thing about the United States. Diversity adds new angles and new dimensions. This helps the creative process because it suggests solutions you wouldn't otherwise have."

Lois Rice, an executive vice-president at Wells Fargo, says, "I love it when we get someone who brings something new to the party. That's exciting to me and it's exciting for the company. To run a company well, you've got to get a mix. Everybody can't come from the same bent. It's much healthier to have a difference of opinion. Surround yourself with people just like yourself and you're going to get stagnant."

"For years," says Nancy Glaser, director of public relations at Avon Products, "everybody was pretty much the same here. We didn't have a lot of diversity in the ranks. And we didn't see a need to change. Because of that, we missed certain demographic shifts."

Since 1977 Avon has been aggressively pursuing diversity, promoting more women and moving toward multicultural diversity. Today 27 percent of the corporation's officers are women, and Laura Lopez, director of Hispanic marketing, says, "Being Hispanic and being a woman, I've been given the opportunity to bring a lot of my own cultural orientation to the job."

Avon's new approach has its roots in business logic. Says Glaser, "The demographics of Avon correlate directly with the demographics of the United States. Whatever percentage of blacks and Hispanics and Asians there are in the United States, that's the percentage of our consumer base. Change is critical because of our labor pool and because of our evolving customer base. For us, diversity becomes a productivity issue.''

Finding a way to draw on the strengths and talents of a diverse populace has been one of America's most successful strategies as a nation. Key Players use the strategy on a smaller scale, valuing multicultural and multiracial teams because they provide a broader, deeper pool of information and experience from which to draw.

STAR QUALITY #5: AN UNDERLYING FAITH IN THE GAME AND IN ONESELF AS A PLAYER

> Every adult gets to a point where she says, ''Okay, given that life's unfair, capricious, and dangerous, do I continue to set goals and take risks and care and hope and dream? Or do I give up?''
>
> Cindy Webster

If I had called Central Casting and asked them to send me someone who embodied the quintessential Key Player, they would have sent me Cindy Webster.

Webster's sense of adventure surfaced in the 1960s. ''A friend called me and said, 'We need more women in Outward Bound. How'd you like to be a mountain-climbing instructor?' I said, 'What's that? Sure.' So he threw me down a cliff on a rope, and two weeks later I was an instructor.''

As one of the first female instructors in the Outward Bound program, Webster discovered two things about herself: she liked being a trail blazer, and she liked being challenged. She went on testing the limits until she found the team she wanted a permanent place on. ''I was working as a forestry crew supervisor. I knew how to run a crew well and handle tools like chain saws and brush hooks. So I tried for forest service seasonal fire fighter. Then I became a hotshot fire fighter for the county. Then a reserve fire fighter. Then a regular.'' And eventually a captain, but not without jumping some high hurdles.

"Everyone assumed the first female fire fighters would be six-foot shot-putters with Olympics potential,'' she says. "Well, I wasn't even a surfer girl. I'm from Indiana. At five feet four, I was shorter than they expected. I was heavier than they expected. And I wore glasses. I certainly did not fit their image of what the first female fire fighter would be. But I had a determination and a willingness to look at the team and figure it out.

"I was the first woman in an all-male world. One of the things that helped me was my background. When I was getting my degree in counseling, I worked at the Kinsey Institute and read abstracts on anthropology. I looked at this all-male world as if I were an anthropologist going to a strange culture. I asked myself, What's the culture? What are the mores? What are the game rules? Then it became fun. Once you understand the culture and the mores, not only do you not make enemies, you can have fun. You can play.''

Once she'd made the team and been accepted by her male colleagues, Webster challenged herself with a new set of tasks. "To get on a male team,'' she says, "you have to start out acting just like the males. But if you stay in this overidentification mode, you ignore your uniqueness. Eventually you have to start asking, 'How can I contribute by bringing what's uniquely mine to this team?' ''

Webster rose to the rank of captain and worked in fire service until a piece of ceiling panel fell on her, injuring her back. To her amazement, she discovered that she would have to fight to get worker's compensation for her injury. "In the late eighties,'' she says, "a new game rule came into effect. The new rule was, 'The county's broke.'

"For the last three years I've been in a survival mode. I've gone from making $40,000 a year as a fire captain to $10,000 a year as a nurse's aide. I've lost almost everything I owned. The injury and the loss of my job didn't beat me, but it came awfully close. I've recently reached a point where I can look at quality of life as well as plain survival. What do I really need to make my life meaningful?''

What would really make her life meaningful, Webster believes, is the right to rejoin the fire service. But until her case makes its way through the legal system, she's forced to live in a state of uncertainty many of us would find intolerable. She hasn't quit playing the game, though. A few months after I interviewed Webster, catastrophic fires swept her region of southern California. Webster, working as a volunteer with the U.S. Forest Service, found herself in a key position. Because she knew the territory, she provided updates and information to the waiting media. She worked sixteen hours the first night, went to work and pulled her regular nursing shift, then returned to another eight hours at her volunteer post.

''What I did wasn't such a big deal,'' she says. ''Doctors who lost their homes performed surgery. When your work is saving lives and property, personal needs come second.''

This isn't a story about winning. For Webster, the game's on hold. But it *is* a story about a winner, a Key Player who has an underlying faith in the game and in herself even when the calls go against her. Though Webster's story is more dramatic than most, her sense of adventure, her desire to get into the game, her ability to keep the play going, her capacity to tolerate both self-doubt and frustration, and her respect for her own playing style are traits common to Key Players in all fields of endeavor.

Before you decide you'll never possess those traits, look back at Webster's story. Notice how infrequently she felt secure, how seldom she was certain she had the required skills. As you read the rest of this section, you'll see the same traces of uncertainty in other women. Key Players don't sail along on a magic carpet of security. They experience anxiety when they face obstacles, they feel discouraged when they face setbacks—but they keep playing the game.

This is what I call "an underlying faith in the game and in oneself as a player," and it goes to the heart of a basic misunderstanding many of us have about self-confidence. How many people do you know who go to seminars or are in therapy to develop self-esteem? I know quite a few. Some of them actually have built up their confidence, but not because of what's gone on in fifty magical minutes. Those who've overcome poor self-images have been lucky enough or wise enough to choose programs or therapists who've forced them out into the arena of life. This is where confidence comes from: it comes from living, not from getting ready to live. Self-esteem develops when you watch yourself succeed in difficult situations, when you pull yourself back up after being tackled, when you realize that you're learning to play better. While a Key Player may lack confidence and feel uncertain, she has enough faith in herself to play the game and enough faith in the game to keep playing, especially when a call goes against her. This is the behavior Key Players showed me over and over again, though they seldom gave themselves credit for their tenacity

Just as we have mistakenly believed that self-confidence precedes achievement, many of us have also mistakenly believed that we have to know where we're going to get there. This isn't true.

Margaret Tutwiler, spokesperson for the U.S. State Department, is *such* a Key Player that I almost didn't get to interview her. The invasion of Kuwait broke the week our original interview was scheduled, and Tutwiler spent the next several weeks holding daily—and sometimes hourly—conferences with an anxious, demanding media. How does someone get herself into such an important slot?

"I never made a 'career' decision," says Tutwiler. "I never knew I'd be doing this job. I never knew I'd be an assistant secretary of the Treasury Department. I didn't know I'd work in the White House. My philosophy has been that if you tell an employer you will do a job, you do it to the best of your ability. You give them a full day's work whatever the task is. I've been very lucky that each experience I've had has opened another door for me."

Like Tutwiler, most of the Key Players I interviewed ended up in careers they hadn't prepared for. Too often, Key Players fail to see this adventurousness as an asset. Rather, they seem chagrined that they'd succeeded without a "grand plan."

"I know lots of people are very thoughtful about their future," says Miya Iwataki, "but all my life, I seem to have fallen into things."

Cathy Hemming, associate publisher at Atlantic Monthly Press, says, "I sort of stumbled into the book business."

"Actually, I'm still trying to figure out what I want to be when I grow up," says Marilyn Weixel, director of human resources for Association Group Insurance Administrators (AGIA).

When I ask Barbara Uehling, chancellor of the University of California at Santa Barbara, "When did you first know you wanted to move into administration?" she answers: "When somebody said, 'Do you want to try being a dean?' "

In response to the question "What did you want to be?" Cheryl Stern, president of The Game Keeper, says, "I had no idea. The only thing I knew was that I didn't want to go to school for the rest of my life. I knew that I was never going to be a 'professional' in that sense of the word, because I wasn't going to go to college ad infinitum and get a ton of degrees. Eventually my husband and I decided we could afford to open a small store and live off his income alone for six months to a year. This was probably the only realistic view we had of retailing: that we would be poor for some undescribed period of time."

Karen Wegmann's original life plan didn't include a career. "I never thought I'd work. I thought I'd get married and have kids and a dog and a station wagon. Talk about picking something that prepares you for nothing— I was a fine arts major. That doesn't even prepare you to be a commercial artist because you can't make money as an artist. Then I got a divorce and I thought, Well, what am I going to do now? Go home to Mother at age twenty-five? And I decided, Well, no. I've always wanted to live in New York. I'll move to New York. I can work in a store. I got a job at Tiffany's. I moved around in retail a bit. I found out that I was good with people, and I was put in charge of managing people. Then I saw an ad in *The New York Times* that said 'Bank Operations.' I'd re-married by then, and I asked my husband, 'Do you think that's sort of like what I do at Bloomingdale's?' '' Wegmann got the job and eventually became a Wells Fargo executive vice-president.

Lois Rice is another woman who was forced into the workplace by financial necessity. "I didn't choose banking as a career," she said. "I was looking for a job. I needed to work. I had two children and I had to support them."

Gerry Cunningham says, "I graduated from college, I got married, I did all the traditional things. And then it hit me: Oh, my God, what can I do? I had no skills. I didn't hone my typing skills because that's not what I wanted to do. But would could I do? Well, I could think well and I could memorize. That's partly why I was a successful Spanish major—I could memorize anything. Luckily there was also this social worker–type person in me, and because of that and because I spoke Spanish, I got a job at Planned Parenthood."

"For me," says Lauraine Brekke, the assistant city manager of Ventura, California, "the hardest thing to face was figuring out what I wanted to do with my life. My senior year in college, everybody was either going to teach or get married or both. I knew I wasn't going to do either of those, but I didn't know what I was going to do. I was in a quandary. Everybody but me had things all figured out. I toyed with the idea of getting an art history degree. I toyed with going to law school. And since I couldn't decide, since I realized I didn't have a clear focus, I decided I'd go to work instead. I panicked about that because I didn't know what kind of work to do. There were different government agencies recruiting on campus. I went to an interview and took a test because I was interested in political stuff.''

These women, like most Key Players, entered the game on the rookie level. They came in as bank tellers and salespeople. Gerry Cunningham was an appointment secretary, in charge of making client appointments and filling out charts. Ann Picciuto worked as a secretary. Many other women couldn't start that high because they didn't know how to type. Yet all these women rose in their careers while their colleagues got stuck many rungs below. Why?

"I took what I thought was going to be a temporary job with the bank as a teller," says Terri Dial. "I won't say I made the decision to have a career in banking. When I decided to be serious about working for the bank, I entered their branch officer training program.''

If there's one advantage women have over men in the workplace, this may be it. We don't enter the game with a sense of entitlement. We're willing to go in as rookies. And once we get on the team, we become energized by the game itself. We "get serious," as Dial did, and get involved in learning to play the game as best as we can. I know many men who never got onto the team because they wouldn't accept a rookie position. I know lots of women who started as rookies and zoomed into the starting lineup.

"When we were tellers," says Lois Rice, "we would play games to see who was the best teller. 'Best' meant who could do the most transactions in a day. We had teller tapes then, so the winner was determined by the length of the teller tape. We would compete to see who could get the most customers in her queuing line, because in a bank people will prefer one teller over another. Queuing lines told who was the most popular, who was the fastest, who did the most work. We had fun. I took pride in trying to be the person that people wanted to see. I thought, We've got to keep these customers coming in. It's important. Even when I didn't totally understand it, I always did that.''

The Key Player, who has an underlying faith in herself and in the game, knows she can score from any position—even an entry-level one. In the process of doing this, the Key Player begins to develop her identity as a player. What are her strengths? In what positions would she be especially good? What skills can she acquire and hone? This is where the sense of play comes on strong: the Key Player is infused with a sense of fun and excitement as she challenges herself with new experiences. Remember how Gerry Cunningham described her job by saying ''I got to do this'' and ''I got to do that''? She was identifying her talents and seeing how far she could take them. When her talents exceeded the limits of her position, she parlayed them into a bigger and better position.

In *The Right Stuff*, Tom Wolfe describes the jet pilot's innate need to ''push the envelope''—to see how high, how far, how fast, and how well he can fly against the ''envelope'' of Earth's atmosphere. The Key Player is constantly testing her own envelope. The testing isn't always comfortable, but the Key Player puts up with it because it's part of the game.

Looking back at an extremely large, complex series of negotiations, Lynn Williams says, ''I thought to myself several times that a person with a weaker stomach would say, 'I can't do this. I need someone else to go to this meeting with me.' I decided it was such a fabulous opportunity, I'd put up with the butterflies. I'd be nervous as hell, but I'd do it. It was an important step for me, and I knew that when it was over I could walk out of the meeting and tell myself, Whew! You made it through another one.''

Lauraine Brekke's first job in city management was as a budget analyst to Seattle's nine-member city council. When she was unexpectedly offered a much higher position involving policy analysis, she grabbed it. "I was terrified," she says. "I was the junior person on the staff. I was the only woman. It hadn't even occurred to me to apply. I took the job and I was scared to death. I was nervous. I worked really, really hard. I was secure after about a year."

In this case Brekke put up with insecurity because she felt the correct play had been made. Earlier, before receiving her promotion, she demonstrated her ability to "play through" a bad call, one she had made herself.

"I'd taken the job with the city council, and for the first six months I thought I'd made a terrible mistake. I thought, Nobody's going to notice me back here. I'm going to die back here in this office and green moss is going to grow on my head. I will get old here. I was stuck behind the scenes, churning out this analysis stuff and reports."

Brekke didn't quit playing. Despite her belief that she'd made a terrible mistake, her underlying and unrecognized faith in the game carried her through. "I stewed about this, and then I did a report that caught everybody's attention. I gave the council a report that, unbeknownst to me, contained information that supported their view on a particular issue. Suddenly I had their attention. I had done some good work for them. They liked what they saw." Not long after that, Brekke was tapped for her promotion.

From the process of testing, trying, and getting past the discomfort, the Key Player eventually develops a respect for her uniqueness. The same women who shared their fears and doubts also gave me these amazing quotes:

> Not only is it okay to be me, I am the best possible me that I can possibly be. And nobody can be me better than me.
>
> Sharon Richardson Jones

I've always found that being myself is the best approach. I can't say I know more than the guys here—

they're amazing—but I can say I know a lot. I've been doing real estate leasing exclusively since 1982. I care about it. I'm a student of it, and I bring a lot of value to the table.

> Lynn Williams

If I want to do something, I get out there and I do it.

> Gwen McCane
> Director of Member Services,
> Oakland Athletic Club

I don't enjoy bureaucratic forms of organization. I can do well in them, but I don't thrive in them. So I've leaped past them. Because of that, I've been able to go ahead and get things done when all the bureaucrats were saying "No."

> Emily Card
> Attorney,
> Independent Financial Consultant

I look at my job at the bank as if I own it, and I've never gone wrong. One of my managers asked, "How do we know we're right?" I told him, "I don't, but this is what I'd be doing if it were my money."

> Lois Rice

When I went for the interview I thought, I'm getting this job and nobody's taking it away from me. Then I moved my plant into the office.

> Ann Picciuto

A Key Player respects her own way of doing things, which often means respecting and appreciating a feminine way of doing things.

As the member services director of the Oakland Athletic Club, Gwen McCane learned to trust her own instincts when it came to discovering what her members wanted. "I did a survey," she says, "but it didn't go over. I tried to get a sense from the members, and that didn't go over either. So I decided to do what I liked to do. I put together a cycling tour in the wine country. The members woke up! They've been calling. It seems as if what I like to do clicks with everybody."

Sharon Maeda, who owns a management and media consulting company, says being a woman gives her a definite advantage. "Our knowledge comes from our own experience or the experience of others around us. Much less comes from 'scientific research.' When we work with people, we're able to look past the surface and make intuitive responses to them."

Ellen Boughn, on a business trip to China, learned a great deal about the country while her male colleagues were talking business. "We were at a formal dinner that went on and on, and although I tried very hard to pay attention, I didn't understand a word that was said or translated because the translation went from Chinese into Japanese before it was translated into English. Very difficult. So my eye wandered around this huge restaurant, a restaurant of perhaps two hundred tables. At one table the local party chiefs were having a birthday party. They were the most powerful people in the room. You could tell. Wherever they went in the room, people got quieter. When they left, there were empty bottles and ribbons and stuff on the table.

"The waitress went to the table, and the first thing I noticed was that she scraped all the food and sorted it. It went back to the kitchen to get reheated and re-served. It didn't disgust me at all. It made sense. This is a country that's very poor.

"No one else in the whole place was watching the waitress. Only me. And then I saw this ribbon that had been on a bottle, and I saw her move it closer and closer to the edge of the table. When it was right on the edge of the table, she opened the pocket of her apron and flicked it in. She stole it.

"I realized, first, that I was in a country so poor that

a young girl has to steal a hair ribbon, and second, that I was in a country that tries so hard for uniformity it doesn't even acknowledge that a young girl wants a hair ribbon. It's trash and she has to steal it. For me, that was China.''

In the space of a few minutes, by observing with a woman's eye, Ellen Boughn learned more about China than her colleagues learned in the course of the entire evening. That's a Key Player.

3 ☆

The Team Advantage

To survive, teams need players. To win, teams need the best and the brightest players—in other words, Key Players. But why do players need teams? During team-building training, I'm often asked a question that goes something like this: "Aren't the weakest players the ones who gain the most from team play? I can see why someone who isn't a peak performer needs a team to pull her along, but I'm not like that. I want to reap the rewards of my hard work."

Often, the person who asks this question is making the mistake of equating "team" with "corporate bureaucracy." The two aren't the same. A corporate bureaucracy does indeed make it possible for weak players to "survive all the way to the top." As the well-known Peter principle states: A person rises to the level of his or her incompetence. This syndrome is exactly the problem teams eradicate. A team is no place for a weak player. Everyone on a team has a specialized task to perform. There's no redundancy, no overlapping, and—most of all—no hiding.

It is the Key Player who gains the most from team play. Just as weak players are spotted for poor play, strong players are noticed for their consistent contributions. More than this, a team is the basic "equipment" you need to play the game. In today's complex world, few of us can escape team play even if we want to. The woman who runs her own catering business may call herself an entrepreneur, but in fact her success depends on the team around her. She needs suppliers who'll sell her quality foods at reasonable prices, a dependable technician to fix equipment in a pinch, an assistant or two, a knowledge-able accountant, and someone to style ads, containers, labels, and business cards.

If we think we can go it alone, we're making a mis-take—a mistake that can keep us from using the Key Player strategy to our advantage.

TEAM PLAY: TWELVE BIG ADVANTAGES

Playing on a Star Team can
1. *stimulate you to a higher level of performance.*
2. *provide a sense of connectedness.*
3. *free you to "play with abandon."*
4. *help you break into the "old boy" network.*
5. *make a stressful effort fun.*
6. *provide you with rapid promotions.*
7. *give you the opportunity to participate in big deals.*
8. *help you achieve a personal goal.*
9. *teach you winning skills and procedures.*
10. *build your self-confidence.*
11. *provide job security.*
12. *help you lay the groundwork for future ad-vancement.*

ADVANTAGE #1: A STAR TEAM CAN STIMULATE YOU TO A HIGHER LEVEL OF PERFORMANCE

It's no accident that the traditional rallying cry shouted by Japanese baseball players before each game is "For the team!" The knowledge that people are counting on us, the heady certitude that our contribution is important and indispensable, is a tremendous catalyst.

Liz Hughes of Hughes on First, a San Francisco–based communications company, calls this effect "team esteem," and despite the current hype, the Japanese don't have a monopoly on it. In the realm of international swimming, for example, Americans aren't always the best. We're among the best—with the Russians and the Germans, we're among the best when it comes to individual events and records. The event in which our opponents fear us, however, is relay swimming. Americans are notorious for coming up with "personal best" times in team events. It isn't deliberate. Our athletes don't consciously save themselves for team competition. In fact, I'm sure they'd prefer to turn in their best performances in individual events. But that's not the way our psychology works. Part of the American character is a mind-set that says, "To the best of my ability, I'm going to see that we all win."

Recently the Japanese have begun to study how U.S. teams work—not for our efficiency, but for our creativity. Overcoming conformist thinking style, many Japanese believe, is their nation's number one challenge. Twenty miles outside Tokyo, Canon has built a "brainstorming" center. "Creativity," says Hajime Mitarai, the company's senior managing director and the lab's creator, "is associated with interacting with colleagues and stimulating each other."

It's that blend of individual thinking and team-inspired motivation that Americans are particularly good at. Sometimes we need someone else to remind us of it.

ADVANTAGE #2: A STAR TEAM CAN PROVIDE A SENSE OF CONNECTEDNESS

"Connectedness" is a word that encompasses such transactions as giving and receiving support, sharing information, learning, and teaching. There are two sides to connectedness: the obvious advantages of being "tied in'' to a network that shares tasks and information and the less obvious but just as important psychological advantages a network provides.

When Sharon Maeda founded her consulting company, Spectra Communications, she looked for partners, not employees. ''I was quite deliberate in wanting to have others as coequals,'' she says. ''When you're the manager, there's often a gap between you and the rest of the staff. It's lonely and it can be isolating. I needed the stimulation of other people on an equal basis, people who would inspire me.''

Maeda didn't want to lead a team because, like all good team leaders, she realized that the leader is the servant of the team. At the same time, she didn't want to play on someone else's team. She compromised by looking for partners, a move that provided both the benefits of ''connectedness'' and the advantages of running her own team.

ADVANTAGE #3: A STAR TEAM FREES YOU TO ''PLAY WITH ABANDON''

The woman who goes it alone has no choice: she must cover all the bases. As a production line of one, she ends up performing many tasks for which she is either unsuited or in which she has little interest. How often have you heard someone complain that although she works constantly, she has no time to do the ''real'' work that's important to her? A gifted salesperson who must take care of correspondence, file reports, make her own travel arrangements, develop client lists, and chart demographic forecasts will feel frustrated and constrained because only a portion of her time is devoted to doing what she does best.

Kay Fredericks is president and CEO of Trend Enterprises of New Brighton, Minnesota, a company she founded over twenty years ago. The company, which produces classroom materials such as decorations, displays, and other teaching aids, has undergone a number of changes over the years. It began as a part-time venture between Fredericks and her husband, grew into a full-time business, and was showing a healthy annual growth rate when, in 1984, the couple divorced and Fredericks bought her husband's share of the business. Fredericks found herself in charge of a burgeoning company (by the time the partnership dissolved, Trend's annual sales were topping $17 million a year); she also found herself responsible for corporate duties she had previously shared with her husband.

Fredericks couldn't fill two full-time-plus positions. Moreover, she didn't want to. Her true talents did not lie in making deals, counting beans, or ferreting out suppliers; they were, and always had been, on the creative side of the business. The company began when Fredericks, a teacher who was confined to bed following an accident, designed cardboard displays to use in her classroom. Sales took off because Fredericks's displays and decorations were imaginative, topical, and contemporary; they caught children's interest in a way that traditional materials did not. Soon Trend was muscling aside such well-established competitors as Hallmark and Milton Bradley.

After assessing the situation, Fredericks decided to delegate a large portion of managerial and administrative duties in order to devote the bulk of her time to product development. Although she introduced new efficiency procedures and cut staff by 40 percent after her husband's departure, she also added a level of general managerships (with a level of supervisors below them) and switched from an entrepreneurial culture to a corporate one.

Once she got out from under the managerial burden and delegated to the team around her, Fredericks was once again free to play her game with abandon. The year she restructured Trend, the company introduced over two hundred new products. One of Fredericks's biggest hits has been the introduction of Stinky Stickers, scratch-and-sniff peel-off stickers that replaced the traditional gold star method of reward.

All of us need a team in order to "play with abandon." We can't turn in our best performance if we're burdened with too many tasks. When you join a team, you won't spend less time working, but you will spend more time doing work that's important to you, work you feel passionate about, work that will keep you energized, not exhausted.

ADVANTAGE #4: A STAR TEAM CAN HELP YOU BREAK INTO THE "OLD BOY" NETWORK

Yes, clannish elitism still exists, more so on some jobs than on others. It can be the "old boy" network, the "old girl" network, or simply a well-established clique that perceives all newcomers as a threat.

In the mid-1980s Virginia Fleming, a manager of personnel relations at The Prudential Insurance Corporation's West Coast office, found herself facing a monumental challenge: changing the status quo. Like many companies at the time, Prudential was a pyramid-style bureaucracy; unlike many companies, Prudential saw the need to change. Under the old system, departments had been near autocracies, with each department head going his or her own way. Prudential wanted an interconnected team system in which the human resources department played a larger role.

Had Fleming tried to go it alone, she almost certainly would have failed: department heads, spotting a perceived interloper on their "turf," would have stonewalled her efforts. But Fleming didn't have to scale the wall alone. Dick Hunt, the vice-president of administrative services in the western office, created a team for Fleming to play on. To head the all-woman crew, Hunt brought in Laura Felberg, naming her director of human resources for the West Coast office. Felberg's background was in marketing, a fact that made Fleming and other team members suspicious at first. "Once we saw that she was going to be fair, that she wasn't out to steal the glory," says Fleming, "we trusted her."

Felberg's marketing expertise turned out to be a plus. Fleming says that Felberg's "approach was to sell [the department heads] on the idea that it was in their best interest to use us, because we could help them meet the company's new goals."

The team moved through the company, converting autocratic departments into star teams. Fleming gained credibility and visibility and was accepted by established department heads, who saw her as a peer because she and her team had helped them survive a period of transition. Dick Hunt's plan paid off for Prudential as well: the team set the wheels of change in motion, allowing the company to change directions with a minimum of chaos.

ADVANTAGE #5: A STAR TEAM CAN MAKE A STRESSFUL EFFORT FUN

While with Olympia & York Properties in New York, Camille Douglas coordinated what was, at the time, the largest commercial mortgage transaction in history. The coup was particularly complex because instead of involving one or two investors, it involved forty. The transaction took months of exhaustive effort yet hit the usual bumps and snags along the way, and it wasn't concluded, as Douglas had planned, in time for her wedding. It could have been a seminar in hell, an energy-draining experience that left Douglas feeling zapped by the corporate hand of fate. It wasn't. "This was a team effort," she later told an interviewer, "people working side by side with me, working day and night for months. There was a wonderful sense of camaraderie. It was exhausting—five nights of intense work and late nights—but I was never tired. The teamwork made it fun and the pioneering aspect made it exciting."

Douglas might have pulled off the same coup without the camaraderie her Star Team provided—but chances are she wouldn't have described it as "fun."

ADVANTAGE #6: A STAR TEAM CAN PROVIDE YOU WITH RAPID PROMOTIONS

"Surround yourself with people who are going somewhere," says Sharon Richardson Jones.

It's a good strategy, and few Key Players have implemented it as successfully as Margaret Tutwiler. Tutwiler graduated with a BA degree from the University of Alabama, worked for two months as a bookkeeper in a Birmingham bank, then found the team she really wanted to play on—she became office manager and executive secretary to the chairman of Alabama's Republican party. She held various state party posts, got onto George Bush's team when he was still ambassador to the UN, played on the campaign teams of both Reagan and Bush, and worked on (now secretary of state) James Baker's Treasury team during the second Reagan administration. Each time Tutwiler's team got promoted, she got promoted with them.

When James Baker became secretary of state under President Bush, he made Tutwiler the department spokeswoman. As often happens when a woman breaks into a new level of play, there was a flap about credentials: Is she qualified? As one newspaper reported, "The skeptics said she was underqualified because she had no foreign policy background; her predecessors had been experts in the field. But the first woman assistant secretary of state for public affairs had a powerful edge that many overlooked. As a longtime aide to Baker, she has access to her boss that has proved influential and helpful."

Tutwiler's credentials may have been an issue to outsiders, but they weren't for James Baker. Because he'd worked with Tutwiler on successive teams, because he'd watched her handle increasing amounts of responsibility, he knew she could fill the post. The skeptics took a wait-and-see approach. By the time Tutwiler had worked her way through a few crises, including the invasion of Panama, she was performing as well as or better than her male predecessors in the role. If she hadn't played on winning teams and leaped ahead with them, she might never have gotten that chance.

ADVANTAGE #7: A STAR TEAM GIVES YOU THE OPPORTUNITY TO PARTICIPATE IN BIG DEALS

- The products development crew at Mary Canican's Horizons, a Boston-based company marketing computerized design programs to architects, created a program capable of using kanji, the written ideographs of the Japanese language. (Because it takes upward of a thousand different kanji to make even a basic, sixth-grade vocabulary, kanji is extremely difficult to computerize.) At a time when many Japanese are marketing their technology to us, Canican is making deals with the Japanese, who haven't yet developed a program of their own.
- Soon after Lynn Williams joined the Cushman Realty team, she was named project manager on First Interstate Bank of California's headquarters relocation; the lease, in downtown Los Angeles' World Trade Center, was for 160,000 square feet of office space—a $75–$85 million deal.
- While serving as a Fellow to the U.S. Senate in the early 1970s, Emily Card took up the issue of equal credit treatment for women. Her team brought the issue to national attention, cultivated legislative support, and got a bill introduced into Congress. The Equal Credit Opportunity Act passed the Senate in 1973 and passed the House to become law in 1974.

Big deals? You bet. Undertakings of this size can't be handled alone. No one individual can do the spadework, get all the balls in the air, and keep them there until the bottom line is duly signed. Big deals happen when a group of peak performers pool their talents, knowledge, and finesse to work as a team. If you get on the team as a Key Player, you're going to get a sizable chunk of the action. Keep in mind: No one makes it to the World Series alone.

ADVANTAGE #8: A STAR TEAM CAN HELP YOU ACHIEVE A PERSONAL GOAL

Even if your goal is one you came up with yourself—getting something into print, establishing your own company, or changing a law—you have a better chance of success if you find others to co-labor with you. Miya Iwataki found that team play was the only way to achieve a compelling personal goal.

"One issue that was very, very important to me was the reparations issue," Miya Iwataki says. "My entire family was in camp." Iwataki's parents were among the many Japanese-Americans living in the western United States during World War II who had their property confiscated and were sent to live in confinement camps for the duration. After the war, these citizens did not have their property returned to them.

"The reason I got involved in the reparations movement," Iwataki explains, "is that I believe all Japanese-Americans, whether they admit it or not, have been affected by the camp experience during World War II."

Iwataki's first step, then, was to join a team that shared her vision.

"I feel that we [the National Coalition for Redress and Reparations, formed in 1980] were special because we were truly a grass-roots, community-oriented organization," she says. "Our goal was clear. It was the successful passage of legislation in both houses to enact our bill into a law mandating monetary compensation for survivors and heirs, a presidential and congressional apology, and the establishment of an educational trust fund."

After a ten-year struggle, the NCRR saw their effort pay off: in October of 1990 the first group of Japanese-American camp survivors received reparations checks and a formal apology from the United States government.

Miya Iwataki achieved her personal goal by joining a team. And when the team wasn't strong enough, her team built bridges with other teams. Iwataki's reparations team worked on behalf of the Latino community, farm workers groups, and the ACLU, and these groups, in turn, supported her team's effort.

ADVANTAGE #9: A STAR TEAM CAN TEACH YOU WINNING SKILLS AND PROCEDURES

Once in a great while, a person rises to the top because she is extraordinarily talented. For most of us, however, success is a matter of tenacity: learning skills and procedures that will take us to the top. Playing on a Star Team is an excellent way to do this, turning what could be a long, fumbling apprenticeship into a short, focused course on how to win the game.

Today, Donna Karan is one of America's top fashion designers, enjoying a rise so meteoric that many think of her as an overnight success, one of those rare individuals born with a winning hand whose only real challenge was finding a way into the game. That's the myth. The reality is, Karan had to learn a lot before hitting her stride as a designer.

At twenty Karan dropped out of Parsons School of Design in New York and went to work full-time for designer Anne Klein. Within nine months Klein fired her because, says Karan, "I couldn't do anything right." Nine months later Karan succeeded in convincing Klein to take her back. By this time Karan was twenty-three, and her job— as a "nondesigning assistant"—was anything but glamorous. Her basic duties were to get coffee, pick up pins, and make charts. What Karan was really doing was learning, from Klein, how to do things right. This time their relationship worked and Karan was given a shot at designing. By the time Klein succumbed to cancer in 1974, Karan was the second-ranking designer on the team.

Klein's death was traumatic for the whole team, especially Karan, who found herself at age twenty-six responsible for the line. She invited Louis Dell'Olio, a connection from Parsons, to join the team, and over the next nine years the two turned in a series of unbroken successes. Anne Klein sales rose steadily, and in 1983 a spinoff line, Anne Klein II, was launched. The new line would feature lower-priced clothes for women with designer tastes and limited budgets.

Karan's apprenticeship was now complete. She began to long for the challenge of starting her own line but, at the same time, was afraid to make a complete break with Anne Klein. Finally her boss, Klein president Frank Mori, made the decision for her by firing her. Karan had little trouble converting her impressive track record into bankable credit: she got backing from Takihyo, Inc., Anne Klein's parent company, and in 1985 debuted her own line.

The move lifted Karan from star to superstar in the design world. Within half a year she'd also moved into accessories: shoes, handbags, belts, gloves, scarves, and jewelry were designed in house. A licensing division was formed and deals were made with Hanes to produce hosiery and Birger Christiensen to do furs.

This kind of rapid expansion is where lots of entrepreneurs flounder. Giving up design control, making deals with outside contractors, and striking up licensing agreements can leave the person in control with no control at all. This didn't happen to Karan. At Anne Klein, Karan had learned more than the intricacies of the fashion business. She'd also learned how large teams can work together to fulfill a common vision. Anne Klein, too, had a thriving accessory business, and Karan had learned how to delegate without losing editorial control. These were the team skills and procedures she needed to make sideline ventures work. First-year sales for Donna Karan Co. were estimated at $12 million.

Successfully launched, Karan next decided to create a high-fashion/moderate-cost line analogous to Anne Klein II. DKNY became a hit, not only because of Karan's design ability, but also because she'd rehearsed the move before, learning what she needed to know while still on the payroll of her previous team.

Had Karan been forced to learn the procedures by trial and error, it would have taken her years longer to make it to the top. Worse, her lack of knowledge might have led her to commit a costly error, one that might have jeopardized her position at the top of the American fashion industry.

ADVANTAGE #10: A STAR TEAM CAN BUILD YOUR SELF-CONFIDENCE

When Allen Neuharth of the Gannett newspaper chain decided to create a national daily paper, *USA Today*, he deliberately put together a mixed staff, one not only racially and sexually balanced, but a blend of big-city types and small-town staffers as well. One of those plucked from a small-town paper and given a shot at the big time was Nancy Woodhull, who was put in charge of one of the paper's four main sections.

The challenge facing Woodhull was more complicated than that facing editors in charge of *USA Today*'s other three sections. Directions had already been established for the "Money," "Sports," and "Life" sections. But how was Woodhull to present her "News" section in a way that would capture—and sustain—the interest of a television generation used to fast-paced, highly compressed jolts of information?

Woodhull's response was to leave deep-analysis reportage to venerables like *The New York Times* and take a different approach completely, hitting the "hot buttons" of the news, leading with stories people were talking about rather than stories that might have far-reaching implications. To outsiders, especially journalists from the old school, the philosophy seemed less than logical, and the paper got a lot of criticism, on its first day, for giving more ink to the death of Princess Grace than it did to the assassination of Bashir Gemayel, Lebanon's president-elect. To Woodhull the decision made perfect sense. Woodhull's "hot button" system hit buttons with the public. The first edition sold out rapidly, and *USA Today* became an American institution.

Ron Martin had helped Neuharth pull the team together, bringing in editors from Gannett papers in small and medium-size towns across the country. Woodhull, brought in from Rochester, New York, was a typical choice: someone from a smaller market who Martin knew could handle the pressure of major league play. Martin knew that confidence might be a problem, especially when other journalists started throwing brickbats at the *USA Today* crew. "I think the enthusiasm of the place and the common bond that we all had . . . helped an awful lot of people through that period," he told the *Chicago Tribune* in 1989. He added that the success the team met with in the marketplace convinced team members "that they were capable of a great deal, that they were able to function in the big leagues."

Nancy Woodhull was one of those who learned, by playing on a Star Team, that she was capable of much more than she herself had imagined. From editor of the paper's news section, she became president of Gannett News Service, the highest-ranking female news executive in the Gannett operation. In 1990 she left Gannett to become executive vice-president at Southern Progress (a unit of Time Warner), a position that makes her editor-in-chief of Southern Progress's five magazines.

ADVANTAGE #11: A STAR TEAM CAN PROVIDE JOB SECURITY

In the first chapter of this book, Deborah Slaner Anderson, executive director of the Women's Sports Foundation, related an incident from her days in advertising. She explained how, when she lost her place during an important client presentation, a teammate stepped in and bailed her out. The presentation went on, Anderson recovered, and the account was won. This kind of recovery play can—and does—happen on a Star Team all the time. When people work together in concert, they know how each play of the game should go. If an emergency arises, teammates have no trouble picking up the ball and moving it down the field without losing the game or highlighting the fact that one team member is temporarily on the sidelines.

In Anderson's case the lapse was momentary; but playing on a Star Team can also safeguard your job if you have to be out of action for weeks or even months. Nancy Kalish had been a senior editor at *Cosmopolitan* magazine for little more than a year when she took time off to have her first baby. On another team, this might have been a risky move. Kalish's career didn't suffer a setback because *Cosmopolitan* is a Star Team whose leader, Helen Gurley Brown, has taught her team to pinch-hit for each other. Senior editors like Kalish regularly develop ideas, make assignments, and fine-tune finished articles; each also knows how to take charge of an assignment in progress and see it through the editorial process, even if she herself did not originate the idea or make the assignment. This meant Kalish could take time off without worrying about her job. While she was on leave her teammates filled in for her, editing articles she had assigned and eliminating the need for a replacement.

ADVANTAGE #12: A STAR TEAM CAN HELP YOU LAY THE GROUNDWORK FOR FUTURE ADVANCEMENT

Every time you work on a team, you have an opportunity to build bridges for the future. Cathy Hemming has zigzagged her way to a top spot in publishing by forming strong links with everyone her teams brought her in contact with. The position Hemming holds today, associate publisher at Atlantic Monthly Press, is a prestigious one, and the traditional way to get it is to enter a publishing house and spend years climbing the ranks. Hemming didn't do this. Her entry into the business was as co-owner of a bookstore. When the partnership dissolved, Hemming went to work for a publisher as a sales rep in the field.

"By far my biggest account was Ingram, in Nashville," Hemming says. She worked so well with Ingram, one of the nation's largest book distributors, that they tapped her for their own team. "They recruited me to come work for them," she says. "That gave me another interesting perspective to see how the book business works. For the next two years, I was buying instead of selling."

Ingram didn't recruit Hemming because they needed to fill a spot and no one else was available. There were plenty of people available, many whose credentials were no doubt more impressive than Hemming's were at the time. Hemming's former client recruited her because she had served so well, demonstrated her ability to build solid bridges to other teams, and impressed them as a Key Player who would benefit the team.

Hemming spent two years with Ingram and continued to build bridges, bridges that spanned the distance from Nashville, where she was based, to New York, where the publishing industry is centered. "Publishers were always flying down from New York to visit us," she says. "I was fortunate to be noticed by a lot of big publishers. I resisted coming to New York, but at some point, if you're in publishing, you don't have a choice. The business is centered here. Eventually there was an offer I decided to take."

The offer was to become the national sales manager for Warner Books, and it didn't come because Hemming was "fortunate" enough to be noticed—it came because playing on Star Teams put her in a visible position and provided her with an opportunity to build bridges that advanced her career.

DON'T JUST STAND THERE—JOIN!

Now you know some of the positive things being a Key Player on a Star Team can do for your career. To reap these advantages, however, you have to join up. Part II of this book will show you how to pick a team and get on the roster.

EXERCISES: ☆

Career Audit

EXERCISE #1

Are You Prepared to Become a Key Player?

The women we interviewed in this book became Key Players by gathering information, by training for special circumstances when their skills would be needed, and by staying keenly aware of trends. They built excellent working relationships with their superiors, customers, suppliers, and teammates at all levels. Their teams had the five star qualities discussed in chapter 1 (see page 26). Ask yourself the following questions to see if you are prepared to be a Key Player. A "Yes" answer indicates you have high potential to be a Key Player. A "No" answer suggests the need for further preparation.

Star Quality #1—I have a sense of mission and a commitment to the common vision.

1 _____ I stayed tuned to the global information that affects my organization. I keep current on issues, customer needs, trends, and innovative practices.

2 _____ I understand the organization's mission statements and know the status of the goals and objectives of other departments, programs, and projects.

3 _____ I volunteer to help other departments overcome obstacles they may have in meeting objectives.

4 _____ I can effectively describe the relationship between the big picture and its related tasks.

5 _____ I focus on the priorities in my own job with minimal guidance.

6 _____ I am willing to put in extra time and effort to help the team accomplish its results.

7 _____ I put the mission and results of the organization ahead of my personal career priorities or preferred tasks.

8 _____ I try to predict what additional skills I will need to remain a Key Player.

STRATEGY:
- Develop a reputation for being informed. Read and learn as much as you can from files, journals, newspapers, and customers. Work hard and keep asking yourself if you are moving in the direction of desired team results. Make time to stay tuned to important information about future skills and talents that will be needed in your field, not just in your company or organization.

Career Killers

- Not understanding why team agreements are important to others
- Having little grasp of real problems that are affecting goals
- Always worrying about the future rather than actively helping your team focus on the future
- Being too busy to stop, look, listen, and understand events occurring around you

Star Quality #2—I love to be challenged by new experiences.

1 _____ I am not afraid to tackle new tasks.

2 _____ I face my fears or inadequacies and take risks anyway.

3 _____ I am not afraid to make honest mistakes or to fail as I tackle what others may perceive as "mission impossible."

4 _____ I am not afraid to present my ideas or to disagree with team leaders.

5 _____ I allocate time to develop my expertise in subjects of high interest to the company, organizational units, or market.

6 _____ I persist rather than give up when confronted with obstacles.

7 _____ I keep cool in a conflict and have strong negotiation skills.

8 _____ I am not influenced by the negative thinking of others.

STRATEGY:

- As retired Navy Admiral Grace Hopper once said, "It is easier to get forgiveness than permission." Don't wait to be invited to take calculated risks. The key word is "calculated." Evaluate the potential positive results of an action, and be realistic about possible consequences.

Career Killers

- Being hesitant to respond to worthwhile opportunities
- Expecting others to look out for you
- Complaining about conflicts to others, but taking no action
- Believing what others tell you without checking the facts

Star Quality #3—I work hard to stay focused and clear about results.

1 _____ I allocate specific time for career development so I can build strong working relationships with members of all the teams.

2 _____ I keep the vision of the mission as I pursue objectives so I don't get sidetracked by crises that are less of a priority.

3 _____ I allocate time to develop my skills and to find special projects in which I can play key roles.

4 _____ I know about important business products, projects, and programs.

5 _____ I initiate new processes of doing things that will lead to better results.

6 _____ I can adapt to necessary changes if midcourse corrections are needed.

7 _____ I make a list of all the priorities I have to perform. Then I evaluate the time each one will take. If scheduling is unrealistic or in conflict, I renegotiate my responsibilities with the team.

STRATEGY:

- Think about what you are trying to do and question the reasons you are not getting things accomplished. As soon as you identify the problems, work on the resolutions. Work with others to keep on the track, and don't be afraid to ask your teammates for help. Avoid getting distracted by other people who might take you off course, and avoid overscheduling your time.

Career Killers

- Going through lots of motions with few results
- Tuning out, feeling overloaded and out of control
- Overcommitment—wearing too many hats
- Rationalizing that details aren't important
- Always being late to meetings or missing deadlines
- Working on "politics" and networking and not getting results

Star Quality #4—I believe consensus is strength and that internal conflicts lead to troubled teams.

1 _____ In team meetings I project a willingness to listen and accept other team members' points of view.

2 _____ I try to work for other team players' objectives in addition to my own.

3 _____ I can mediate differences between players and weave diverse viewpoints into a win-win proposal.

4 _____ In a conflict I try to help players focus on points of agreement so problems can be solved.

5 _____ I avoid destructive gossip.

6 _____ I respect other team members, despite differences in style.

7 _____ I question my own thinking so I can explore fresh ideas.

8 _____ I empower others by encouraging them to participate in team discussions and decisions.

STRATEGY:

- Become a great listener. Anticipate difficulties. Help the players on your team resolve issues before they become conflicts by making sure information and critical resources are being shared. Stop sabotage and secrecy, and encourage team players to bring conflicts into the open where they can be dealt with.

Career Killers

- Avoiding conflicts
- Soothing people's wounded feelings but not resolving the conflict
- Not accepting responsibility for errors and blaming others
- Hoarding information or power

Star Quality #5—I have faith in the game and in myself as a player.

1 _____ I play by the rules and do not sabotage others in the performance of their tasks.

2 _____ I keep commitments.

3 _____ I am always looking for new information, and I pursue continuous learning in fields or aspects of my work that are changing rapidly.

4 _____ I laugh at my mistakes and use appropriate humor to help me over the tensions of a crisis situation.

5 _____ I keep myself mentally and physically fit so I can face stress with sufficient energy.

6 _____ I let difficult events energize me and drive me toward goals rather than derail me from my purpose.

7 _____ I am respected by others for the quality of my work.

8 _____ I influence changes in the rules, rituals, or roles of the game if they are moving the team away from its goals.

STRATEGY:

• Keep building your mind, physical stamina, and sense of humor to offset what will be predictable stress. Key Players are not "workaholics"—they are driven to achieve their goals but spend time resting, reflecting, and recharging their energy with healthy diets, exercise, mental conditioning, and personal retreats. Most of the interviewees placed a high value on personal relationships, hobbies, and free play. Many commented that regular recreation sharpened their dulled wits.

Career Killers

- Getting a reputation as a "workaholic" rather than as a peak performer
- Failing to set goals on a daily basis
- Feeling unappreciated or victimized
- Failing to eat healthful, energy-building meals
- Dwelling on past mistakes
- Believing you are in a dead-end job

Your Move Now

If you did well on this exercise, you are positioned for opportunity.

1. Start working on the questions you answered "No" to as soon as possible.
2. Start broadcasting that you are looking for new challenges.
3. When tackling assignments, bring fresh energy and strong commitment to the team.
4. Communicate frequently with other team members. Sometimes this is known as "management by walking around." Other people say, "Spend as much time out of your cage as in it."
5. Don't overcommit; exceed the expectations given you.
6. Build alliances with other Key Players, teams, customers, and suppliers of services to your projects.
7. Avoid strong identification with "toxic players." Their thinly veiled disloyalty, hostility, and skepticism could contaminate your own reputation.

Most important, express gratitude for the little things people do for you. Many "spectators" are in powerful positions and will want to help you get ahead.

EXERCISE #2

Rating Your Reputation as a Key Player

These are actual remarks made about real Key Players from a variety of businesses and industries. How many of these statements would describe you?

1. "She initiates and completes a project with minimal direction."
2. "She can work miracles with limited resources."
3. "I can always count on her when the pressure is on."
4. "She is perceptive and quickly sees solutions to problems."
5. "She goes out of her way to help others improve and succeed."
6. "She's not into 'we-they' talk and always takes responsibility for mistakes or problems she's created."
7. "She picks up the ball quickly if someone drops it."
8. "She never steals the credit or claims it personally. She always credits the team."
9. "She always focuses on the customer and on our long-range plans to serve them."
10. "She's not afraid to speak up and disagree with the boss."
11. "She is good at breaking a big project into smaller pieces so we can organize our actions."
12. "She finds cheaper, better ways to do things."
13. "She knows all about products, services, and issues."
14. "She has a great sense of humor and can laugh at her own mistakes and learn from them."
15. "She is knowledgeable, patient, and easy to work with."
16. "She can make a decision and the subdecisions necessary to make it stick."
17. "She is reliable and on time to meetings, meets deadlines, and informs us of changes and problems."

18. "She never talks down to people even though she is one of the elites around here."
19. "She is willing to do some dirty work."
20. "She is flexible and can let go of the need to control events. She trusts her teammates and supports them if changes are recommended. She also knows when not to be flexible."
21. "She's a critical thinker and won't be rushed into a decision."
22. "She tries to build consensus."
23. "She can hold her own in confrontations without losing control."
24. "She can keep several balls in the air without complaining."
25. "She is service-oriented rather than success-oriented—that's why she is successful."
26. "She has a high energy level and is enthusiastic about the mission and challenged by problems."
27. "She has a good grasp of history and applies it well to current problems."
28. "She admits when she doesn't know something. And then she learns it."
29. "She pushes hard and is demanding but is considerate of the needs of others."
30. "She's confident and focused on the success of this team. She's a real Key Player."

PART II ☆

PART II

4 ☆

Team Types

In chapter 1 I told you that a Star Team accomplishes its task with a high degree of enthusiasm and provides its members with opportunities for advancement and growth. Now, let's expand our definition.

WHAT'S A TEAM?

As executive vice-president in charge of Wells Fargo's northern California division, Terri Dial is responsible for 1,200 employees at 104 branches and deposits in excess of $6 billion. Dial is a high-level Key Player who directs a powerful team. Yet when I attempt to place her experience in the team framework, she resists.

"It's a question of good management," she insists. "To me, it's like asking 'Can you do your job?' "

Frequently women play on—and even lead—teams without being consciously aware they are working in a team-dominated structure. Some, like Dial, fly by instinct, doing the right things and manipulating the system without having to learn, analyze, or plan. Most of us, however, need more specific guidelines. For us, learning to recognize teams, understand their workings, and decipher their rules is a necessary task.

To put the Key Players system to work for us, we must become aware of the teams around us and, in particular, the team (or teams) we're currently playing on. This isn't always easy. Teams in the workplace don't wear colorful jerseys or share the same locker room. As we'll see, team members may not even be based in the same geographical location or employed by the same firm.

STAR TEAM

A Star Team is a collection of individuals who co-labor to complete a project. On a team, players freely exchange information, pool time, and apply talent to get the job done. When a player has made her contribution and can't advance the project further, she hands off to another team member who can. On a sports team you literally see players handing off to each other to advance the ball to scoring position. In business the handing-off process is invisible because players divide tasks and work simultaneously toward the goal.

In the process of day-to-day work, team transactions become so familiar to us, we aren't aware of the team dynamics. Yet almost everything we accomplish is the result of team play. Successful careers and outstanding performances happen because there is a team supporting the individual, supplying her with information, and giving her the feedback she needs to succeed.

In understanding the teams around you, your first task is to identify the smallest—not the largest—team you play on. This is where your greatest power is. The smaller the team, the more cohesive the players. And the more cohesive the team, the greater the responsibility, power, and potential impact of each player, regardless of rank within the organization. The power of the individual diminishes in proportion to the size of the team. Therefore, if you see only the larger teams you play on, you will find yourself trying to influence processes over which you may have little control and teammates with whom you may have limited contact.

Where you draw the line for your team depends on the level at which you are playing. Terri Dial, who's playing at a high level within a large organization, directs such an extensive operation that it is difficult for her to conceptualize it as a team. Sharon Richardson Jones, director of Outreach Activities for the Oakland A's baseball team, does see herself as part of a team—the team she directs. And someone who works for Jones may identify herself as part of an even smaller team within that team— say, as part of the crew that works to provide free transportation and discount tickets to elderly or handicapped fans.

TEAM TYPES

When we think of teams in business, we usually think of a unit that can be represented as a neat package on the office flow chart: a team whose members share office space and interact on a daily basis to carry on a vital part of the company's business. This is one kind of team, certainly, but it isn't the only kind. As the economic playing field has expanded, letting new contestants into the game and challenging us to compete, many types have come into existence. Here are some teams you may find yourself playing on in the years to come.

The Traditional Team

Terri Dial has spent most of her career playing on—and now leading—*traditional teams*. The traditional team exists within a division or department of the corporation, is subordinate to the corporation's rules, and handles a specific unit of company business.

Innovation and unpredictability are not the hallmarks of a traditional team. Rules are well established, as are methodologies, use of resources, and player roles. Players know in advance what's expected of them: how many hours they'll have to work, what they'll be expected to accomplish and how they'll be expected to accomplish it, whom they'll have to report to and interface with, and what it will take to succeed on the team. Being courteous, respecting role boundaries, and knowing the rules are extremely important if you play on a traditional team, though how tradition-bound your team actually is will vary from corporation to corporation—some companies give traditional teams much more room to maneuver and improvise than other companies do.

The advantage of the traditional team lies in its stability and predictability. The rules are clear-cut and easy to understand. Often there's a formalized pathway to success, such as a management training program. For players with handicaps to overcome (players who are new to the game, who lack experience, who have educational deficits or deficits of self-confidence), the traditional team can provide a supportive environment and a chance to learn the ground rules. But tradition also has its drawbacks: change may be hard to effect, and the pace may seem maddeningly slow to players who yearn for a faster, riskier game.

The Matrix Team

Ann Hartman and Kerry Andrade head their own teams at ABC Clio Publishers, a privately held company specializing in reference books and professional publishing. Hartman is the company's vice-president/publisher; Andrade, the human resources manager. In addition to leading their own teams, both serve on a core management team, a task force composed of team leaders throughout the company. The core management team is a prime example of a *matrix team*.

Kerry Andrade describes the purpose and function of this special team: ''Our core management team meetings consist of the heads of each functional unit. The team brings the issue of accountability to the table. Each person on the team wears two hats; this promotes follow-through and provides excellent leadership training. Wearing those two hats means you have to think beyond your own operation; you have to see other points of view. What has come out of this matrix is that all members have developed new skills in areas different from their usual jobs and have become a resource to other players in ways that were never anticipated.''

The pitfall awaiting all matrix teams is that turf wars can easily develop. Team members become too focused on promoting the interests of their own teams, often losing sight of what's good for the corporation. If you serve on a matrix team, you will be constantly challenged to maintain this delicate and difficult balance. The rewards, however, are well worth the challenge: members of matrix teams have high visibility, get an inside look at what's going on in departments across the company, and, best of all, get to participate in policy setting and leadership at a high level.

The Intrapreneurial Team

In 1986 Robin Wolaner pulled off an unusual coup: she convinced media giant Time Warner, Inc., to be her partner in a new magazine venture. Wolaner, with fifteen years of experience in the magazine industry, came up with her idea in 1984 and spent two years developing, testing, and refining her product. The result: *Parenting*, a magazine aimed at upscale, well-educated baby boomers. When direct-mail feelers got an impressively high 5.7 percent response rate, Wolaner began her search for a partner with deep pockets: she would need at least $5 million to launch the magazine.

Meanwhile, Time Warner had been working on a similar project of its own. Christopher Meigher, executive vice-president of the *Time* magazine group, agreed to meet with Wolaner. Aware that new magazines carry a high failure rate, Meigher was wary at first. However, it soon became apparent that Wolaner was nine to twelve months ahead of the Time Warner Group and had a better understanding of both the customer and the competition. Ultimately a deal was made. Wolaner came on board as publisher of the magazine and retained 51 percent ownership of the magazine, a point she insisted on as a condition of the deal. With this arrangement, Wolaner became part of an *intrapreneurial team*, a team that functions with a high degree of independence under the umbrella of a parent corporation.

Though Time Warner brought Wolaner in from the outside, intrapreneurial teams are more often created from within the corporation. The mission of the intrapreneurial team is to create: a new product or concept, a fresh marketing strategy, improved internal operations, a drastically different approach to customer relations. Because their imperative is to create the new and different, intrapreneurial teams work outside the formal organization, usually in "skunk works" (the term popularized by management consultant and author Tom Peters), think tanks, or research-and-development enclaves. These teams have freedom and autonomy, as do the individuals who play on them. On an intrapreneurial team, it's more important to think creatively than to follow all the rules. This means gifted thinkers can rise faster in a corporate setting than they could on traditional teams, where pathways to success tend to be fixed.

The pressure on an intrapreneurial team to show results is enormous. There is no middle ground here. The team operates on a pass-fail basis: either it produces something new and different or it doesn't. Players on an intrapreneurial team must be Key Players, ready to go beyond the limits of their job descriptions and give their all to the group. If a player isn't prepared to do this, the team will quickly turn on her. Intrapreneurial teams travel fast and light, and players who can't keep up threaten the survival of the entire team.

The Transition Team

When Wells Fargo took over Crocker Bank, it was the biggest bank acquisition ever made in the United States. What made the situation different from most takeovers was the fact that the two companies were approximately the same size. In one tremendous swallow, Wells Fargo doubled its dimensions—and Key Players like Karen Wegmann, then head of the Customer Transactions Division for Wells, had to hammer out a smooth transition.

"I had a discussion with my old boss about how long it would take," recalls Wegmann, now an executive vice-president. "I was thinking of all the mechanical things we had to do—notify customers, issue new checks for them, change all the signs, retrain employees—and I was arguing for more time. I gave him an estimate. He said, 'It has to be done in half that time.' We brought Crocker and Wells employees together. We'd get together with various people in the room about once a week. It was a grass-roots way to do it, and it worked. Toward the end we were converting thirty branches at a time, over a weekend. Once they were converted, we sent people out to train the branches, which took about three days. There were some mistakes and some things went awry, but almost everyone got into the swing of things and became 'Wells' people.''

Wegmann is absolutely right when she cites speed as a factor of takeover success. One of the main tasks of a *transition team* like hers is to make people comfortable in the midst of a potentially difficult change. By getting the Crocker people to see themselves as part of the Wells Fargo team, Wegmann substantially decreased their anxiety level; by quickly training them in Wells Fargo procedures, she ensured smooth running for the bank's business and gave new employees visible assurance that they would fit in with Wells Fargo culture.

When a transition team moves in and helps during a takeover, it does more than provide simple "how to" advice. Executives like Wegmann also teach the rules of the acquiring company and promote acceptance of those rules. Often, transition team members are also there to fire people who aren't coming on board and to identify players who aren't cooperating with the new organization. If you work for the acquiring company and are asked to be on the transition team, it is a compliment: only Key Players are put in roles where they can teach—and thereby influence—new players. If you work for the acquired company, getting on the transition team can boost and solidify your position. Though the team will dissolve as soon as things are running smoothly, the alliances and reputations formed in the process are long lasting.

The Temporary Team

A transition team is one kind of a *temporary team*, a crew that comes together to complete a certain project or solve a particular problem. Task forces and quality circles are both good examples of temporary teams. The temporary team is growing in popularity for two reasons. First, it is extremely efficient for the company—team members pull double duty, joining the temporary team in addition to, not in place of, their regular jobs. Also, combining people on temporary teams is a good way of getting them to know each other in different contexts. On temporary teams, the company can see how players perform in a variety of situations.

Temporary teams are among the most diverse in their employee mix. A temporary team can be full-time staffers from one department within the corporation, a mix of staffers from several departments, or a mix of staffers and free-lancers from outside the corporation. Temporary teams can also form outside the corporation, drawing together people from several organizations or people who ordinarily operate as entrepreneurs.

Emily Card, attorney, financial consultant, and author of *The Ms. Money Book*, has spent her career playing on temporary teams. If you're married and have a credit card in your own name rather than in your husband's name, you're enjoying the benefits of one of Card's earliest team experiences. As a university professor in the early 1970s, Card ran into a wall of sex discrimination when she tried to obtain credit and buy a house. "So I hired an attorney. Eventually I negotiated to get the house in my own name, but it took a lot of work and cost me more money." Before Card could take possession of the house, she was appointed a Fellow in the U.S. Senate and relocated to Washington, D.C. She gave up the house she had fought to buy, but she ended up with a compelling issue: ensuring equal credit opportunities for women.

"I started working on that issue even though I had other work," she says. "I wrote a huge research paper and turned it in to Senator William Brock [R., Tenn.], who agreed to support the legislation. There wasn't a women's movement organized like there is now around Washington. There weren't official lobbyists. Each organization had one person who filled many jobs. We would get together. There were lots of people who worked on getting that legislation through. I arrived in Washington in January, turned in the research paper in February, and the legislation passed the Senate in late July of 1973 by a vote of ninety-seven to zero. Our team operated over a short period of intense activity."

Card left Washington in 1974, but the temporary team she'd put together worked to make sure the Equal Credit Opportunity Act passed the House and became law. "There were people who took over after I left," she says. Present or not, Card remains known as the mother of equal credit for women.

As Card discovered, the temporary team can be a "farm team"—an excellent training ground for players new to the game. It provides opportunity, a manageable focus, and access to established Key Players. A temporary team is a good way to get involved, get noticed, and start forging links with other teams. If your temporary team succeeds, your worth as a player jumps, allowing you to join another team at a higher level.

The drawback of playing on a temporary team is fatigue. Big demands will be made on your time and energy, and these demands may interfere with your schedule, making it difficult to concentrate on your regular work. Nevertheless, playing on temporary teams is an essential step in most careers.

The Transorganizational Team

Southern Californians are accustomed to fire, an event as seasonal on the West Coast as hurricanes are in the East. Mountain brush habitats are usually the hardest hit, but in the summer of 1990 raging firestorms swept the residential area around Santa Barbara.

"The fire broke out on Wednesday night," says Ron Keller, a Sears store manager. "On Thursday morning a man came into the store. 'Can you help me?' he asked. 'I've lost everything. I don't know where my wife is. I don't have a wallet. I don't have any money. I don't have a driver's license. I don't have a credit card.' Our employees jumped to take care of the many, many victims who came in here. It was nice to be able to do that."

Nice, yes, but also the work of a *transorganizational team*. Though affiliated for many years, Sears and its Allstate Insurance subsidiary failed to take full advantage of the alliance. According to Keller, "Somebody finally understood what should have been an obvious idea. They said, 'Why don't we use Sears on some of the claims and catastrophes?' What evolved from that is the Allstate Synergy Program. We processed lots of them after the fire. When an Allstate customer has a claim, an in-store representative contacts the customer and sets up an appointment for the replacement of all those items, or as many as possible, through Sears. One of the staff helps the customer collect the needed items, and it's billed to Allstate. Obviously it's good for business, but it's also good for the customers. We make it convenient for them, often scheduling appointments before regular store hours, and we mix in a discount."

Transorganizational teams link two or more companies

together. They form when organizations can exchange one commodity for another or when they can bond together to do something that couldn't be done efficiently alone. In Keller's situation, Sears gets extra customers from Allstate, and Allstate, in turn, gets specialized service from Sears.

As business moves onto a global playing field, transorganizational teams are becoming more and more common. Quite often I see three or four corporations form a team to negotiate their way into a new territory and establish themselves in the new market. In this case they may pool legal resources, exchange market research information, and combine public relations efforts. These world-trade teams negotiate agreements so that all companies on the team can get into a certain country.

Getting on this type of team puts you in a powerful position. Transorganizational teams open up many opportunities for you, give you high visibility, allow you to meet other corporations' Key Players, and lay the foundation for profitable networking. However, this is also a difficult type of team to play on. Corporate cultures are likely to be in conflict, and secrecy is almost always a concern. Players from diverse companies won't risk divulging trade secrets or sensitive financial information to "outsiders," so information sharing is commonly thwarted. Often the information that's held back is critical; without it, the team may not be able to get its job done.

The Outpost Team

Today, Seyril Seigal's title is an impressive mouthful: she's the resident representative of the United Nations development programs and resident coordinator of the United Nations System for Economic and Social Cooperation to Venezuela. In the 1970s, when she first began working for the UN, her title was much shorter—clerk.

"They liked my work and kept giving me greater opportunities, but I discovered that there was this distinction between 'general service' and 'professional,' and never the twain shall meet. Then I became really ambitious. I wanted to jump this hurdle, this wall. They were hiring men with the same qualifications I had and giving them professional jobs, and here I was, a clerk.''

Seigal's way over the hurdle was to work on an *outpost team*. With the help of a mentor, Seigal got a field post assignment. ''They persuaded our office in Chile to take me on as the fourth person on a four-person staff. I learned Spanish quickly. I got my proficiency, and I started on the professional ladder. I've moved far in this system. Tremendously far.''

At one time, anyone on an outpost team was probably, like Seigal, involved in international politics or a government employee. Diplomats, ambassadors, military personnel, foreign intelligence officers, and Peace Corps volunteers were the Americans most likely to work abroad. That's no longer the case. With increasing frequency, private enterprise is sending its own profit-making delegations farther and farther afield. In order for McDonald's to open its Pushkin Square branch in Moscow, for example, an outpost team had to establish a base, get the franchise up and running, and recruit and train local Muscovites for the team. The onetime rare experience of serving on an outpost team may, in the future, be no more than a routine step on the ladder as more and more companies send teams abroad to do business.

As Seyril Seigal discovered, joining an outpost team can be an effective way to overcome a bureaucratic hurdle. That's because the outpost team, like the intrapreneurial team described earlier, exists outside the formal organization. Far from home, rules become more relaxed. Invariably home office rules must be adapted to fit the new situation, and helping create the new rules can be valuable experience. Because an outpost team has greater freedom than a corporation-based team, it can offer greater autonomy to each player. In this microcosm of the company, Key Players can test and develop leadership skills, and the corporation, in turn, can see how well they perform.

The flip side of freedom and autonomy, however, is the lack of a supportive hierarchy. The outpost team has to be self-reliant—it has no choice. It's on the front lines at all times and is operating as the corporation. A player who has trouble with her outpost team is in an especially difficult situation. There's no higher authority to appeal to, and transferring home, even for legitimate reasons, is often perceived as failure.

The Scattered Team

"I've got the only geographically decent district," says Margaret Rush of the United Methodist Church. "I oversee forty-seven churches and it's only a ninety-mile spread. A colleague of mine has a really unwieldy district—the whole state of Utah and Colorado from the Great Divide west." As a district superintendent, or pastor to pastors, Margaret Rush works on a *scattered team*—a team whose members are physically separated from each other. Isolation, she says, is the biggest obstacle to overcome.

In Rush's case, the isolation is imposed by geography. Despite this obstacle, her network of churches is close-knit, with each church having a clear perception of the community to which it belongs. That isn't always the case. Often, members of scattered teams will be geographically close, working in the same corporate headquarters, but they will be isolated by divisional lines. They may be working on different facets of the same project—design, testing, marketing, packaging, and so on—but fail to see themselves as part of the same team. If the company doesn't knock down the barriers and encourage team play among these members, the results can be damaging to everyone. Communications errors cause endless technological foul-ups. Valuable resources are wasted when players repeat each other's work. Costly mistakes are made because there's no forum for ordinary suggestion making. A friend of mine once told me about a pedestrian overpass in Minneapolis that's a monument to the dangers of the scattered team. Like most pedestrian overpasses, this one was designed in a gentle arch to throw off rainwater. For some reason the building crew got the plans upside down. Instead of arching, the overpass dips in the middle, collecting rainwater and providing a breeding ground for mosquitoes. Had the architect who designed the overpass been on site, he would have pointed out the error; so would the engineer who worked on the specs. But the team was scattered. There was no dialogue and no opportunity for the architect or the engineer to participate in the execution of the work.

As you may have guessed, playing on a scattered team is a difficult assignment. You have to have the nerves and spirit of an entrepreneur and the tenacious will to communicate over, under, around, and through a variety of obstacles. You have to stop looking for support and start giving it. If you can do this successfully, however, you're in a strong position. Although the scattered team doesn't have visibility, it does have clout. The person who can play under these circumstances isn't easy to replace, as corporations have learned through bitter experience. Because of this, it's easier to build your reputation as an individual here than on many other teams. Often, players who thrive on scattered teams are invited to become leaders on other teams; the path can lead all the way to CEO.

The All-Entrepreneurial Team

When you watch someone like Martina Navratilova compete, you may think you are watching a lone entrepreneur, someone far removed from team strategy and interplay. If you ask the entrepreneur, however, you'll get a different story. Athletes, performers, and other "lone stars" are often even more attuned to the team approach than the rest of us. I remember hearing Navratilova humorously describing herself, early in her career, as "the great wide hope" of tennis. To transform her physique, her psyche, and her game, Navratilova brought a number of entrepreneurs together, a coaching and support team that has included personalities as diverse as Billie Jean King and diet guru Robert Haas. Craig Kardon, Navratilova's current coach, emphasizes independence above all. "You can't get coaching in the middle of a match," he says. "In an individual sport, you have to accept total responsibility for yourself in competition."

Kardon could just as easily have been talking about business. If you're an entrepreneur, you have to take responsibility for yourself in competition—but that doesn't mean you can't benefit from a team in the background.

Invariably, an *all-entrepreneurial team* is a support group. The support can be financial, emotional, or social. It can mean sharing information, office space, equipment, personnel, or client lists. Often it means sharing experiences and small talk, an effective antidote against the isolation many self-employed people feel.

Not surprisingly, a team made up of entrepreneurs is at high risk for developing deep splits and conflicts. Because the members aren't team players by nature, they often have a hard time putting mutual interests ahead of their own.

Another hazard for the all-entrepreneurial team is that it is independent. Because it isn't accountable to a higher authority, it can easily drift off in the wrong direction. Team members can become mistakenly supportive, telling each other what they want to hear and buying into a mutual fantasy. Entrepreneurs working together on a project may convince each other their product is marketable when it isn't; professionals renting an office together may convince themselves that business will be brisk enough to cover the costs, even though there are no facts to support this. When mutual delusion occurs, the whole team goes down the primrose path together.

If you join an all-entrepreneurial team, make sure you're getting honest business feedback: you want real facts, figures, and advice, not wishful thinking and hopeful forecasts.

The Family Team

When Mary Baim, Robert Lance, and a silent partner bought Plywood Minnesota, a chain of home remodeling stores, the organization was losing $1 million a year. Baim became president, CEO, and personnel director; Lance became the operations manager. By instituting wide-ranging administrative changes and getting rid of middle management, the failing retail chain was in the black within one year; within two years the Baim-Lance team could point to positive growth.

In private life Baim and Lance are married, and their venture is one of many *family teams* flourishing in America today. It's a new twist on the old theme, the modern version of the family-run farm or the mom-and-pop neighborhood store. Family teams often succeed because of the strong emotional ties members have to each other, ties that foster uncommon commitment and extraordinary incentive to make the venture a success. A family team can also eliminate the problem of the spouse who "just doesn't understand" why you have to work late or make an unexpected business trip.

When family teams hit a snag, however, the effect can be devastating. Relationships are pushed to the breaking point, spouses bring their office feuds home with them, parents turn on their children and vice versa. I once counseled a client whose mother, part of her family team, insisted on maintaining a "Mother knows best" role in the business. Mother didn't know best, and the organization almost went bankrupt. Forcing Mom out—the only action that could save the venture—created bitter feelings on both sides.

Because teams are living organisms, they're seldom as tidy in real life as they are on paper. The team you play on may be a hybrid of two or more of the team types described above; you may find yourself playing simultaneously on a layer of teams, or you may find your team situation shifting constantly. This isn't a disadvantage. The greater your team experience, the broader your reach and visibility within the organization. Being able to play on a variety of teams is one of the traits that lifts you to Key Player status because it broadens your experience, provides you with resources for future challenges, and adds to your worth as a player.

5 ☆

How Star Teams Work

Teams can be weak or strong, winners or losers, effective or ineffective. The team personality comes in part from the interplay of the individual personalities of the players. It also comes from the rules, rituals, and traditions the team has evolved to offset personality conflicts.

A friend recently told me about returning, as a consultant, to a company she'd worked for twenty years earlier. The small organization had tripled in size, gone multinational, and acquired a new personnel mix from top to bottom. In my friend's era, the employee lunchroom had been an especially egalitarian place, where the head of the company sat elbow to elbow with the lowest-ranking employees. Since the company had grown so much in size and no one from my friend's era was still working there, she was surprised to discover the atmosphere in the lunchroom unchanged. The new CEO still ate with his manufacturing crew, and business difficulties were still freely aired and frequently resolved. None of this was accounted for by the official operating rules of the company. Yet clearly there were rules in place—rules that maintained the special atmosphere of the employees' lunchroom.

As individuals move in and out of social systems, they pass along a complex welter of information—information that is both written and unwritten, information that is absorbed both consciously and unconsciously. Team personality is the result of the subtle culture that is passed from individual to individual. Even when teams are broken up and replaced, the new teams that form in their stead are composed of players who pass along bits and pieces of previous team cultures. If the team in question is a Star Team, this passing-along process is positive and success-building. But if the team is non-productive, team members have a monumental task on their hands. They must do more than recruit Key Players: they must examine and restructure the inner workings of the team itself.

HOW TEAMS OPERATE: THE FOUR R'S

You can learn about any team by looking at its operating style: What does it predictably do, and why? When I ask my clients to analyze their teams this way, they often tell me they can't. Because teams do work that is complex and multifaceted in nature, finding the hows and whys may seem impossibly daunting—a job, as one woman told me, "for systems analysts only."

The trick is to look beyond the work itself. Forget for the moment that your team is an intrapreneurial research and development crew, that you are second in command in a large office that reviews dubious insurance claims, or that you're a traveling sales rep marketing a new type of double-density recording tape for a globally scattered team. The operating style of all teams, regardless of the type of work they do, is the outcome of four components. I call these components the *four R's*, to make them easy to remember; they are *results*, *rules*, *rituals*, and *roles*. If you look carefully, you will see that all teams operate from these four R's. Star Teams add a fifth R—*recognition*—for individual members of the team.

Star Teams take care to get the order right. They agree on results first, then they set ground rules and settle on procedures; finally they discuss the roles each member will play. Only after the mission has been completed successfully do they enjoy recognition—for the team and for individual players.

Following this order reduces misunderstandings and facilitates smooth and successful team play. When I'm called on by a company and asked to improve its operations, I show management how to establish this results-to-recognition flow. Janice Witmer Howell is the manager of human resources at Wavefront Technologies, a California-based, international software graphics company in a growth mode. She says, "Knowing the rules and the actual procedures before we agree on roles has reduced time that used to be wasted in extra meetings and eliminated conflicts among team players. With the four R's we know what the roles need to be and can agree on timing. It greatly speeds up the attainment of goals."

RESULTS

Results are the "work" the team envisions. If the team is part of a larger organization, results are assigned by the parent company: design this, market that, develop a new system for a set of procedures, train people, and so on. If the team is entrepreneurial, results are dictated by the team's clients.

THE FOUR R'S

- *RESULTS: the goals the team envisions*
- *RULES: the code that governs team members' behavior*
- *RITUALS: the methods and procedures of team members*
- *ROLES: the positions players fill and the timelines*

AND THE FIFTH R

- *RECOGNITION: what Star Teams give Key Players for their efforts*

---

* * *

A good way to see the results your team is working for is to ask yourself, In six months or a year, what do we want to show for our effort? You should be able to answer in a dozen words or less. If your answer takes longer, think again: you may have lost focus and gotten bogged down in procedures, which can be dangerous. In fact, substituting procedures for goals is the most common reason teams—and individuals—fail.

Failure to establish clear goals can cripple a team and cause the corporation to withdraw or limit support. The year NASA put a man on the moon, 1969, its funding constituted 4 percent of the annual federal budget. For several years it had maintained a goal list that most Americans understood and supported. By 1990 Americans were no longer certain what NASA was doing. That year it received only one percent of the federal budget, a slippage of support that Senator Albert Gore, in a CNN interview, attributed to the agency's lack of "focused goals." For NASA, it was one more round in a downward spiral: as support diminished and its operating budget sank, it became harder and harder to set goals, produce impressive results, and reinvigorate its image.

Star Teams are results-driven. They operate on the premise that results aren't negotiable: you can't redefine your mission to make it easier to accomplish, nor can you pick your goals first and accept whatever results come your way. While the other R's—rules, roles, and rituals—are changeable, results are not. Once the mission is set, there are only two things the team can do: achieve them or fail to achieve them. Occasionally a team will be handed a "mission impossible." If the results truly aren't attainable, the team must come up with convincing proof that this is so, or its track record will suffer.

In setting decisive goals, a Star Team also considers—and states—the "shadow" side of the situation: the results it doesn't want to produce. Knowing what results are to be avoided helps the team steer clear of unproductive and even disastrous rules, rituals, and roles.

A Star Team has a clear understanding of the desired results and pitfalls at all times. "Show a 15 percent annual growth," "cut operating costs by $250,000," and "improve information transfer between departments" are all good examples of desired results. As you see, they're broad. To get a significant result, teams establish a series of smaller, more manageable, and much more precise goals.

When Mary Baim and Robert Lance bought Plywood Minnesota, the result they wanted to produce was to turn the company around: stop the fiscal hemorrhaging and start bringing in profits. Here are goals they established to bring the results about:

- *Design and implement administrative systems:* When Baim and Lance took over, "administration" consisted of two desks and a secretary.
- *Make better use of information:* Under the previous owner, there was no procedure for trapping information or using it.
- *Eliminate payroll deadwood:* "In order to be profitable, one must be lean," Baim says. She eliminated middle managers and took a hands-on approach, having store managers report directly to her.

The accomplishment of these goals got the company out of the red. Everything had been done to cut costs on the internal side of the organization. Baim and Lance now looked at the second part of the desired results—increasing sales volume. For this stage, they decided to

- *find out what customers want.* Baim commissioned a market survey of customer buying patterns and preferences.
- *change the store image.* Plywood Minnesota began as a center for home handymen with emphasis on lumber. Since women are the prime buyers of home remodeling

products, Baim redesigned stores to create an environment that would appeal to women.

- *place greater emphasis on customer service.* Customers in the market survey put this at the top of the list. Baim strengthened emphasis on customer support services throughout the chain.
- *boost the product line.* Previously, stores had stocked a fairly narrow product mix; the selection of appliances, cabinets, vanities, sinks, paneling, carpeting, and wall coverings was expanded.
- *regain customer confidence.* An advertising and promotional campaign was launched to make buyers aware of the new-and-improved Plywood Minnesota stores.
- *plan for growth.* Based on the results of the marketing survey, Baim and her husband spotted locations for new stores.

Baim's goals were well chosen: they produced the desired result of turning Plywood Minnesota back into a profit-making company.

RULES

What would you do if you found this posted on your office wall?

THE RULES

Rule #1: The female always makes the rules.

Rule #2: The rules are subject to change at any time without prior notification.

Rule #3: No male can possibly know all the rules.

Rule #4: The female is never wrong.

Sergeant Karen Krizan, head of New York's Ninety-fourth Precinct Detective Squad, turned to her team and said, ''Read 'em, memorize 'em—and live by 'em!'' Krizan's substitute for the old rules made her point.

A remarkable team leader, Krizan knows that teams can't operate without rules. A team without rules quickly becomes a mob. Whenever a revolution occurs, throwing out the old team and its rules, there is usually a period of anarchy and confusion until new rules can be established.

Krizan, the subject of a 1990 cover story for *New York* magazine, is one of only five female commanders for New York's seventy-five detective squads. Before she became team leader in the Ninety-fourth Precinct, she was second in command in one of the city's toughest precincts—the seventy-ninth in Bedford-Stuyvesant, Brooklyn. As *New York* reported, Krizan lost little time putting the rules in motion: ''Some of the detectives of the seventy-nine were known as the Bad Boys. They had no experience with bosses like Krizan. Suddenly, the Bad Boys had to remember not to swear, since to Krizan swearing isn't professional and undermines her authority. They found their orders on Post-it notes.'' Krizan also banned vulgar, *Hustler* magazine–style humor from the office, launched an office cleanup campaign, and made detectives rid their reports of jargon, bad grammar, and groundless speculation.

Not everyone accepted the rules at once. At least one detective habitually threw the Post-it orders away. Krizan was persistent and kept enforcing the rules. By the time she was promoted to detective squad commander in the Ninety-fourth Precinct, the Bad Boys were sorry to see her go.

Rules are the laws of the team. Some rules are written down; most are not. To facilitate team play at her chain of retail stores, Cheryl Stern provides a ''minimal performance handbook'' for employees. ''This is the bible for everyone,'' she says. ''If you're not performing to this standard, you don't get to be on our team.''

To be a Key Player, you must know both the written and unwritten rules that govern your team. Cindy Webster gives a graphic example of learning one of the unwritten rules of conduct. "Some of the game rules are fun," she says. "One of the things men do differently is make it look easy. I was told this by veteran guys on the Los Angeles County fire crew. They didn't mind helping me because they knew I was going somewhere else to be hired and promoted. I wasn't going to be in competition with them. So they told me, 'When you see guys cruising through the job, know that they are faking it. Inside, they're busting their balls, but they were taught to make it look easy.' "

Knowing this rule helped Webster get on the team. "When I took my first agility test, there was one other woman, me, and several guys. There was a young, rookie fire fighter who was there demonstrating how different parts of the test should be done. One of the things he demonstrated was how to pull a hose."

A fire hose bears no resemblance even to the most heavy-duty garden hose. It's a cumbersome, fireproof piece of equipment that weighs as much as, and often more than, the average person. "The rookie was young and naive," Webster continues. "He ran down the field pulling the hose, all 180 pounds of it. He exaggerated how hard it was, even pretending to collapse. I picked the hose up, whipped around the same course, and beat his time. Then I laid the hose down, said nonchalantly, 'Piece of cake'—and went around to the other side of the fire engine and collapsed where no one could see me."

Team rules do more than spell out the punishable offenses. They also delineate the paths to success. Knowing your team's rules should tell you what you'll have to do to succeed on the team. Suppose the unwritten rule is, "Our team shares information," and you come into possession of knowledge that, although irrelevant to you, could help a team member perform her job. If it's later discovered that you failed to pass along this information, you'll get a black mark. On the other hand, if you're consistently seen gathering and disseminating information of importance to your colleagues, you'll be perceived as one of the team's most valuable players.

On a Star Team, rules also include by-laws that function as a Bill of Rights to individual team members. These rules, usually of the unwritten variety, may guarantee team members freedom from personal attack and the right to be treated with politeness and respect, or assure them that they will not be made scapegoats if the team gets into trouble.

Rules are designed to keep the team running smoothly and to see that results and goals are met. For these reasons, rules allow for the apportionment of resources: they direct and/or limit how time, money, people, and other assets are to be deployed. Unlike results, team rules aren't fixed. They can—and often do—change during the course of the game, whenever a new situation must be dealt with. In fact, willingness to change the rules is one of the hallmarks of a Star Team. A team that won't change its rules is handicapped. In a world characterized by change, rule-bound teams lack the flexibility and responsiveness needed to survive.

One of the biggest rule changes going on in companies today is the switch from multilayered management hierarchies to hands-on management. The old rule was, "Don't bother the people at the top, report to middle management." The new rule is, "There is no middle management, report to the top."

Executive Vice-President Lois Rice says, "If you work for me and I'm not around to answer your question, call my boss. Call all the way to the top. You will never get in trouble for trying to get a question answered. What you'll get in trouble for is not trying." If you want to be a Key Player on Rice's team, you'd better understand this rule.

Tolstoi opens his masterpiece *Anna Karenina* with the deceptively simple, ultimately profound observation: "Happy families are all alike; every unhappy family is unhappy in its own way." A like observation can be made of teams. Star Teams employ similar rules—rules that promote efficient, harmonious teamwork and provide for the rights of individual players. The rules on weak teams vary from team to team. The rule on one weak team might be, "Make the boss look good at all costs"; on another it might be, "John and Mary get all the credit"; on still another it could be, "Cliques have the real power on this team."

Here are the rules that guide Star Teams and their Key Players:

STAR TEAM RULES

Star Teams

- *honor their commitment to work faster, smarter, and better than other teams.*
- *keep the goals clear.*
- *don't make decisions on impulse; information is gathered from all team members before a decision is made.*
- *work together; once a decision is made and goals are set, everyone pitches in 100 percent—even those who originally opposed the plan.*
- *allow rules to be challenged and changed as the need arises.*
- *are democratic; they do not permit cliques to divide the team.*
- *don't have sacred cows; no one's place on the team is guaranteed, not even the leader's.*
- *confront problems head on.*
- *impose standards of etiquette and ethics on all team members.*
- *protect the personal feelings of players by banning personal attacks.*
- *share responsibility: if the team makes a mistake, the team takes the blame and works together to correct the situation; no one on the team is made a scapegoat.*

- *share glory: when the team scores a victory, everyone on the team is recognized and rewarded.*
- *freely share information. (See "Communication Rules for Key Players," chapter 7, page 164.)*

Besides knowing and following the rules, a Key Player also has to know when to break a rule. A rule can be broken if it helps the team achieve a particular goal. When Anne Adams was a product manager at Qume, she broke the rules by "getting task force groups together to make things happen." She didn't have the authority to do this, but she didn't get into trouble, either. The reason she retained—and enhanced—her Key Player status while breaking the rules can be found in her own words. She pulled skunk works teams together to make things happen. She produced results and she earned respect and recognition for the players on her teams; in going beyond the written rules of her job description, she was following an unwritten rule: "It's okay to break the rules if you produce results with the fewest undesirable side effects."

RITUALS

What does the interdepartmental softball rivalry have to do with the Monday morning sales meeting? They're both team rituals, and, if you notice, many of the same Key Players will appear on both. Rituals are the "how to" aspect of teamwork rules, the actions a team takes to meet goals and produce results. Any time you put a question in the framework—How does this happen?—you are asking about rituals.

Some rituals are designed to produce the desired results. *Cosmopolitan* magazine, an exceptionally well run team led by Helen Gurley Brown, has a number of rituals that promote the desired result—a monthly magazine with high reader appeal. One ritual mandates that every Friday editors submit a number of ideas for articles. Brown reviews the ideas herself and adds her own comments to the ones she finds promising. The accepted ideas are then sorted into general categories and clipped into idea notebooks. When it's time for story assignments to go out, editors and writers both have a treasure trove of ideas to choose from.

Like all well-designed rituals, this one is simple, sensible, and promotes team success in a number of ways. First, it ensures a steady flow of fresh, current ideas into the magazine. Once accepted, article ideas become the shared resource of everybody on the team: any editor can assign any article. This prevents turf wars, which can—and do—occur at magazines whose editors compete with each other to get their own story ideas into print. Above all, the ritual promotes team efficiency. Unpromising ideas are eliminated quickly, before a great deal of time has been spent on development. Assignments are made on the basis of what the magazine really wants, which is much more efficient than choosing from whatever happens to come in over the transom.

Teams also engage in rituals that have nothing to do with business but, instead, serve to foster esprit de corps on the team. The company picnic, weekly softball or volleyball game, annual corporate retreat—all these rituals are important not only for the pleasure they provide, but for the team bonding they effect in the process. Star Teams keep these rituals gender neutral to bring both men and women into the loop. When Avon, a pace setter in breaking the glass ceiling, started bringing women into management in the late 1970s, then-CEO David Mitchell became concerned that "President's Golf Day" was underattended by women. He changed the title of the event to "President's Day" and added tennis and swimming to the roster of activities.

Cheryl Stern has always been a firm believer in extracurricular team events. "For our tenth anniversary, we took everyone who'd been with us for a certain length of time on a three-day cruise to Ensenada, Mexico. We did it again in 1986, because that was the year Trivial Pursuit hit the market and we had a good year. We went through some hard times, but now we're healthier than we've been in three or four years, so in conjunction with our fifteenth year, we're taking all employees with three or more years in to Club Med for a week."

Employees with less than the requisite time in, Stern says, don't feel left out. "First of all, they know it's coming up for them. Also, we have a manager's meeting every year and everyone gets to come to that. We talk business for a few hours during the day. There are social events at night."

Such jaunts are expensive, especially for a company recovering from a bad spell, but Stern says, "I can't imagine $15,000 more well spent. Everyone comes back so energized. Just as we're heading into our big season, they're ready to go, team-oriented, with lots of spirit."

To be a Key Player on your team, you have to know what the rituals are and you have to participate in them. Don't forget that both kinds of rituals—those that address the team's business and those that build the team's esprit de corps—are equally important. If you're not around when the team kicks back, loosens up, and relaxes, you're going to miss a lot: tidbits of vital information, insights into your teammates' personalities, and a chance to build the kind of person-to-person bridges that exist between Key Players.

ROLES

As you learned from chapter 2, part of what individual players do is strictly business, the tasks and activities likely to be found in formal job descriptions. This, the job title, is one kind of role.

What your job title is influences the work you do, your status on the team, and even how other teams perceive you. Catherine Morrison, second in command to California State Assemblywoman Cathie Wright, realizes the power a job title can have. That's why she got her team leader's okay to change hers.

"My actual title is 'administrative assistant,' " Morrison explains. "In the state legislature, there's a hierarchy of titles, and in terms of personal staff, administrative assistant is as high as it goes. Years ago this title had a specific meaning; even now, in certain fields, it has a specific meaning. But many people tend to confuse it with being a secretary. I observed that men who have the same position I do were calling themselves 'chief of staff.' I told Cathie [Wright], "I'm going to call myself 'chief of staff.' She said, 'Oh, fine.' "

Morrison didn't make the change only to keep her title in line with her duties. "When I am at a meeting representing Cathie," she says, "people need to know that the most senior staff person was sent. I could be in a meeting with two men who have the same position I do. If they introduced themselves as chiefs of staff and I introduced myself as an administrative assistant, it would seem as if Cathie had sent a junior staff person. That wouldn't be politically appropriate."

Morrison sensitively and correctly perceives that to be competitive, her team must fill the chief of staff position. Key Players on Star Teams must be sensitive to a second level of roles as well—roles that nurture the team and take care of its survival needs. For a team to perform efficiently, both job description roles and the roles that promote team survival must be competently filled. (For more on roles see chapter 9, "Key Roles for Key Players," p. 205.)

On a Star Team, roles—like rules—are mutable: they can be redesigned, shared, multiplied, and combined as needed. When players aren't able to fill in for each other, when they feel their roles are guaranteed, or when they regard roles as nothing more than ladders in a personal power climb, the team loses momentum. Sometimes this is the fault of the team for not making its demands clear, sometimes its the fault of individual players, and more often it's a combination of both.

On a Star Team, no one's role is guaranteed, not even the leader's, and team members are expected to slide into and out of position as needed. This can mean switch hitting, it can mean handing off your role to a teammate in scoring position, it can mean taking on an extra role if there's an emergency or a temporary vacancy. Often, when a large project is in the works, official role boundaries dissolve completely as everyone on the team pitches in to get the job done.

RECOGNITION, THE FIFTH R

Ordinary teams operate out of the four R's—results, rules, rituals, and roles. Star Teams always include a fifth R in the formula—recognition for the team. In describing the new team approach to success outlined in chapter 1, I told you about Paul Miller and Kristie Wilde, television journalists who created a new department at a small station in Salinas, California. I began to recognize these people as Star Team builders when Kristie Wilde remarked that she planned to use lots of reporters on the set because "they sound and feel good when they get to be out there." This is a fine example of team-style recognition.

One of the things Helen Gurley Brown likes best about heading the team at *Cosmopolitan* is the ability to award recognition. "When you're the person in charge, you don't need credit from anybody. You've already got the top job. You don't have to say, 'That was my idea.' You can give all the credit to the people working with you."

Lauraine Brekke sees getting recognition for her teammates as a matter of fairness. "They take the blame if something goes wrong. It's right that they take the credit when there's success. It goes both ways. I've always tried to push my subordinates into the spotlight. I like to let them shine." Brekke pauses, then adds, "Because I know how much fun it is."

These sentiments are typical of Star Team leaders, who realize that Key Players thrive on recognition. You've already seen some examples of this: in Lynn Williams, whose team leader at Cushman Realty named her project manager on the First Interstate Bank deal; in Margaret Tutwiler, whose team leader, James Baker, gave her opportunities and promotions even as critics challenged her lack of formal credentials; in Ann Picciuto, whose team leader at a fortune 500 electronics manufacturer responded to her need for change by putting her in charge of a newly created organization.

THE BIG MO

Teams are subject to the laws of momentum. On a Star Team, only the results are fixed. Rules, roles, and rituals flow from the need to meet the goals that produce desired results. Because there is interplay among these three elements (rules can influence roles, roles can influence rules, and so on), team play is fluid. Energy and effort aren't "blocked" but flow freely back and forth across the team. This constant flow of energy produces momentum. The team becomes excited by its own work and is stimulated to higher levels of performance. This is what I call team synergy, the optimum performance level.

Even a large, unwieldy, and previously troubled team's performance can be positively affected by momentum. In 1985 Constance Horner succeeded Donald Devine as head of the Office of Personnel Management, the agency that oversees three million federal employees. Under Devine, the department had been reorganized four times in as many years, and morale was so low that performance was at a virtual halt. The chief challenge facing Horner: how to improve synergy on her five-thousand-person team.

Many thought the task was impossible. "She took a job which is a walking opportunity to make enemies," former *Wall Street Journal* columnist Suzanne Garment told business writer Sal Vittolino. The job, Garment continued, "is a living, breathing invitation to disaster."

After a few years in office, however, many were touting Horner for boosting the esteem—and the productivity—

of her team. Horner improved team performance by creating more flexible rules, giving staffers more dynamic roles, and providing new avenues for recognition.

One of Horner's first moves was to overhaul ''the overly rigid system of rules and regulations that govern federal personnel, so that public employees can see a job that needs to be done and do it—without the delays and frustration and excessive regulation of their activity.''

Creating flexible rules is one way of empowering members of the team. Another way is decentralizing authority. Donald Devine, Horner's predecessor, had been described by at least one union leader as ''dictatorial.'' Horner, on the other hand, delegated authority to agencies under OPM's umbrella. Claudia Cooley, OPM's associate director of personnel systems, describes Horner as someone who ''understood the importance of giving line managers the authority to get their jobs done.''

Concerned that employees avoided innovation and risk because there was no reward system in place, Horner worked to institute pay increases based on performance rather than tenure. She also promoted a number of team members—career civil servants—to positions previously awarded to political appointees.

Horner didn't turn the elephant around completely, but by 1989, when her term at OPM was up, her team had developed recommendations for a host of reforms, including simplification of the personnel guidelines for federal employees; development of a comprehensive and compassionate AIDS policy for government workers; reduction in the number of civil service pay grades, elimination of automatic increases, and provision of increases based only on merit; and privatization of many federal services, a move that, if adopted, would trim the payroll by six hundred thousand and save an estimated $20 billion a year.

Failure to get the four R's in the right order is the single most common reason teams fail to become Star Teams. When a team gets the order right, sharing a common vision of results serves as a platform on which to build. If the other R's are put in place accordingly, the team gathers momentum and creates the synergy necessary to work out difficulties and achieve the desired results fueled by continuous recognition.

6 ☆

Choosing a Team and Joining

Many of us hesitate to join teams. Sometimes it's because we fear we'll be taken advantage of, that our hard work and effort will be credited to someone else. More often we resist teams because we feel we aren't ready to hold down a first-string position. We don't want to find ourselves in the spotlight until we know every move and are confident that we can give an error-free performance.

Players who take this point of view end up spending most of their careers in the bull pen warming up. The fact is, no one joins a team 100 percent confident of her abilities to play, and for good reason—you need to get into the game to mature as a player. You can warm up all you like, you can read and study and practice, but there are some things that can be learned only by joining a team and becoming part of the starting lineup.

All of us wonder whether or not we're ready to play, whether we have what it takes, whether we will make a costly error or blunder, and, above all, whether we are trying to join a team that plays above our skill level. Ironically, the opposite is more likely to be true. Women tend to place themselves on teams below, rather than above, their actual skill levels.

If I ask an administrative assistant to identify the team she plays on, she is apt to tell me she's ''just'' part of the ''secretarial team'' at present but hopes to advance in the future. This woman, not yet a Key Player but with the potential to become one, is holding herself back by only seeing herself as part of a "secretarial team." To become a Key Player, this woman must stop aligning herself with other secretaries; she must stop seeing herself as one of many interchangeable players in the secretarial bull pen.

In the 1960s Helen Gurley Brown set her sights on joining a magazine team. She had an impressive track record as the author of the best-selling *Sex and the Single Girl*, and her newspaper advice column was a favorite with young career women. Brown was convinced that a magazine geared to this young, curious, newly liberated audience would fly, and when she was given the chance to revamp the ailing *Cosmopolitan*, she didn't hesitate to join the team. Yet despite her strong track record and her conviction that her instincts were correct, Brown wasn't certain she was "ready" for the *Cosmo* team: years later she told an interviewer that on the eve of her first day at work, she'd been so scared she stood on Park Avenue and cried.

Many Key Players, like Brown, head into the game full of uncertainty. Unlike Brown, they don't always remember that they were afraid. Instead they remember feeling "challenged" and "stimulated" by the new opportunity that lay before them. Indeed, the need to be challenged by new experiences—one of the five star qualities shared by Key Players—is the positive reframing of the initial self-doubt and apprehension experienced when joining a team. The difference between women who remain players and women who become Key Players is that Key Players don't let the uncertainty stop them. Instead they pick a team, join up, and get into the action.

TEAMING UP

You don't have to wait until you change jobs to join a team. In fact, you shouldn't wait. No matter what job you currently hold, no matter what your career plans are, you can—and should—begin to develop your team strategy.

Joining a team isn't automatic. To become a full-fledged member of any team, you must do more than fill a job description. To see how true this is, try a quick experiment. Make a list of the players on your immediate work team, the vital people without whom you could not perform your own job. No doubt there will be one or two names you overlooked, people who could and should be on your list but remain on the shadowy sidelines. These people have failed to join the team, not because they are lazy or incompetent, but because no one has yet shown them how to go about it.

Since the idea of using teams to advance your career is relatively new, you yourself may be in this category. If you've been at your job for some time, turning in an excellent performance and watching others around you advance while you remained stuck, the reason may be that you've never joined your team. Players who bond with their jobs rather than with their teams stay in those jobs. Players who bond with their teams have more latitude: teammates open doors for each other, provide each other with opportunities, and move ahead together.

What if the team you currently belong to isn't a Star Team? There's no law that says you can only play on one team at a time. In fact, as we'll see, playing on more than one team will help you become a Key Player. If your job places you on a team that doesn't provide you with recognition or opportunity, look for an auxiliary team to join, such as a temporary team or a transition team—both can provide you with visibility as well as connections with other Key Players.

No matter what your situation, whether you are joining a team you are already familiar with or are switching jobs and linking up with a whole new team, joining up is, or should be, a five stage process. Skip any of the stages and you may find you've made a bad match. Invariably, women who make good team matches—matches that get them onto Star Teams—move through the five stages listed below. They aren't always aware of passing through each stage, but when I question them closely, I see the same pattern emerge.

THE FIVE STAGES OF JOINING A TEAM

- *STAGE #1: Scout the team.*
- *STAGE #2: Decide to join.*
- *STAGE #3: Put yourself in the picture.*
- *STAGE #4: Get on the roster.*
- *STAGE #5: Pass the initiation.*

STAGE #1: SCOUT THE TEAM

"When I'm interviewing people," says Lois Rice, "I find that most of them have read a lot about the company. They can spout back what they've read about us, so I'm careful to ask questions that can't be answered from memory."

What Rice, as a team leader, is looking for is proof that candidates have done more than research the corporation. She wants people who know how her team functions on a day-to-day basis and have a clear understanding of what the position they're applying for entails. For this reason she advises players intent on joining her team to "interview people [in the company] before you come to your interview. If you're a candidate for personal banker or business banker, talk to people who hold those positions. Find out what the reality of the job is, what they like and what they don't like."

The scouting procedure, Rice believes, should continue right through the interview. "People find it intimidating to ask questions during an interview," she says. "Most people would rather be questioned themselves. But I'm looking for people who ask the right questions."

From a team leader's point of view, Rice has found that the more understanding a candidate has about the team, the better. Employee dissatisfaction and turnover, she says, are much lower when people's expectations fit reality.

Before you can join any team successfully, you must understand it thoroughly. Here's a checklist of facts you should know about any team you're thinking of playing on:

Team Facts: A Twenty-Point Checklist

To assess a team, you should discover

- what type of team it is.
- the team history: teams have track records just as individuals do; it's important to know whether the team is a rising or a falling star.
- the team's current status: is the team in a viable, expanding, profitable division of the company or industry, or is its future limited by factors over which it has no control?
- personnel changes: who's been dropped from the roster and why.
- what the reward system is: are Key Players given recognition, new opportunity, promotions, or salary increases?
- what the penalty system is: is the team flexible enough to allow for some mistakes?
- who's currently in the starting lineup: know every player on the team and what his or her job is.
- who fills the roles: know which of the key roles (described in chapter 9: "Key Roles for Key Players") are filled and identify the players who fill them.
- what the expected results are: what the corporation expects the team to accomplish, or in the case of an entrepreneurial team, what results are necessary for the team to remain in business.

- what the team's goals are (unless goals promote desirable results, the team isn't a Star Team).
- what the team's rules are: know both the written and the unwritten rules (see chapter 5, "How Star Teams Work," page 113, to learn more about team rules).
- what the team rituals are (see chapter 5, "How Star Teams Work," to learn more about team rituals).
- what it takes to play on the team: study the Key Players on the team to discover what skills and experiences are necessary to become a Key Player yourself.
- what it takes to play each position: find out exactly what's involved in the job you would fill on the team; what's written in the formal job description may bear only a loose resemblance to reality.
- what learning experiences you will have on the team: what the team does that would add to your knowledge and experience.
- how the team deals with setbacks and difficulties.
- how disputes are settled.
- what team members say is positive about the team.
- what team members find fault with on the team.
- where other members of this team have gone after leaving the team: did playing on the team help their careers? Were they in higher demand for having played on the team?

STAGE #2: DECIDE TO JOIN

Players join the first team they come across; Key Players decide which teams to join.

"I chose that team," says Ellen Boughn of her recent move from self-employed entrepreneur to team leader on an intrapreneurial crew. When her photo stock company, After Image, needed an infusion of capital, Boughn had a few alternatives open to her. She could sell her company outright, sell it and stay on as a manager, or, she says, "I could have gathered the resources and the capital to continue on my own, even though I was pretty tired of doing it on my own."

Boughn was ambivalent about the choices open to her. Tired of going it alone, she was also uncertain about working for someone else. Her personality and background left her with an antiteam bias, and only recently, through her course work at the John Anderson Graduate School of Management at UCLA, has she learned the positive value of teamwork. Could Boughn take what she'd learned in school into the "real" world of business? She wasn't at all certain. "I had an honest conversation with myself," she says. "I began by asking myself, 'Can you have a boss? Can you work on a team?' "

Boughn decided she could play on a team if the conditions were right. Being in charge—the team leader—and retaining a degree of autonomy was important for her, and she began looking for the right team to join. "All the way along the line," she says, "I did a lot of footwork and homework."

Knowing what she needed from a team paid off for Boughn: she sold her company to London-based Tony Stone Worldwide and became an intrapreneur. Still in charge of the company she created, Boughn also has the backing of a large, international team. "I feel lucky," Boughn says, then corrects herself. "No, I don't feel lucky. I created this for myself. I knew what environment I wanted, and also I knew what I would have to have to make it work."

Boughn's right. She wasn't lucky, she was smart. She looked at her needs, examined various teams to see what they were offering, and made the best-possible match for herself.

In the course of the corporate steeplechase, many of us forget to examine our own needs. A successful match is a two-way street: it isn't only a question of whether you fit the team: it's also a question of whether the team fits you. Before you put yourself through the ordeal of trying out, make sure you've examined both sides of the question. Decide to join a team only if it meets some of your career needs. If it doesn't, look elsewhere.

Before you decide to join a team, sit down—as Ellen

Boughn did—and ask yourself some searchingly honest questions. Here are some good ones to start with:

Are You Right for the Team?

1. Is there an open position? (If all the jobs are filled, the team doesn't need you.)
2. Why can you fill the position better than another candidate? (You'd better know how to answer.)
3. Can you embrace the team goals? Are they in sync with your own?
4. Can you support the team rules?
5. Are you willing to join the team in its rituals?

Is the Team Right for You?

1. Is the team a Star Team?
2. If the team isn't a Star Team, can it contribute to your career anyway? How will you gain an important experience or opportunity by playing on it?
3. Who are the Key Players on the team with whom you want to work?
4. What good work can you yourself do on the team?
5. What about the team excites you?

I wish all of us could join Star Teams all the time. I believe that as teams continue to proliferate in the workplace and Star Teams win the race for survival of the fittest, there will indeed be more and more Star Teams at all levels and in all fields. Now, while the corporate elephant is still turning itself around, we're living—and working—in a time of transition. Some of the teams surrounding us may be Star Teams; some are not.

If there isn't a Star Team for you to play on, don't lose heart: playing on a mediocre team is almost always better than playing on no team at all. You'll learn the basics of team play, you'll make connections with people who may figure in your future, and—if you choose wisely and play well—you'll be able to increase your worth as a player.

I once encountered a unique group of women who had

met each other while working, in different capacities, for a small book packager. In publishing a packager is someone who creates a book idea, sells the idea to an interested publisher, then hires the writers and editors needed to create a finished product. What struck me about these women was that they were all Key Players, yet the team they had played on together was anything but a Star Team. Salaries were small, tensions were high, recognition was virtually nonexistent, and the team leader—who owned the company—had a known talent for burning people out.

Since these women were talented enough to get jobs elsewhere and smart enough to know what they were getting into, I wondered why each had joined such a team. Each, as it turned out, had a perfectly logical answer. One of the women, a novelist, wanted to build up her credits in nonfiction writing. A second woman, previously an editor at a large publishing house, wanted the chance to develop book ideas of her own. The third woman, fresh from college, chose to join this small, troubled team as an editor rather than signing on as an editorial assistant at a larger house and waiting for advancement.

Each of these women stayed on the team long enough to get what she needed, then moved on. Each moved to a better position on a better team; each sought—and received—a better salary. While the team they'd played on together hadn't been a Star Team, they went on to form an informal transorganizational Star Team of their own, bouncing ideas off each other, throwing opportunities each other's way, and giving each other excellent word-of-mouth publicity in their field.

STEP #3: PUT YOURSELF IN THE PICTURE

Once you choose a team, you need to begin mentally reshaping that team: seeing—and planning—how the team will perform differently because of your presence. The fact is, the team with you on it had better be different from the team without you on it. If the team performs exactly the same after you join as before, it means you aren't making an impact. You haven't succeeded in making yourself an essential part of the team.

Putting yourself in the picture means seeing, before you join, exactly where you will fit in: what work you will do, what roles you will fill, what players you will work most closely with, and what connections you will need to make. In a way, it's like preparing a military strategy map—only in this case your mission is not to attack, destroy, or conquer, but to integrate and merge, enhance and strengthen.

According to Cheryl Stern, entry-level players and players who come on board at a higher level have two very different tasks facing them. Entry-level jobs tend to be defined by the corporation: there are set tasks the employee is expected to perform. The question isn't so much how the employee will fit into the team today, but where that "fit" will lead to tomorrow. "The beginning team player," Stern says, "has to say, 'Is there a role in that job that I would like to play somewhere down the line?' " The entry-level player needs to get a picture of where she wants to go on the team in order to start working in the right direction.

The player who joins the team at a higher level, however, has a different responsibility. The higher you go, the less "pre-set" the job is. "If you're coming in at a middle level," says Stern, "you've got to bring in something that doesn't already exist." The higher up the ladder you go, the more a job is the product of the individual who fills it. A coach in the NFL is expected to win, but beyond that, there are very few givens. He can call all the plays himself, rely on his offensive and defensive coaches, or let the quarterback call the plays from the huddle. He can encourage his team to interact with reporters or make themselves unavailable. He can require a practice session the day before the Super Bowl or tell his players to take the day off and enjoy themselves. He can do just about anything he wants, but if his presence doesn't significantly lift the level of team play, he'll find out that NFL can also stand for "Not for Long."

What happens if you skip this stage, counting on your instincts to lead you once you get on the team? First, you may not be able to convince the team to take you on if you don't demonstrate an awareness of what you can do once you get there. Even if you do get on the team, you may find yourself in trouble. Michael Dukakis, a talented and capable player, was able to get onto the Democratic team at the highest position available. Once there, he floundered: not because he was intellectually or politically inadequate, but because he wasn't prepared. He hadn't devoted sufficient time or energy to putting himself in the picture.

STAGE #4: GET ON THE ROSTER

The invitation to join the team usually comes from the team leader. To get this invitation, you need to demonstrate your mastery of Stages #1, #2, and #3, as Gwen McCane did when she approached a potential client whose team she wanted very much to join.

Before Gwen McCane became the director of member services at the Oakland Athletic Club, she worked as a color consultant. "I had learned how colors can be used to project images and influence mood," she says. When McCane learned that the transit system was having problems with their employees, she knew she had the information she needed to try out for the team. (Notice that "getting on the team" doesn't always mean becoming an employee; it can mean, as it does here, connecting with a new client.)

McCane designed a new color scheme for transit system employees, choosing blue, burgundy, off white, and blue gray. "The next day," she says, "I called the assistant general manager's office and asked if I could have a meeting with him. I went into his office and told him, up-front, what I was there for. I pointed out that his own appearance was picture perfect. This man was a very sharp dresser. I asked him why his drivers didn't look the way he looked. When I finished talking with him, I walked out of there with a contract to design new uniforms.''

McCane knew her client was an avid sports fan. As a real estate agent, she had sold many houses to professional baseball players in the area. She could have played off her prospective client's interest in sports and spent the first part of the interview talking baseball. She chose not to. Instead she focused immediately on her goal—presenting her idea about the new uniforms. McCane might have made the deal even if she had started out talking baseball, but she might also have conveyed the idea that her plan for new uniforms was little more than an afterthought, something she was just toying with. She might have lost her client's interest, since attention span is limited; or she might simply have run out of time and found herself shuffled out of the office before she'd approached her subject.

Notice, too, the order in which McCane made her points. Although she came to the interview with a color scheme in mind, she didn't begin by saying, ''I think your employees would look terrific in these blue, burgundy, and white uniforms.'' Instead she demonstrated her knowledge of the team. She discussed the behavioral problems the team leader was having with his employees. In other words, she identified a ''hole'' in the team, a way in which the team was being held back because no one was effectively filling the role of harmonizer. McCane showed how she could fill that role by designing a uniform whose calming yet businesslike colors would lift employee morale. In doing this, she was showing how her presence would help the team work better.

In identifying the problems facing the transit system, McCane didn't present new information. The assistant general manager was well aware of the problems facing him. What McCane presented was an understanding of the team and a unique contribution that would improve team play. It isn't hard to see why she landed the contract.

If you're joining a team that's entirely new to you, the

invitation will be formal—the offer of a job, landing a contract, or being named to a task force or quality circle. If you're joining a team that's existed around you for some time, a team you should have linked up with some time ago, the "invitation" will be subtle. If your team leader begins asking you to more meetings, gives you more challenging work to do, encourages or facilitates your relationship with other members of the team, begins speaking in terms of the future, asks your opinion, or puts you in charge of other members of the team, make no mistake about it—you're on the roster.

STAGE #5: PASS THE INITIATION

Being chosen by the team leader is one thing; being accepted by your teammates is another. All of us have an inherent suspicion of strangers. The same impulses that led us, as children, to ostracize and tease the new kid in class have been tamed only slightly. When we join a team, we go through a probationary period with our teammates during which they will test, observe, and make up their minds about us in their own fashion. If we join predominantly male teams, as many of us do, this probationary period often takes the form of a series of baffling and inscrutably adolescent pranks.

When Karen Krizan began her career as one of New York's Finest, on foot patrol in East Harlem, the guys on her team hazed her mercilessly. They referred to her as "sweetheart," the same term they use for prostitutes; they stepped up the level of swearing and vulgarity when she walked into a room; when she wanted to leave her beat to use the bathroom, one sergeant insisted that she call in the request over her radio, alerting every squad car and fellow cop that she needed to "take a personal."

Joining the team at a high level won't keep you from being hazed, either. When Krizan, now a sergeant, took over the Ninety-fourth Precinct Detective Squad, she went through another probationary phase. Sometimes the pranks had a point—like the picture of a witch posted on her door in response to her yelling at someone—but just as often they seemed pointless. One day an envelope marked "Rattlesnake Eggs" was left on her desk. When Krizan picked up the envelope, the eggs rattled. Startled, Krizan dropped the envelope. The boys thought this was hilarious. Next came the "coordination test," in which a detective asked Krizan to roll the edge of a quarter over her face with one hand. Since the edge of the quarter had been heavily marked with lead, Krizan was left with pencil tracks over her face. Once again the boys thought it was hilarious.

Krizan didn't get too upset over these incidents. Instead she surprised her new teammates by laughing with them.

But what's behind these *Animal House*-style pranks? Deborah Slaner Anderson says, "People test each other, and men and women do it in different ways. My experience has been that when women get into environments with men, they feel the men are testing them because they're women. We're not as quick to understand that men test each other, too. Whether it's about their virility, their competence, or their looks, they test each other. If a man grows a mustache, another man will say, 'What's that caterpillar on your lip?' Anything to see how the person will react.

"When a woman comes into the room, they may call her a girl or they may say something derogatory. They're doing it to see how she will react. Can she stand the pressure? Does she know the rules of the game? And the rules of the game, on most teams, are about testing each other. People aren't supposed to take it personally. It's part of the initiation."

Cindy Webster expresses a similar point of view. "When you are in an unfamiliar team environment, innocuous actions can be mistaken for personal attacks. Joining the team looks impossible. And, indeed, it is frustrating and difficult." To join the previously all-male culture of the fire service, Webster made an "objective inquiry," looking at her new team as if she were an anthropologist. "I asked myself, 'What's the culture here? What are the game rules? Let me explore this new culture.' I realized I wouldn't be accepted immediately because I was in a new culture. When people join a team in a fire station or a bank or any kind of new environment, they should not take it personally if people won't relate to them right away. You'll be more successful if you take an objective approach. To be accepted, you have to see the structure of the team and learn what the rules are."

Krizan sensed this and passed the test by not taking the pranks personally. Instead of getting mad or feeling victimized, she laughed it off and went back to work.

This was exactly the right thing to do. "Men," says Anderson, "like to show they can roll with the punches. They like to prove that they can take it and give it back. Then they're part of the team. They assume that everybody knows these rules, and they get very confused when women don't know how to play [their] game."

To pass initiation rites devised by men, you have to maintain a sense of humor and "play through" the prank by getting on with your work. "If you react by getting flustered or distracted," Anderson says, "you won't get on the team."

Krizan didn't get distracted by the pranks her teammates pulled. She kept her sense of humor and her focus and didn't let their hazing interfere with her job performance. Despite the witch picture left on her door, she continued to take detectives to task whenever the need arose. Like Cindy Webster, Krizan demonstrated a willingness to look at the team, figure out its rules, and adapt to them. Displaying another Key Player trait, she demonstrated her ability to stay focused on goals and results.

Besides checking your sense of humor and your understanding of the rules, men haze for another reason: to determine whether the newcomer will stand her ground or if she can, in fact, be pushed around.

One of the most common tests women are given is what I call the "coffee test"—as in, "Honey, get us some coffee.'' Gerry Cunningham, now a plant manager with Jostens, had just come on board the company when she was given the test. "I had been there probably three months," she says. "I was walking down the hall one day and I passed by one of the bosses' offices. He was in there with another man, a man who also ranked above me. He called out, 'Cunningham, get me a cup of coffee,' and tossed a quarter at me. For a minute I just looked at him. On one hand, I was new and he was my boss. On the other hand, I wanted to set a tone. I explained, 'If you had a broken leg and couldn't get up, I would graciously get you a cup of coffee. Or if you said to me, "Gerry, I'm so busy right now. Are you busy? Would you mind getting me a cup of coffee?" then I probably would get you a cup of coffee. But I don't do it otherwise.' Then I walked away.''

Cunningham never suffered reprisals for her firm stand. Just the opposite. "I'm sure he told all the guys that I did that,'' she says, "and that got the point across, that the rules were going to be the same for me as they were for everybody else.''

Even if your team is highly civilized and free of the obvious pranks described above, you will have to prove to your teammates that you belong on the team. When Gerry Cunningham became a plant manager, she was viewed with skepticism. "The men were very frank about it,'' she says. "They would openly ask me, 'How did a woman get to be a plant manager?' I told them, 'Well, I'm very smart. I've worked hard and I'm the best person for the job. You have faith in my predecessor, don't you?' The men would say yes because my predecessor, who is still my boss, was very highly respected. Then I'd say, 'He was the one who chose me, so I must be pretty good.' They were completely satisfied with this answer.''

You can pass the initiation rites and make the team if you, like the Key Players above, maintain your sense of humor, refuse to be distracted, and stand your ground on the important points.

NOW THAT YOU'RE ON—MOVE UP

Once you're on the team, your next step is to move up to Key Player position. You can do this from any spot on the team, and you can do it without receiving a formal promotion. To become a Key Player, you must know how to do more than just perform your job—you must know how to help the team succeed. The next chapter will show you how to hone your team skills.

7 ☆

Honing Your Team Skills

> **WANTED**
>
> *Young, skinny, wiry fellows not over 18.*
>
> *Must be expert riders*
>
> *willing to face death daily.*
>
> *Orphans preferred.*

This is what it took to be a Pony Express rider in 1860. What it takes to join a Star Team of today is quite a bit different.

"Work should be a playground, an inspiration, an aesthetic thing, not a Monday-to-Friday sort of death," says Anita Roddick, co-founder and chief executive of Body Shop International, a London-based, environmentally conscious cosmetics firm with franchises in more than three dozen countries. When it's time to hire, Roddick and her managers say they look for individuals with enthusiasm, empathy, concern for the community, and creativity.

At first glance this sounds a lot like what I call "recruit speak," the virtually meaningless language that fills book after book of business advice: "Be enthusiastic!" "Be creative!" "Care about your company!"

As opposed to what? Do any of us think that unenthusiastic, uncreative, and uncaring might be the way to go? The problem with recruit-speak advice is that it's too obviously right.

As I interviewed Key Players in team-building positions, quite a few of them echoed Roddick. I was told that Key Players should be "enthusiastic," "ethical," "flexible," and "able to communicate." Yet as I listened, I became convinced that what I was hearing wasn't mere recruit speak. It was a new—and important—criteria for getting into the workplace.

EXCELLENCE PLUS

Key Players are no longer talking about the bottom-line-conscious "personal excellence" skills touted in past decades—not because these skills are no longer important, but because at Key Player level it's a given that you'll perform your job faster, better, and smarter than your colleagues. (If you're not up to speed on what it takes to excel in your field—brush up! See "Are You Prepared to Become a Key Player?" exercise on page 75).

"I need expertise in whatever the function is," says Karen Wegmann. "I look for people who have very good common sense. People who are well grounded. People who are adaptable."

Though this sounds like recruit speak, it isn't. Karen Wegmann and the other Key Players I interviewed are sharp, tough-minded businesswomen. When they look at potential players, they're looking for a lot more than corporate pep.

What Wegmann is doing is shorthanding—summing up a complex sequence of thoughts into an end result of one or two words. You've already seen a good example of shorthanding in the case of Key Players who strive to perceive their work as fun because they realize fun is a tremendously useful stimulus. Decoded, Wegmann's message is tougher—and smarter—than it seems. First, she tells us that only peak performers can try out for her team: "I need expertise in whatever the function is." Then she lists a number of capabilities that go above and beyond job expertise. In demanding common sense, stability, and adaptability, Wegmann is saying, "You must have a certain range of team skills to play for me. If you aren't going to make our team stronger, I'm not going to take you on."

Wegmann didn't arrive at this decision because she thought it would be "nice" to have a harmonious team. Rather, she knows that team disharmony is expensive. In today's highly competitive business climate, interpersonal conflicts, missed communications, and enfant terrible geniuses represent a waste of resources. Getting "lean" extends far beyond slashing expense accounts and firing middle managers. Once business gets lean, it has to learn to operate lean, and operating lean means creating efficient teams.

Key Players in team-building positions demand a combination of job skills and team capabilities. Players who don't come to the game with the right package aren't going to get onto the team.

STAR SEARCH: THE FIVE REQUIREMENTS

#1: You must be ready to play at all times.
#2: You must promote team performance.
#3: You must keep the level of the game high.
#4: You must be reliable in the huddle.
#5: You must know how to score from any position.

This is the message I heard over and over again, though it was often shorthanded to me in requests for "enthusiastic," "ethical," and "flexible" employees. When I filled in the blanks, listening and observing carefully to catch the meaning behind each word, I discovered there are five requirements Key Players look for in potential teammates, each of them above and beyond expertise on the job.

Understanding what these requirements are and why they're valued can get you onto a Star Team in starting position. Dismissing them as recruit speak can keep you on the bench forever.

#1: YOU MUST BE READY TO PLAY AT ALL TIMES

"I advise women to stay on top of their health," says Sharon Richardson Jones. "We can't make the mistake of thinking the second half of life is going to be easy. For women who have energy, there will be new opportunities and new challenges."

On a sports team, being ready to play means being mentally and physically in shape for the game; it means being suited up and ready to go; it means being eager to get out of the clubhouse and off the bench and onto the playing field. Being ready to play in business means the same thing. You must be well rested, well nourished, and fit for the game every day. You must dress as the players on your team dress. You must know the plays because, in the heat of action, no one is going to call time out and wait for you to catch up. Above all, you must want to be part of the game.

In the realm of professional sports, clock watching is virtually unknown. Players become so involved in the game, they forget what quarter, period, or inning it is. If someone has to sit out for a few minutes, you'll see him pacing the sidelines as if being out of the game were the greatest punishment in the world. This player is absolutely convinced that his team can't win without him. He sees himself and his team as one, and watching the game flow on without him is painful.

If we could transfer this attitude from the world of professional sports to the world of business—if we could clear the benches of the clock watchers and the not-my-jobbers—America's productivity problem would be solved. We'd be on our way to building a nation of Star Teams and Key Players. If you have any doubts about how far this attitude can take us, look at the level of professional sports in America. It's ironic that sports teams have produced a superlative product by applying principles that businesses should use, but seldom do.

If you're not ready to play the game, someone on your team will have to get you in shape to play. If you don't keep yourself mentally and physically healthy every day, your performance will drop and one of your teammates will have to cover for you. Team leaders know this, but none of them articulate it precisely this way. Instead they shorthand the information by asking for "energy," "enthusiasm," and "self-motivation."

"When I interview a person, I look for a willingness to go the extra mile," says Lois Rice. "I am not looking for the smartest person in the world. There's more to life than grades. I am looking for the person who is willing to step out and make a difference every day. If a person has that willingness, then I can provide her with opportunity."

Rice says she discovers whether a candidate has the necessary energy "through questioning that has nothing to do with the bank. For example, I notice if someone's worked her way through college. I look at the energy and forthrightness with which they answer questions. You can find out a lot if you're so inclined." Rice adds that her company had learned "the hard way" that extensive screening keeps costly employee turnover to a minimum.

By the time a candidate reaches Rice, she has had at least four other interviews. "What I don't want, and what I tell them I don't want," says Rice, "is someone whose concept of the job doesn't match reality. Banking used to be a world in which you did what you were told and that was that. You never had to think. Now, you've got to think. This is a time of tremendous change. People can't be content to let things go on around them. They have got to take ownership of their actions and make things happen."

The emphasis on players who can "make things happen" ("self-starter" in entry-level placement lingo) came up often, possibly because it's a concept we still haven't grasped. I see far too many women who've bought into the notion that if you perform well and study the play book diligently, the coach will realize you're ready to play and pick you for the team.

Remember how choosing up sides worked in grade school? Whoever got to be captain quickly filled her team with friends. Her best friends were picked first, second best next, and so on down the line. If you weren't friends with the captain, you experienced the humiliation of being the last chosen, even if as a player you were as good as—or better than—the captain's friends.

Well, business works in much the same way. As women we haven't always had time to get to know the captains. When it's time to choose sides, they sometimes don't see us in the crowd of faces. Though this has been called the "old boy network," it's really just an old network, a collection of familiar names and faces. If we have a let-things-happen attitude, if we wait to be chosen, we're going to spend our whole careers waiting to get onto a Star Team.

"I tell women that if you want something, go out and get it," says Ann Picciuto, who teaches a workshop in corporate gamesmanship in addition to her position with a Fortune 500 electronics company. "No one is going to tap you on the shoulder and say, 'Oh, by the way, you've been selected.' You've got to break down the door and say, 'Hey! I'm here and I'm going to play.' "

There's one important advantage we have now that we didn't have in the schoolyard: Business isn't a game. The stakes are real and very high. When you were eleven and didn't know the captain, no amount of effort could get you on the team. Now, you can make things happen. By showing up ready to play, you can win a spot on the team.

Key Players are quick to notice—and demonstrate—determination to play. Lois Rice says, "It's easy to be better than average. You come in early, you work late a few times. You show that you're able to do more than your fair share. People who are interested in total equality will not thrive here. Life is not equal. We're a performance-oriented company. People who work harder and smarter get ahead quicker.''

When I ask Pastor Margaret Rush to name the Key Players on her team at Denver's Emmanuel Methodist Church, her post immediately before moving up to district superintendent, she names her secretary. "Nancy was more than I bargained for. She had enormous self-motivation. If I mentioned producing a brochure for new members, she wouldn't wait until I had time to get the project going. She would come back to me and say, 'I tried this on the computer. How does it look to you?' ''

Key Players in team-building positions want people with zest, energy, and a willingness to go the extra mile. What they don't want is workaholics. Many of them went out of their way to tell me this, and a few of them cited workaholic periods in their own careers as pitfalls.

Lauraine Brekke worked for the city of Seattle and for Seattle's King County before moving south. "The county executive I worked for was a workaholic, so I became a workaholic. I worked my tail off. I never worked harder than I worked there. When I look back on that period now, I say, 'That was crazy. Nobody should have to work like that.' ''

Cheryl Stern goes out of her way to avoid hiring workaholics. "I think working eighty hours a week is a myth," she says. "I think anybody who's working that many hours needs to figure out what she's doing. I am very suspicious about people who work like that in a corporate structure. They're not doing it right. And I am not in business to burn anybody out. I am very conscientious about that, always. The business we're in is a front-line, customer-service one. People can get tired. Stale. Burnout can cause a lot of damage.''

Workaholism, as many of us have learned firsthand, produces fallout: disrupted and fragmented personal lives, a nagging feeling that we've "missed out," and burnout on the job. If your performance drops because you're mentally and physically fatigued, if you have to take a leave of absence, if you're so exhausted you have to switch professions entirely, your whole team loses. The kind of burning ambition vaunted in the eighties didn't help individuals or their employers. Perhaps for this reason, I never once heard the word *ambition* during the course of my interviews. Instead Key Players told me they want people whose lives are well balanced and satisfied.

Sharon Maeda regularly counsels people who are no longer in playing condition. Her job is to pull them off the bench and get them ready to play again.

"Right now," she says, "we're working with a department of the city [of Seattle] that is being reorganized. Part of this department will go to a newly created department. Part of the staff will be absorbed into another department. Nobody's going to lose their job per se, but there's a lot of anxiety over the changes that are taking place. Our job is to help them cope with these changes over which they have no control and show them how to survive, personally and professionally, what may be a twelve-month period of uncertainty.

"The first thing I did with these people was sit them down in a group and make each of them tell me what they did to relax and ease the stress. Most people said, 'I don't have time to relax.' Two people, however, said, 'I don't take my work home with me. I enjoy my family. I'm busy with activities.' Of the people in the department, these two people had, by far, the most interests outside their work. These two people were not stressed out or exhausted by the situation. They accepted it as par for the course, as a new administration coming in and making changes. Their attitude was, 'This is yet another change, not that different from other changes.' "

Key Players know that people who live only to work lose their resilience and their zest. They go on showing up day after day, but they're no longer in shape to play the game.

I expected Key Players to tell me they stayed in shape for the game by physically relaxing, by taking time off to do nothing, by going on retreats and giving their minds a lot of "down time." Nothing could have been farther from the truth.

For Key Players, staying fresh means staying involved. "You must put balance in your life," says Gerry Cunningham. "You must find a way to get out of your job and broaden your horizons."

Cunningham practices what she preaches, serving on the local board of the United Way and on the board of an industrial association. She isn't an exception. A majority of Key Players I interviewed are active in volunteer work or in professional organizations. Lois Rice's "hobby" is real estate development. "I have two partners who work full-time," she says, "and I work on the weekends. On our first project, I sold all sixty-eight houses myself. I love to sell."

These Key Players aren't unique. Rather, they mirror the tendency of bright, well-educated, high-achieving Americans to use their leisure time productively. In *On Photography*, Susan Sontag speculated that people from high work-ethic cultures see leisure time as the opportunity to do something pleasurably stimulating and satisfying. In *Megatrends 2000*, John Naisbitt and Patricia Aburdene found so many of us attending the symphony, going to museums, and participating in regional theater that they cite "renaissance in the arts" as one of their ten trends for the future.

Key Players are already part of the trend. They believe in contributing to the community and expanding personal horizons. Their unspoken belief that a whole person is a better employee prompts them to seek out players who are similarly involved. Listen to the words of Karen Wegmann:

"We have many employees all across the state of California who are involved in their communities. They have families, they have kids, and they find time to do volunteer work. They have an energy level that's extraordinary. It acts as a catalyst to the rest of the company. It makes us successful.''

#2: YOU MUST PROMOTE TEAM PERFORMANCE

Like many Key Players in team-building positions, Karen Wegmann uses deceptively gentle adjectives to describe what she wants in her employees. After telling me she looks for people who are ''flexible'' and ''adaptable,'' she adds, ''I look for people who genuinely care about the company.'' Then, couched between the comfort words, she delivers the hard message: ''I am not interested in somebody who wants a career at the expense of the company or other employees. I do not like, nor does Wells support, the concept of individual stars.''

There it is, the message of the 1990s. If you don't listen carefully, you're going to miss it. Many players have already been penalized for the oversight. In 1989 Douglas Aircraft, a subsidiary of McDonnell Douglas located in Long Beach, California, let five thousand managers go. Four thousand of the managers were rehired, but only after successfully passing personality tests that measured their ''team player'' abilities. In today's workplace you must facilitate the performance of the team you play on. Key Players value and protect the Star Teams they play on. They scout for players who will make the team stronger, who will help the whole team perform better and more efficiently.

When I ask Marilyn Weixel, human resources director at AGIA, to name the type of player she's tried hardest to avoid in her career, she says, ''The prima donna. You can't always spot a prima donna right away. But very quickly, as soon as you start working with her, you can tell. Then I think it's critical to admit that a mistake's been made. You need to say, 'This isn't right. This isn't working. This is not what we thought we were getting into. Let's talk about this and bail out if necessary.' ''

"The first question I ask when I interview," says Lois Rice, "is, 'Why Wells Fargo? Why do you want to work here?' My next question is, 'How do you think you're going to add value?' You've got to perform to get on board here, but performance is more than just numbers. Performance is also fitting in with a team, recognizing that you are just part of a team. If you want to succeed here, accepting and being accepted is crucial."

Rice echoes the team sentiments of a great many Key Players. This is why, when I talk to top executives, I hear the words *flexible* and *adaptable* so often. Playing effectively on a team requires compliance. The ability to co-operate is, as Carl Sagan points out in *The Dragons of Eden*, a sophisticated evolutionary development. It requires the individual to suppress his or her impulses long enough to communicate with the group, arrive at a consensus, and follow it through.

To play on a team, you must see yourself as a part of the universe, not the center of it. This is why managers seek employees who are "well grounded" and who don't have "egos." A player who is caught up in herself, who worries constantly about her career and her issues, is not going to promote team performance, she's going to impair it.

"People who have ego problems," says Gerry Cunningham, "are not good team players. When they see the team somehow compromising their personal interests, they can't see the big picture. They're more worried about what someone else is going to get or what they're not going to get. They're shortsighted. It's a killer."

Cunningham goes out of her way to make sure these people don't end up in positions that can affect the bottom line. When she assembles a special projects group, she says, the first thing she looks for after job expertise is "people who can work within a team and enjoy themselves within that team."

When a player is caught up in personal ego issues, she weakens her team by switching from a "we" position to an "I versus you" position. When one person on a team sees herself as separate, she divides the entire team. As women, we often think men have a lock on "ego" issues, but this isn't the case. Key Players I talked to cited one particularly female ego problem that often gets in the way of team play: seeing ourselves as part of an oppressed minority.

As a black woman in the predominantly white male world of professional baseball management, Sharon Richardson Jones could see herself as a minority. She doesn't. Instead she says, "Certainly there is racism. There is sexism. There is ageism. But all these 'isms,' including amateurism, are kicking us in the rear. We must accept being women, or being third-world women, and move on with it." Jones sees her team not as part of the problem, but as part of the solution. "The way to get over these hurdles is to arm yourself with a good education, a creative mind, and good people."

Remember how many Key Players emphasized the importance of picking your battles? This is the reason. If you fight every battle, you channel much of your time, energy, and talent away from your team and its goals. Knowing how to overlook unimportant issues and being able to focus on teamwork is part of flexibility, too.

As I listened to team leaders talk about the need for flexibility, I realized they were talking about more than being able to be part of a group. They were also talking about the ability to change directions with the team. I began this book by discussing the many changes now shaping the business world. Change is the order of the day, and team leaders are ever mindful of the fact. Once upon a time, an obsolete team might have been permitted to continue within the corporation. Today that isn't the case. Teams are regularly remade, broken up, and recombined, "refitted" with new procedures, and asked to perform a completely new task.

Lois Rice, who's been with Wells Fargo for more than twenty years and risen from teller to executive vice-president, credits her longevity and success to her ability to change. "The reason I haven't had to change companies,'' she says, ''is because I've changed. That's the key. Flexibility is one of the most important things I look for when I interview people. If you aren't flexible and adaptable, this is the wrong company for you. Things are going to change every single day. You've got to be able to change with the environment. That is the world of the nineties.''

Gerry Cunningham says, ''I look for people who are open to learning something else, an enhancement to the skills they already have. An engineer cannot function solely because he or she is a great engineer. This person has to be open to learning how the department works. He or she has to be able to integrate production knowledge with office technology like computer entry. I look for someone who's open-minded in that way.''

Sharon Richardson Jones prides herself on her open-mindedness. ''I am teachable,'' she says. Maintaining this kind of flexibility, Jones believes, is the ticket to job security in the future. ''We've got to be able to be activated at the age of fifty to try something new. Instead of being on the down side, we have to be as enthusiastic and energetic as anyone who is entering the work force.''

When you're able to switch directions, embrace new goals, and learn with ease, you strengthen your team. Players who can't—or won't—adapt to a changed environment weaken their teams. They slow efficiency because someone must now coax them to change, deal with their disgruntled feelings, and walk them through the process. A lot of time and energy that should be going into the team's product is now being funneled into one team player. Even worse, the resistant player undermines team spirit by opposing the team. You may have seen this happen a few times yourself. The team is shown a new procedure or given a new assignment, and an unhappy coalition wastes weeks grumbling about how ''unfair,'' ''difficult,'' or ''stupid'' the new directive is.

Karen Wegmann's hard-line attitude sums up the team-first position Key Players maintain. ''We don't placate people in this company. Someone who is miserable makes other people miserable. I feel no remorse when that person goes. I have found out that anyone can have a job. There are a million jobs out there, and I don't know anyone who's left here who hasn't found a job. No one has to work here. I tell people that. I try to say it more gently, but that's what I tell them. I feel very strongly that everyone has a choice to make. I've made many choices in my life. Some of them have been good and some of them haven't been so good. It's up to the individual. If you don't like it here, don't whine every day. Leave. Go find something you like.''

Key Players are extremely aware of the fact that esprit de corps is at the heart of team performance. To this end, they seek out players whose personalities will nurture the team and keep it strong.

Sharon Maeda, who founded Spectra Communications with three other women, tells an interesting story about the demise of her team. Despite the fact that her partners were bright and accomplished, one by one they left the company. Maeda remained, took sole possession of Spectra, and went on to create a new team. To Maeda's surprise, the company's business adviser had picked her out as the ''survivor'' months earlier.

''He said he knew I would be the one who lasted the first time he met with all four of us,'' she says. ''When I pointed out that my partners were talented and experienced, he said, 'Skills are one thing. But you are the one who can convince people. That's probably why they agreed to be partners with you so quickly. You convinced them and they believed you. They didn't stop to think of what the down side would be or that their personal needs would get in the way. They were swept away by what you told them. They loved the idea without thinking how difficult it was going to be or the price they were going to have to pay in order to make it work.''

Though the team ran into insurmountable differences, the force of Maeda's personality brought it together and held it together for some time. This is leadership, something Key Players look for in every person they recruit.

You can provide it in a number of ways. First, like Maeda, you can maintain an infectious "can do" attitude. "You have to go into something with a positive attitude," says Gwen McCane. "You have to keep saying 'I can do it. I can do it.'" McCane believes the one reason people gravitate to her is because she is able to project a positive image. "It has to be genuine, too," she adds. "You can't fool people."

Another way to promote team well-being is to remain calm in a crisis. When a setback occurs, the whole team receives an emotional shock. People who are ordinarily competent do things they would not ordinarily do: they express doubts, they talk about the "terrible" thing that has happened, they blame each other for the disaster that has occurred. Unless someone stays calm, the whole team will end up in a feeding frenzy of despair. One calm voice, however, can stop the tailspin. You don't have to have a recovery plan up your sleeve—you just have to insist that recovery is possible. This is usually enough to get the team back on track.

One of the most overlooked ways to strengthen your team is to lessen tension and create esprit de corps with the careful use of humor. "In church work," says Pastor Margaret Rush, "you deal with family problems, deaths, all kinds of crises. If ministers and other church workers can't break the tension and laugh together, you're in trouble. When I was choosing an associate minister, we wrote 'sense of humor' into the qualifications."

The value of humor isn't confined to high-tension fields like the ministry. A friend of mine who ran a midsize printing company in Atlanta recently hired a new sales manager. He narrowed down the pool of applicants to three—all women and all excellently qualified. One he ruled out on the basis of her appearance. Sloppily dressed, she was all wrong for a position that required heavy contact with customers—she didn't present a "ready to play at all times" appearance. The other two were impossible to choose between. Both were ready to play, and both had an impressive track record at their previous jobs. In a quandary, my friend called an executive recruiter female acquaintance of his and asked for help. "Easy," the headhunter said. "Hire the one who makes you laugh." My friend took the advice and has never regretted it.

Shared laughter is one of the rituals that converts a group of strangers into a team of comrades. It makes people comfortable with each other, and comfort is a tremendous stimulant to team productivity. "I don't think I'm charismatic," say Lauraine Brekke, "but I project friendliness."

Lauraine Brekke is a team leader in a powerful position, but you don't have to be a manager to lead your team emotionally. It's important to remember that leadership doesn't always mean directing people or being "in charge." It means influencing—keeping team spirit high and team efficiency strong by "leading" with your attitude. If you can do this, you'll be respected as a leader—and a Key Player—regardless of your official position on the team.

#3: YOU MUST KEEP THE LEVEL OF THE GAME HIGH

"Keeping the level of the game high" means doing top-quality work and keeping team spirit strong. It also means sharing your team's values. While Key Players often expressed the desirability of a culturally diverse team, they also emphasized the importance of shared values.

Catherine Morrison says, "Cathie [Assemblywoman Wright] and I complement each other. Culturally, she has a volatile, classically Italian approach to life. I have a restrained English approach. Professionally we meet somewhere in the middle, and that's proven effective. We share the same basic values. Our approaches are different, and that makes our work dynamic."

What "shared values" means is ethics. To understand why ethics matter to team leaders, think back to how and why ethical codes developed in the first place. Without standards for behavior, the group devolves into a mob and it's every woman for herself. Ethics free people to function and achieve as a team.

Ethics are also important for practical reasons. If one person on the team doesn't keep the standard of the game high, suspicion will fall on the entire team. The team will be regarded throughout the department, the corporation, and the industry as not to be trusted. The team will have a tarnished reputation, and everyone on the team will suffer. Team leaders have a primary obligation to protect their teams and keep team reputation intact. When they evaluate individual players, they demand players who will share these values and maintain high standards of gamesmanship.

"Integrity is the first characteristic I look for," says Barbara Uehling, chancellor of UCSB. "I've learned that you can't impose values on people. You've got to start where they are." Uehling wants to make sure everyone on her team "starts" from the same high level.

"You cannot develop a new set of ethics to fit each new situation," says Ann Picciuto. "Ethics are consistent and permanent." In the course of working for an electronics company, Picciuto has frequently been in charge of on-site audits of subsidiary companies. "My ethics have been tested many times," she continues. "I've had a company president say to me, 'Don't come audit us. Here are tickets to New York. Go enjoy yourself. See some shows. Go out to dinner. We'll pick up the tab. We'll cover for you.' If you compromise your ethics once, it's all over. You must keep yourself above reproach."

In the notoriously cutthroat world of commercial real estate, Lynn Williams takes pride in playing on a team that maintains high ethical standards. "There is a set of ethics Cushman Realty adheres to that I am comfortable with," she says. "There was one very large transaction that John Cushman and I worked on together. We were very close to the end of negotiations and had worked out the major points." At the last minute, she says, the client got greedy. He felt the landlord was so anxious for a deal, he could be pressed for one more concession. "That would have been going back on our word," Williams says. "Real estate is a very small community. All we have is our reputation and our integrity. I spoke with John Cushman and we both decided we wouldn't do it. Resigning from the deal meant sacrificing a commission worth hundreds of thousands of dollars. I was happy that I got support all the way to the top of the company. Ultimately, about three weeks later, the client called, apologized, and asked us to work for him again. We were hired back. We closed the transaction and were paid."

Williams's reasons for keeping the level of the game high is based in practicality. She points out that real estate is a "very small community" where reputation and integrity are important assets. This, in fact, is true of virtually all industries. Once you rise above the entry-level tier, all industries are small industries, and a team or player who devalues the game is going to be ostracized from the business community.

"It's far more important to me to make sure my clients are pleased than to close a deal and get paid," says Williams. "Maybe I'll make less money, but I'll be happier at the end of the day. I know that if my clients are pleased and a deal doesn't close and I go without a paycheck for six months, it's okay. There will be more deals and more paychecks coming from those clients in the future because I've kept their best interests in mind. I've listened to them. They have trust in me. That's another key to the team approach."

Hand in hand with ethics goes etiquette. On a team, good manners prevent people from offending and alienating each other. Manners allow people to interact, compromise, and work together despite personal differences.

"You must treat people with respect," says Ann Picciuto. "Humans are emotional beings. We have feelings and a sense of personal dignity. I develop rapport by treating the janitor with the same respect as I treat the president of the company."

Picciuto, like all effective team leaders, has a strong sense of democracy. By treating everyone with respect and dignity, she makes it easy for her teammates to operate out of a "we" position. If an important chart is lost in the computer system, with only the hard copy remaining, the secretary will gladly reenter the data if he's been made to feel he's an equal member of the team.

One of the smartest women I know is a self-employed copywriter. Though she doesn't have a formal team, she fosters a sense of team spirit with everyone she interacts with. She's gone out of her way to learn the names of the regular UPS and Express Mail carriers who handle her route. She's told them what kind of work she does and has made it clear that she couldn't do her job well without them. All this paid off one day when she had to pick up her sick child at school, even though she was expecting an important delivery. Knowing that the woman's work frequently involved overnight turnarounds and feeling himself to be part of her team, the UPS man didn't toss her parcel back into his truck when he learned she wasn't home. Instead he climbed over a locked fence to slide the envelope under her door. If he hadn't done this, the woman would not have had the information she needed for a presentation scheduled to take place the next morning.

If a team leader doesn't insist that members treat each other politely, the team becomes an aristocracy. In an aristocracy, people don't treat each other equally. Some people believe they are more important than others and freely trample on the rights and feelings of those they perceive as beneath them. This leads to feelings of "I versus you" on both sides, and although the team's self-styled elite may be perfectly content with the status quo, the "peasants" conspire and often launch a revolt. Revolutions bring productivity to a halt, sometimes destroying the team in the process.

Leona Helmsley made a fortune in the New York hotel and real estate game; she even managed to beat many of the income tax charges brought against her. Yet throughout her trials no one thought of her as a winner; instead we learned that the self-styled queen of the Palace had alienated employees and ruled by fear and intimidation. When she got into trouble, there was no team to back her. Her dynasty fell apart, disgruntled employees rushed to testify against her, and she earned a lonely reputation as "the Queen of Mean." Leona Helmsley won many battles but lost the war: her hotel business dropped so drastically that she had to launch an expensive publicity campaign to get back into the game.

As women we often pride ourselves on our sensitivity to others. Many of us are deft when it comes to tuning in to a co-worker's mood and saying the words that let the person know we've noticed and that we care. This is an important ability, and as with other acts of courtesy that come from one-on-one interaction, we're generally on the mark. Acts of courtesy born of team play don't come quite so easily to us. One shortcoming we have that has been sighted by many Key Players I've talked to is that we don't know how to let a fellow player save face.

"Men are competitive," says Barbara Uehling, "but they almost always manage to let the other person save face. They're good at that. Women are not as good at this skill. Sometimes a woman tries to prove herself by defeating a man." All this proves, says Uehling, is that "the woman needs to learn the skill of letting people save face."

"You have to exercise diplomacy," says Ann Picciuto. "Once you challenge a man head on, you may lose him as an ally. Other men may take his side and they may, collectively, try to get even with you. Lots of women make this mistake."

I know of one woman who set her career back several years by making this mistake. The woman belonged to a research-and-development team whose leader, nearing retirement, was no longer interested in creating new or innovative products. He was widely unpopular and the subject of much behind-the-scenes criticism. When the leader squashed one of the team's most promising projects, the woman challenged him openly. She demanded that the project be continued and implied that the team leader was growing overly cautious. Since these were the sentiments she had been hearing from her teammates for months, she thought they would be grateful to her for bringing the matter into the open. She was certain that she would have their support. She didn't get it. Embarrassed silence filled the conference room. No one came to her defense. Her project was discontinued. Within months the all-male team turned against her and she was forced to quit the team.

This woman failed to realize that while her teammates might complain bitterly about their leader in private, they had no intention of challenging him openly. He had been a Key Player in the organization for many years and had earned a degree of respect. True, he was no longer an effective leader, but his imminent retirement would resolve the problem diplomatically. To her male teammates, this woman's act seemed crudely aggressive and needlessly cruel. They began to view her as someone who couldn't be trusted. They became cautious around her, on guard lest she do to them what she had done to the team leader. Before she knew it, she was out of the information loop. No longer able to perform effectively, she resigned.

Turn on any football game and you'll see opponents helping each other up after the most bone-crunching tackles. There's tremendous meaning packed into this gesture. It's a way of saying "I won this particular play, but I respect you as a player; my goal isn't to grind you into the dirt, but to play the best game I can."

When players don't let each other save face, personal rivalries replace team effort. In an athletic event, when pushing and shoving matches break out between individuals, the whole team is penalized. The level of the entire game goes down.

Much the same thing occurs in business. A team member who will not let another team member save face is competing on a personal level. When personal rivalries blossom, people stop acting as a team. They don't share information and ideas freely; they become overly focused on whether or not they will receive personal credit for their efforts.

Key Players make a point of letting their teammates save face. As a Key Player in a predominantly male environment, it's a lesson Mary Haddenham, a high-level manager at a government engineering laboratory, learned early in her career. "Two of us were competing for the manager's spot," she says. "When I found out that I got the job and my opponent didn't, I went to him and said, 'It was competitive and a very close call. I hope we can have a good working relationship and that we can incorporate some of your goals.' I left his office and didn't talk to him for about a week because I knew he was emotional about the whole thing. About a week later I invited him into my office. 'Come in and sit down,' I said. 'You have a lot to do with this program and I value your input.' He turned around and became one of the most important members of the team."

This is an example of a Key Player at work. Haddenham exercised the "male" characteristic by letting her former rival save face, but notice that she employed the "female" characteristic in correctly perceiving his feelings. "He was emotional about the whole thing," she says. Too often we fall into the trap of thinking that because they exhibit emotions in a different way, men don't have any feelings in the workplace. When Cindy Webster became a fire fighter, she found that masculine sensitivity played a large part in the men's resistance to having women on the team.

"Men were uncomfortable sharing a communal bathroom with me," she says. "They were uncomfortable that we were in one dorm with no partitions. They were uncomfortable about running around in their underwear. Men are more modest in a coed situation than we give them credit for. When I joined the team, they were embarrassed, and men don't like being embarrassed. When men are embarrassed, that feeling comes to us as anger."

Wise words. Key Players insist on team members who practice etiquette toward each other because it defuses the anger, embarrassment, and ruffled feelings that block effective team play.

#4: YOU MUST BE RELIABLE IN THE HUDDLE

On a foggy night early in 1989, an Avianca airliner descended in eerie silence through layers of clouds and crash-landed in a wealthy community of Long Island, New York. The crash, which killed many of the people on board, wasn't due to the weather, mechanical failure, or terrorism. It was attributed to a breakdown in communications. Inclement weather had caused delays all over the New York metropolitan area that night. Planes were stacked up and circling the skies over LaGuardia, Kennedy, and Newark airports. The Avianca, like many airplanes in the sky that night, was running low on fuel. Instead of relaying this information to the air traffic controllers, instead of declaring an emergency, the pilots circled patiently until the fuel ran out.

The story may sound incredible, but it isn't. Late in 1990 the Federal Aviation Administration issued a report naming "missed communications" as the culprit in most fatal air crashes. To remedy the situation and improve air safety, the FAA went on to recommend stronger focus on "teamwork" among members of the flight crew.

Communications are at the heart of all team play. You can have any number of highly skilled and highly motivated players, but unless they know how to communicate effectively with each other, you will never have a team.

Cheryl Stern, president of The Game Keeper stores, says, "My impression of corporate America is that people spend too much time in cubicles. Not only do they not talk to their neighbor, they're discouraged from sharing ideas and points of view. We don't have cubicles here. We find errors or problems and share insights into what's going on just by talking. Someone walks into my office and says, 'Did you know this?' or, 'Did you see this?'

If I'm sitting in a little cubicle not sharing information with anybody, I'm going to die.''

Sharing information with your teammates is only one part of communicating effectively. Like being good at your job, it's considered a given, and most team leaders waste little time justifying its importance. It goes without saying that if you play on a team, you'll share information. Regarding information as private property, guarding it jealously, or—worse—feeding it to someone outside your team for your own personal gain is a major offense.

Margaret Tutwiler came to prominence as a Key Player on her team because of her ability to communicate effectively. Lee Atwater described her as "one of the best message deliverers in the business." She knew how to convey information from one team member to another without scrambling the message; and, just as important, she knew how to get a quick response. This skill made her an indispensable link on her team.

Developing and sharing official information (market analyses, research, reports, and so on) isn't the only way to contribute to your team. Gerry Cunningham says, "I cultivate 'grapevine' sources. I need people who will come into my office and say, 'You didn't hear this from me, but . . .' Then, when I'm out on the floor or in someone's office and the issue comes up, I already know about it. That allows me to operate from a position of strength.''

If you're in a good position to provide grapevine information to your team, make sure of a few things before you become your team's "mole." First, make sure that you're passing along useful information, not corporate gossip. Next, make sure your team leader understands that you're only passing on what you have heard, not vouching for its absolute validity. Finally, make sure your team leader will protect your privacy as a source.

Interestingly, women I interviewed placed much more emphasis on listening as a form of communication than men usually do. The flip side of passing grapevine information along is listening for it. And remember Lynn Williams's comment on ethics on page 156? "I've listened to them," she says of her clients. "They have trust in me. That's another key to the team approach."

According to Cheryl Stern, "Many managers aren't being trained to stop and listen. What's really going on? If they don't know, there's a problem."

Lauraine Brekke says, "Listening is one of the most important team values I've developed. Being able to understand someone else's point of view is essential. My style is collaborative, not dictatorial."

Brekke's statement goes to the heart of an essential difference between men and women. In *You Just Don't Understand: Women and Men in Conversation*, linguist Deborah Tannen relates a series of experiments performed by Elizabeth Aries, a psychology professor at Amherst College. Aries studied women and men in small groups and discovered that the sexes had different conversational styles. "The men," writes Tannen, "tended to set the agenda by offering opinions, suggestions, and information. The women tended to react, offering agreement or disagreement."

We listen carefully because our conversational style depends on assimilating what someone else is saying and reacting to it, either in agreement or disagreement. This transaction leads to a leadership style Brekke identifies as "collaborative." Men's conversational style may cause them to listen less attentively—if you are going to present your own "opinions, suggestions, and information," you do not need to be a particularly attentive listener.

It would be a mistake to interpret "listening" as a passive act. As Tannen pointed out, women's reactions included both agreement and disagreement.

"Avoiding conflict is a pitfall," says Barbara Uehling. "I have watched what happens when administrators avoid conflict, and what I've found is that the institution doesn't get anyplace. People would much rather have a resolution to a problem, even if it's unfavorable, than have the problem avoided."

COMMUNICATION RULES FOR KEY PLAYERS

- *Allocate time to become informed.*
- *Share information. If other people spend time and energy getting information you already have, you've done nothing for the team and have lost an opportunity to perform as a Key Player.*
- *If you don't have solid facts or information, don't bluff, buy time to research the issue.*
- *Never talk over the heads of your teammates: stay clear, concrete, and concise. Check for understanding.*
- *Be ready, willing, and able to explain unclear messages and answer questions.*
- *Tell it like it is diplomatically, especially if it's bad news.*
- *If you hear something outside the team, get the news as rapidly as you can to the person on your team who needs it.*
- *Respect your team's "rules of relay" when you pass along information. Make sure everyone who needs the information gets it. If a team member ends up in an embarrassing spot because she wasn't "in the loop," you've made a mistake.*
- *Be an approachable listener: don't dismiss ideas or information as irrelevant (even if they are), and let people know you can keep confidences if necessary.*
- *Don't respond to unexpected information or feedback emotionally. Take a break to adjust and regroup.*
- *If you disagree with a point of view or a plan of action, criticize the act or issue, never the person.*
- *If you have to confront someone on your team, pick the time and place carefully; don't embarrass or alienate teammates by criticizing them in public or going directly to the team leader with your complaint.*

Uehling sees voicing disagreement as vital to team unity. Lois Rice sees it as vital for team success.

"I want people who think on their own," she says, "people with a spark of entrepreneurial spirit in them. I don't want people who are not going to speak up. I want people who will say, 'Wait a minute. Why are we doing this?' I want people who question. I'm not hiring people to come on board and say, 'Yes, yes, yes.' I want people who have enough guts to step up and say, 'Hey, we shouldn't do that.' I don't want people who agree with me. In fact, I encourage my team members to disagree with me."

Of course, not all team leaders encourage disagreement. In fact, quite a few leaders will punish you for contradicting them, no matter how correct you are. These team leaders aren't Key Players, and their teams will never be Star Teams. On a Star Team, well-thought-out disagreement is an essential success tool, and Key Players value it as such.

If you're going to play on a Star Team, you need to master the art of communication. Of course, this means speaking and writing effectively, but solid communication doesn't stop there. On these pages you'll find guidelines to ensure effective communication with your team.

#5: YOU MUST KNOW HOW TO SCORE FROM ANY POSITION

In chapter 2, I noted that Key Players can score from any position. When these same Key Players become team leaders, they want teammates who can do the same. As one woman executive said in the course of an informal seminar, "You can't count on your whole team to be there all the time. If it's an all-night-project situation, your mailroom people will have gone home. You have the higher-ups, the so-called executives and idea people. But if no one knows how to call the messenger service to get the project picked up at three A.M. and delivered to the out-of-town client for the next day's meeting, you're all dead.''

There's nothing ''executive'' about not knowing how to run your office word processor; there's nothing ''key'' about not being able to fill out a purchase order or a shipping manifest. In a business the most crucial projects often are completed in the middle of the night by skeleton crews. If the people on the skeleton crew can't fill in for missing members of the team, no one is going to score. Everyone involved will look foolish and incompetent because they couldn't supply the most basic of basic skills: they didn't know which overnight express company to call, they couldn't access important information in the company computer, they didn't know how to print out an impressive report.

If you want to be a Key Player, you have to know the basic skills needed to take a project from start to finish. ''One of the most important pieces of advice I can give women,'' says Barbara Uehling, ''is 'Be prepared.' '' When I ask her what she finds particularly annoying in a team member, she cites, ''People who have lots of rhetoric and little ability to implement.''

Beginning in 1989, Hyatt Hotels Corporation launched its annual ''In Touch Day,'' sending executive staff into the field to join domestic staff. The company's president, Darryl Hartley-Leonard, initiated the program when he realized that most of the company's 430 corporate employees had never worked in a hotel. Dan Azark, vice-president of Hyatt's hotel development unit, says, ''This gets us back in touch with our customers and our employees.'' A Hyatt competitor, the Marriott Corporation, gives executives courses in basic hotel work before they take their jobs, then sends them back into the field for periodic refreshers.

Being prepared and filling in for teammates are forms of pinch hitting, a basic team maneuver.

Mary Canican is the founder of Graphic Horizons, a

Boston-based firm that develops CAD (computer-aided design) systems for architects. Her status doesn't keep her from acting as on-site technician to her clients, though. She routinely carries two screwdrivers in her purse and says that, in a small company, "you have to be able to do everything."

Team leaders know how to play every position and want players who can do the same. "I do not tolerate people who have an 'it's not my job' attitude," says Cheryl Stern. "The person who feels that way isn't going to be around long. We are a cohesive team. We cross-train. People who work on the operations side know how to do at least three different jobs. They will be at their desk for the first three to six months here, but by the end of the first year they will have been cross-trained in many different parts of the organization. This is a small company. When somebody goes on vacation, I don't want her desk to be empty."

I often find that women are reluctant to acquire extra basic skills or demonstrate proficiency in the basics they already have. Their reasons are legitimate: too often, being a good secretary has meant staying a good secretary; performing extra tasks has meant getting stuck with them on a full-time basis. If you're on a team that exploits you this way, you're not on a Star Team. Team leaders who are Key Players won't let you languish, they'll reward you.

Ann Picciuto used expertise in basic skills to get onto her company's team. "I was applying for a high-level secretarial slot at this company but the executive was looking for someone with more expertise. He didn't see anyone he liked, so I said, 'Hey, look at me—I can take shorthand a million miles an hour and I can type. I can do this job.' He hired me, and after two years in that position I got a call from the chairman of the board's office. I was asked to interview to be an administrative secretary in the corporate headquarters office."

Wells Fargo executive vice-president Karen Wegmann says, "One of the ways you become successful in this company is for people to see your work. I can think of several people, women and men, who have excellent reputations for doing their own work well. Credit is given to them by the more senior people, and then they're asked to do more. There's a woman in our credit card department, Barbara Brady Smith, who's superb. She's an excellent manager. And she's a good businessperson. If I get a raving customer and I call her and say, 'Barbara, tell me what to say. I have this guy on the phone, what can I do?' She will say, 'No, no, give him to me. I'll deal with him.' I'm not trying to hand him to her, but she's saying, 'Let me do it because I know I can do this well.' So we are both, in effect, trying to do it. We have a rule that customers cannot be transferred more than two times. To a customer, everybody at Wells *is* Wells. Saying 'It's not my department' doesn't work here. And it shouldn't work here. Ours is a 'fix it' culture.''

This is what Key Players in leadership positions look for in their teammates: people who have a ''fix it'' attitude, people who are ready, willing, and able to score from any position. When the game is on and the clock is ticking, team leaders want to see points going up on the board—they don't want to hear players talking about how they would have scored if only they'd been in the right position. That's what sportscasters commonly refer to as ''woulda coulda shoulda'' talk—talk that always goes on in the locker room of the losing team.

EXERCISES: ☆

Star Team Criteria

EXERCISE #1

Identify the Teams you Play On

Perhaps you haven't thought of your work with others as teamwork. However, most of us play on not only one, but several teams as we complete our daily tasks and plan future projects. Remember, a team is any group of two or more people who actively care about helping each other achieve excellence.

The first step in learning how to be a Key Player is to identify the teams you play on. After you make this determination, you can assess the quality of the work and the working relationships that characterize each team.

For this exercise, identifying the teams you play on, you will need a large sheet of blank paper on which you will draw a map of your current team relationships.

In the center of the paper, draw a small circle and put your name in it.

Traditional Teams (see page 89).

Draw a ring around the center ring. This first ring is your traditional team and will include people in your work life with whom you have face-to-face contact on a daily basis. Draw similar circles inside the ring and put the names

169

of those people in the circles. Do not include people you do not see every day or who work independently from you.

NOTE:
- You should draw circles for all the following teams even if you cannot name any players on them.

Matrix Teams (see page 90).

Draw a concentric ring; this is for the people who work on common tasks with you but who do not work in your geographic area or who work with you infrequently. These may be people who supply you with the materials or support you need to get the job done, or it may include people who produce a different part of the task after your traditional team has performed. These teams are called *matrix teams*.

As with all the circles, place smaller circles inside the ring and label the circles with the names of the players on this team.

HINT:
A good way to identify your matrix team is to look at your phone messages or consult your calendar to check your interdepartmental meeting schedule.

Intrapreneurial Teams (see page 91).

Draw a third concentric circle, fill it with inner circles, and label these circles with the names of the people who are players on this type of team.

HINT:
This type of team may be composed of people inside or outside the organization, but it is a team that is composed of experts in specific fields who are brought together to develop a particular program or product. Within a company it may be the team that is assembled from several

departments to develop a prototype of a new computer system. In a different kind of setting, it may be a team of community volunteers who are assembled by the town council to draft new zoning laws.

Transition Teams (see page 93).

Draw a fourth ring. It and its corresponding smaller, named circles are for the teams that are formed after reorganizations, mergers, or takeovers.

HINT:

Do you serve on any task forces or committees to aid in employee relocation or the plan to integrate two sets of identical departments into a new company? Have you worked with people in dismantling a division or shifting workloads from one department to another? These are transition teams.

Temporary Teams (see page 94).

Draw a fifth ring to represent the group of people who come together for an assignment that has a specific, finite life span.

HINT:

This team may have met only once at a weekend retreat, such as an interdepartmental managers' meeting to set goals and objectives for the new year, or a group of church members who came together to provide emergency services for a family whose house had burned down.

Transorganizational Teams (see page 96).

Draw a sixth ring, and see if you can spot the players to write in the inner circles.

HINT:

These are the teams that are formed between your company or organization and organizations on the outside.

Examples are national and international trade associations, sister cities, companies in related fields or industries, private foundations and nonprofit programs that may be supported by your company, political groups or lobbyists, or joint ventures your company may have with other companies.

Outpost Teams (see page 97).

The seventh ring to be drawn is for far-flung team members. These are teams with Key Players who are doing their time ''in the field.''

HINT:
These are sales forces or distributors in cities or regions apart from the national office, chapters of organizations, people assigned to tasks at the customer or client location.

Scattered Teams (see page 99).

Differing from outpost teams in that there is no central office, scattered teams comprise the eighth ring and its corresponding named circles. These are for people who work together on a central goal—remember the definition of a team—but who do not work in the same location and may never see each other.

HINT:
Political campaigns and church programs are good examples of scattered teams.

The All-Entrepreneurial Team (see page 100).

All the players named in the ninth circle, in their regular work lives, head their own kingdoms. The team may also be a temporary team or a transition team or even a scattered team, but we have a separate category for it because the strongly independent nature of each player changes the nature of the team play.

HINT:

If you are pursuing a new business, it's a good idea to form a team of other entrepreneurs for support.

The Family Team (see page 102).

Finally, the tenth ring is for the family business. The names of these players should come quickly to you if you are involved in such a venture!

Now that you have identified the teams you play on (or may have played on in the past), let's rate your experiences.

STEP 1.

To evaluate what strengths or opportunities you may need to develop in order to become a Key Player, note the rings on your map that have no "named circles"—in other words, teams on which you have never played.

STEP 2.

On the teams with named rings, place a + (for a good working relationship), a − (for a negative working relationship, or a ? (for an unknown quality of relationship) next to each name. Notice the way the teams may balance (a majority of + relationships, a few negatives) or tilt toward failure. When we examine the needs and characteristics of individual players, you may want to refer to your map to determine if you are playing with problem players, if you can improve the working relationships of your teams, or if *you* are the problem player. (We've all been there!)

STEP 3.

Answer the following questions about your own work and career goals, and relate those goals to the teams on which you do—and do not—play.

1. In addition to your regular work, are you willing to take on extra responsibilities, often without additional compensation?
2. Are you interested in developing a reputation as someone who can positively influence others to accept change?
3. Do you have excellent interpersonal skills?
4. Are you an entrepreneur or interested in becoming an entrepreneur?
5. Do you have expertise in a technical field or a specific skill?
6. Do you want to develop—or demonstrate—effective leadership skills?
7. Are you adept at conflict resolution?
8. Do you manage meetings well?
9. Are you quick to make decisions?
10. Do you enjoy lengthy processes and procedures?
11. Are you interested in working on international or global projects?
12. Do you prefer working alone?
13. Are you challenged by the opportunity to test new ideas and products?
14. Can you maintain strong communication links with people who work at great distances?
15. Do you have good negotiation skills?
16. Is long-term loyalty and commitment to other people with whom you work of strong importance to you?

Let's correlate these questions and your answers with the types of teams we have identified.

1. If you answered "No" to this question, you are limited to working primarily with traditional and matrix teams—the basic teams on which you must play to accomplish your tasks.
2. While many teams may offer you the opportunity to develop or demonstrate this skill, the transition team, assembled at the point of change, has the highest profile on this subject within an organization.

3. Interpersonal skills can be developed on a variety of teams and are critical to players on all teams. However, if this is a skill you already have, you can quickly become a Key Player on a transition team (where sensitivity and diplomacy are essential to successfully completing the job), temporary team, and, of course, family team.

4. The all-entrepreneurial team and the scattered team are the most likely teams on which an entrepreneur would play (in your work life—in your personal life, you may play on volunteer teams on which you have many different roles). If you are interested in becoming an entrepreneur, seek out temporary and transition teams on which to serve. The projects and the time periods that are the framework for these teams provide excellent experiences for future entrepreneurs.

5. If you answered ''Yes'' to this question, you have the opportunity to become a Key Player on an intrapreneurial team and transorganizational team.

6. You can demonstrate these skills on a transition or a temporary team; outpost teams will give you the best opportunity to develop these skills.

7. ''Yes'' makes you a good candidate for Key Player status on almost any team, but you are particularly valuable to the family team, the transition team, and the all-entrepreneurial team.

8. A good manager of meetings is a valuable asset to any team that requires frequent meetings: traditional teams, matrix teams, and especially temporary teams, where an immediate goal requires skillful handling of the limited amount of time.

9. The temporary team is a good spot for a quick decision maker. If you need to strengthen your decision-making skills, look for a temporary team to join.

10. The process-oriented player will do well on transorganizational teams, where procedures and following protocol is extremely important.

11. The transorganizational team may offer the best opportunity to make international or global connec-

tions, but look carefully at some other possibilities. The matrix team in your organization may include suppliers from another country, outpost teams may be in international locations, scattered teams may include people working around the globe.

12. Surprise! Loners can still be Key Players on a variety of teams. Best possibilities: scattered teams and outpost teams. Just remember that working alone means that excellent communication links must be maintained with other players.

13. The outpost team is a good spot for someone who wants to experiment with new ideas and projects with a minimum of risk. "In the field," far from the constraints of politics and policies, you can prove—or disprove—new theories and processes. Your fellow players will be customers and other people in the community where your business is being conducted.

14. Good communication links—and creative communication links—are requirements for Key Players on transorganizational teams, outpost teams, scattered teams, all-entrepreneurial teams, and temporary teams. All teams need players with a commitment to keeping each other informed; however, the specific types of teams listed will go out of business without an emphasis on communication.

15. Negotiation skills are especially important in the all-entrepreneurial team (where independent egos are strong) and on transition teams (where the status quo has changed and people are feeling threatened).

16. Although loyalty and commitment are cornerstones for Key Players on all types of teams, they are numbers one and two (and three and four and so on) on a family team.

STEP 4.
Watch your company and your community for opportunities to join the teams that will give you a chance to be a Key Player or that will help you learn new skills. Inside your organization and out, volunteer to play on these teams.

EXERCISE #2

Are You on a Star Team?

Review your map of the teams on which you are a player. Then assess each team, asking the questions listed below. If you are a team leader, a "no" answer to any of the questions indicates a challenge to solve. If you are a player on a team that has any "no" answers, you may consider coaching fellow players in constructive team play, improving elements of your own play, or, in the worst-case scenario, looking for a new team.

1. Is every player committed to the desired results and clear about the undesired results?
2. Are there common and shared values about the quality of the work to be performed?
3. Is there mutual respect and acceptance for differences among players in terms of background, experience, style, and methods?
4. Are all players willing to improve their play?
5. Do players try to help each other by coaching rather than by criticizing?
6. Are players willing to accept final decisions without resentment?
7. Are all the players reliable?
8. Does every player agree to follow the rules that were agreed upon?
9. Do players face conflicts openly and appropriately?
10. Is the team fun—not just functional?

EXERCISE #3

Role Assessment: Will Your Role on a Team Be Powerful?

Before accepting a role on a team, be sure this role will provide you with important skill training, access to Key Players, and experiences that will advance your career. Analyze the power of your role by answering these questions.

Yes or No:

1. Your participation is highly visible to the market.
2. Your role has clear and simple rules to follow, and you have a lot of latitude when taking action.
3. Your role has few paper or reporting requirements.
4. Your role is essential to the company and is tied to revenue-generating projects or the success of the organizational vision.
5. Your role will enhance the company or organization's growth potential or effectiveness (government).
6. Your role involves a lot of time and interaction with other Key Players.
7. Your role includes authority to implement decisions after team meetings.
8. Your team has direct contact with top executives or Key Player/coaches.
9. The team has a history of success.
10. Your role involves presentations or interactions with top customers or other high-level players.

NOTE:
Many of these items can be influenced by redesigning your role (such as getting more visibility with important customers). Be careful about taking on a role on a team where most of the answers are "no." This could be a traditional trap. You will work hard, spend lots of time, and get little recognition or skill out of your participation.

PART III ☆

8 ☆

Your Move to Key Player Position

By now you should be developing a mental index of your Key Player qualities and skills. (Exercises to help you do this can be found in the career audit section beginning on page 75.) Don't expect to have all the skills in place at the outset, and above all, don't wait to start playing the game until you do. Athena, goddess of wisdom, may have sprung fully formed from the forehead of Zeus, but Key Players don't spring fully formed into the workplace. They develop wisdom as they go along, advancing, learning, and using what they have learned to advance again.

To make the move from talented rookie to Key Player, players must take certain steps. If you saw the movie *The Right Stuff*, you've already witnessed a dramatic example of rookies moving into Key Player position. Alone together, momentarily isolated from their trainers as well as from the press, the seven Mercury astronauts are having a showdown. Some members of the team have been using their celebrity status as a springboard into the beds of bedazzled young women. John Glenn is objecting to this vociferously, and the bad boys, led by Alan Shepard, are just as vociferously insisting that it's none of Glenn's business.

To understand the tension of the moment, understand something about the individuals involved. None of these men is a team player by nature. In fact, they've been picked because they can think and act independently in stressful situations (the same expectations placed on the Key Player in business today). Moreover, these men come from different branches of the service and adhere to a not-so-subtle spirit of navy vs. air force vs. marines. Finally, like most test pilots, they possess large amounts of boyish defiance and disregard for rules.

Shepard views womanizing as one of the perks of a dangerous, poorly paying job. He accuses Glenn of being "way out of line" in his attempt at moral policing. Glenn responds by telling Shepard that morals are not the issue. In John Glenn's view the Mercury astronauts are sitting on the opportunity of a lifetime—the opportunity to become national heroes. He isn't about to let unfavorable team publicity destroy that opportunity.

For Shepard and the bad boys, two things are now at stake: womanizing and backing down. The long, tense moment is broken when Shepard and his supporters swing to Glenn's point of view.

If you saw this scene, you witnessed individual players take the first step to becoming Key Players. In real life the struggle lasted for weeks, but the end result was the same. Author Tom Wolfe, whose book inspired the movie, aptly described the transformation when he wrote that the astronauts might have "their rivalries, their differences in backgrounds and temperaments and approaches to the job at hand, but they should be able to arrive at firm decisions as a group, no matter how acrimonious the debate might be, and then close ranks and pull together, one for all, all for one."

Let's look at exactly what happened here.

At the beginning of the scene the astronauts saw themselves as individual peak performers: "I'm going into space" rather than "We're going into space." To embrace Glenn's point of view, Shepard and his supporters had to do three things. First, they had to accept the idea that there was a team goal. Next, they had to acknowledge that this goal could be achieved only through cooperation. Finally, they had to be willing to subordinate conflicting personal goals to the team goal.

Having opposed Glenn openly, it must have been especially difficult for Shepard to back down. Because he relented and brought his supporters into line with him, the team became a Star Team.

It's not hard to see that Shepard earned his Key Player spot, but what about John Glenn? Glenn, an intensely moral man who disapproved of his teammates' carousing, didn't have to adjust his point of view. Just the opposite. He made his personal goal—acting like a hero—the goal of the entire team. Was he a Key Player or just a likeable manipulator?

Never overlook the importance of being right. If Glenn had promoted a goal detrimental to the team, he wouldn't have been a Key Player. In correctly identifying what was needed for the team to succeed, he was a Key Player.

In the course of a ball game, everybody gets a chance to do a little winning and a little losing on the personal front. Glenn and Shepard switched winner-loser positions when NASA announced the Mercury flight schedule. Glenn, like most of his teammates, had assumed that he was the front-runner for the first launch. Instead the nod went to Shepard with Glenn designated backup. Shepard must have felt a tremendous sense of personal triumph, yet he swallowed the impulse to play "I'm number one." As for Glenn, he set aside his personal disappointment and threw himself enthusiastically into the supporting role, even good-naturedly shouldering Shepard's luggage when Shepard was besieged by autograph seekers at airports.

Embracing team goals is just one of several steps you must take to become a Key Player on your team. As I've worked with women over the years, I've had the opportunity to observe both winners and losers. The difference between them isn't as great as you would think. Often it isn't a question of intelligence, talent, or even effort. Lots of us are educated, bright, qualified, and hardworking—but we aren't making it to the top because we're climbing the wrong staircase.

Although the Key Player strategy can be used by both men and women, it is a uniquely female route to success because it is designed to overcome the underlying difficulties and prejudices we face. When you perform in the workplace as an individual, the men around you tend to see you as a woman first and a co-worker second. When you ''plug into'' your team as a Key Player, you reverse the perception: the men around you see you first and foremost as a teammate, an equal, and a peer.

This chapter will show you the right steps to take to get into Key Player position and which pitfalls to avoid.

STEP #1: EMBRACE YOUR TEAM'S VISION AND GOALS

''When I look at Key Players, I see commitment,'' says Gerry Cunningham. ''I see people who are saying, 'I'm going to put my energies, my intelligence, and everything I've got into achieving the goals of the organization, whatever the stated goals are.' That shared commitment by team players is what makes business successful. A person can't be a Key Player unless she embraces the team's goals.''

To become a Key Player, you must embrace your team's goals and make them your first priority. In doing this, it's important to remember that team goals are not the same as results the team is assigned to produce. These assignments come from outside the team, when the organization or the client asks the team to produce a specific result. Goals come from within the team. Their aim is to produce results in a way beneficial to the team and its players. For example, the assignment given to the Mercury astronauts by NASA was ''Go into space.'' The goal John Glenn argued for was to create a positive, heroic team image in the process of going into space. As often happens, the team's goal was more farsighted than the assignment it had been given.

BECOMING KEY: THE TEN STEPS TO TAKE

1. *Embrace your team's vision and goals.*
2. *Make sure everyone knows you're on the team.*
3. *Know the traditional route to success in your field.*
4. *Play every point of the game.*
5. *Learn the micro and the macro.*
6. *Share what you know.*
7. *Manage sideways.*
8. *Extend your reach beyond your team.*
9. *Join extra teams.*
10. *Keep improving your job.*

On a Star Team, team goals are in harmony to promote team success, and this benefits the corporation as a whole. On a Star Team, goals also promote the success of the team's members. If your team doesn't support you by providing you with opportunities and challenges, if it doesn't recognize and reward your achievement, you aren't playing on a Star Team. Whenever your team's goals don't support your goals or provide you with the opportunities you need, you have only two choices: you must either redefine your goals or change teams. If you don't, you will be constantly swimming against the current, trying to do enough of the team's work to get by and enough of your own work to feel satisfied. But as we've seen, "getting by" is a catch-22 position. It is an attitude that leaders don't want on teams. You won't be valued or rewarded for your personal achievements, you'll be overlooked—or dumped—because you're not giving your full attention to the team. If your goals are out of sync with the goals of your team and you aren't willing to change them, you must change teams. You will never become a Key Player on a team whose goals you can't embrace as your own.

STEP #2: MAKE SURE EVERYONE KNOWS YOU'RE ON THE TEAM

Being on the team on the organizational map isn't good enough; you'll end up sitting on the bench waiting for your turn at bat. To become a Key Player, you must make sure your teammates and team leader know you're part of the starting lineup.

We humans are a tribal lot. If we perceive someone as "one of us"—a member of our family, clan, or team—we go out of our way to notice and praise her achievements, we interpret her actions in a favorable light, we extend the benefit of the doubt to her more readily than we would to a stranger. If your teammates see you as an independent player, your accomplishments may go unnoticed. Worse, they may be misread. Unless you make sure your teammates know you're on their side, working to enhance their status as well as your own, they may think you're trying to upstage them and grab the glory for yourself. If this happens, your team will turn against you—even if you're the team leader.

How do you get people to see that you're part of the team? One way is to wear the team uniform. Look at the teams around you and you'll soon notice that people who play on the same team dress in a similar fashion. Law and banking teams wear unadorned, conservative clothing, teams in advertising adopt a more relaxed style, and retailing teams favor a polished, avant-garde look. Being "in uniform" means being approachable for team business; it's a visual cue that you're in harmony with the team and ready to play.

If your job involves heavy client contact or interaction with members of other teams, you become the team representative: the team uniform will help position the team correctly in the client's mind and identify you as a Key Player on the team.

People will also see you as part of the team if you follow the "team routine." Whenever there's a team meeting, make sure you're part of the huddle; if the team takes the playing field at eight-thirty every morning, don't show up at nine—the day's game has already begun. If the team stays on after the regular work force goes home, stay with them: this is often when Key Players meet, mingle, compare notes, and form alliances. If your team doesn't work late, however, don't make the mistake of being the only team member to stay on. Instead of being recognized as a Key Player, you'll become the team doormat.

Still another way to make people see you as a teammate is to identify a hitherto vacant slot and fill it. Mary Haddenham got her team transformed into a department by doing this on a grand scale. She says, "I translated the customer's requirements into what the lab could do. No one had made that bridge before. By making myself a valuable player in the program, I brought in a lot of new income. The program went from nothing to something significant. That's one of the reasons it became a department."

In filling a vacancy, you can either take on tasks no one else is doing or fill roles no one else has taken on. Haddenham did both, filling the job slot of customer liaisons officer and acting as a visionary who created projects for the lab staff to implement.

STEP #3: KNOW THE TRADITIONAL ROUTE TO SUCCESS IN YOUR FIELD

As we've seen, it's important to have a sense of improvisation. All the Key Players I've talked to have had a marvelous sense of adventure, an ability to pursue their interests and seize the opportunities that came their way. But once they found a path that appealed to them, they all acquired the traditional skills and experiences needed for success. Improvisational ability will help you explore and discover. It will not make you a Key Player.

Barbara Uehling says that women, no matter what their career ambitions, should be impeccably prepared. "I've had lots of women come up to me over the years," she says, "and ask, 'How can I be a dean?' or, 'How can I be a provost?' Usually these women don't realize there is a set of experiences you have to go through to be credentialed and credible. You don't suddenly wake up one day and decide, 'I'm going to be a dean.' Women need to be analytical about the skills they need and the experiences they need, and they have to set out to get them."

To emphasize her point, she relates an anecdote about a woman who came to her for advice. "The other day I had a fascinating conversation with a bright woman with good credentials. She's a faculty member in another institution, and her question to herself was, 'Do I want to stay around here and do the work that's required to get tenure, or do I want to go into administration?' She was perfectly aware that her administrative possibilities would be limited because she had never gotten tenure, and she was struggling to evaluate exactly what the consequences would be. I thought her approach was healthy. Some women would have expected to get into administration without investigating what the traditional route was."

In 1980 Stephenville, Newfoundland, was a town of ten thousand with a high unemployment rate. Cheryl Stagg's idea to reenergize the economy by staging an annual arts festival in the town's leading cultural asset, a 450-seat theater, seemed idealistic at best. But Stagg and her board of directors made the project work, first by getting box office receipts into the respectable zone and next by appealing to corporate sponsors for support. "I researched the corporate-giving policies of major companies," Stagg explained to an interviewer from *Savvy* magazine. She then used her research to put together press kits loaded with clippings, photographs, and press releases. The strategy worked and sponsors began opening their checkbooks. Stagg also researched endowment programs available through the Canadian government. She was often turned down because the Stephenville Festival didn't meet a particular requirement. "But after I studied the guidelines," she says, "I could tailor our work to fit the official requirements." By the time the festival was five years old, it was bringing half a million tourist dollars into the town every summer.

If you want to become a Key Player, you have to know what success on the job calls for and be able to demonstrate that you have the skills and experience needed to play the game.

STEP #4: PLAY EVERY POINT OF THE GAME

I once heard a top-seeded tennis player explaining how he lost a world championship. One minute, he said, he was well ahead of his opponent and mentally savoring his victory; the next minute he was at the net congratulating his opponent, who'd come from behind to beat him. The moral: Every player plays the match point; Key Players play every point as if it were the match point.

In business I often see players who have all the makings of a Key Player but, for some reason, are saving their talents for a play they consider important. They perform halfheartedly, waiting—and hoping—for a project they can give their all to. Then, their thinking goes, they will astonish their teammates and bosses with their talent and hard work.

To the team leader who sets the agenda and assigns the tasks, all work is important. Every task on the agenda must be done and done well for the team to succeed. The player who holds back, waiting for an assignment she finds more interesting, is sending out the message "I don't feel this is important, so I'm not going to waste much energy on it." The message the team leader expects from a Key Player, however, is much different: "I will promote the team's success in any way I can." Players who pick and choose are labeled "dispensable" and relegated to the bench. Team leaders don't see them as long-term members of the team and, as a result, don't pick them for the very projects these players are saving their talents for.

CBS's Connie Chung became a Key Player by playing every point of the game. In 1973 Chung was a relatively unknown reporter working for CBS News in Washington. Of all the juicy assignments that came out of the Watergate scandal, Chung, as a rookie, drew one of the least juicy: staking out the home of former Nixon aide H. R. Haldeman in hopes of getting her questions answered. Chung perched on Haldeman's doorstep for days, shouting questions and getting the usual cold shoulder. Finally the network sent her to follow the Haldemans to church. "I knew it was reprehensible," Chung told columnist James Brady seventeen years later. "His wife asked me, 'Have you no shame?' But because I'd been there so long, in front of his door, he said, 'Look, I'll meet you after church. And talk to you.' " Chung got her interview, a coup that boosted her to prominence at CBS.

Proving her ability to play the minor points of the game earned Chung a shot at the major points: first as news anchor at KNXT-TV, CBS's Los Angeles affiliate, then as an NBC weekend anchor, and finally back to CBS to host her own prime-time interview show. When, in 1990, she asked for a massive cutback in her schedule to pursue her personal goal of becoming a first-time mother, CBS agreed to let her do so without cutting her $1.3-million-a-year salary. To Chung, the Haldeman assignment was much more than a "lucky break"—it was a formative experience. "Watergate," she says, "developed my doggedness." Doggedness, in this case, is synonymous with playing every point.

In business, know-how is important—but "do-how" is even more important. Gerry Cunningham was promoted to plant manager by her own team leader, the previous manager who had himself been promoted to a position at Jostens corporate headquarters. When I ask why her boss defied the company's predominantly male culture and picked her to succeed him, she says, "I have always put out one-hundred-plus percent, and I have always kept the company's interests at heart."

In sports, rookies and players new to the team are continually performance-tested in minor-league games and in exhibition contests. A responsible team leader wants to get a feel for an individual's capabilities before thrusting the player into a do-or-die situation. The same thing happens in business. Unless the circumstances are unusual, responsible leaders don't bring in an unknown to execute a project crucial to the entire team's success. Instead they first observe how players perform on less-than-crucial projects.

When Pastor Margaret Rush needs someone to take charge of a large project, she looks to see who performed well on the previous play. "I watch to see how people function in small groups and on small tasks," she says. "I know if someone organized one project, she can organize a more complex project. If someone did a lesser task well, she can do a larger task well. One of our members is a teacher who is going back to school for her master's degree. Last year she taught a vacation Bible school class. Anyone who watched her work could see that she had tremendous organizational ability. This year our associate minister recruited her to take charge of the Bible school program. Early in the year, the woman had already recruited her teachers and her helpers and her refreshment crew."

In observing the woman work, Rush says, she spotted other leadership qualities as well. "People are drawn to her. They like to be with her and they want to work with her. That's another thing I look for, even in small social groups. Whom are people drawn to and whom do people say 'Yes' to?"

If you think some plays are more important than others, you're wrong. For a Key Player, every down is an opportunity. This book is studded with Key Players who've risen to the ranks of play callers by giving every play the best they had to offer.

STEP #5: LEARN THE MICRO AND THE MACRO

As I interviewed Key Players, one thing became startlingly clear to me. While some women were getting stuck midway in their careers, while much legitimate complaining was being done about the numbing effects of the "glass ceiling," Key Players were getting to the top. Not only were they getting to the top, they were getting there fast: many in less than six job moves, and some in as few as three. What facilitated their rise?

With few exceptions, the Key Players I interviewed all took the time to "learn" their organizations, not just their jobs. They invested time in understanding how they fit into the team, how the team fit into the department, how the department fit into the company, and how the company saw itself in the world.

Lois Rice says, "If you work for a company, you have to get to know the people who work for it. You have to take the time. You have to think about your positioning in the marketplace."

Mary Haddenham succeeded in a vast and dauntingly bureaucratic organization because she did "take the time." When her team generated so much increased income that a new department was created, Haddenham was one of three candidates in contention for the managerial slot. How did she distinguish herself as a Key Player who deserved the position? "That was the first job I ever sought," she says. "I said to myself, 'I'm getting it.' The two males I was working with didn't try very hard. One in particular thought he was a shoo-in. His attitude was, 'I'm a guy, it's in the bag.' He learned a hard lesson. I did grass-roots information gathering. I talked to technicians, to the division director, to the customer. I knew more about that department than my department head. When he had a question, I could answer it. If I couldn't answer it immediately, I could get the answer for him in the next half hour. I gave up a lot of my own time. I put a lot of time into information assessment. It was a learning experience for me, but it was interesting. It was fun, too."

When you know your organization from top to bottom, you're in position to plot a successful path for yourself. This is the way to discover where the opportunities are, which teams are the winning ones, and who the company's top players are. One of the best steps to take is to interview the organization's Key Players to find out what the career paths are in their fields of expertise.

Gerry Cunningham believes that asking questions is a vital success strategy. "Asking questions is crucial," she says. "Don't stop at your department lines. Ask, 'How did this get this way? Why is this procedure done like this?' When I first came to work at Jostens, I asked questions of anybody and everybody. That's how you get to see the whole picture."

Team leaders who are Key Players value players who want to know about the company. "I encourage my people to call all the way to the top if they've got a question," says Lois Rice. "I want them to feel free to find out, to keep questioning until they know what the answer is."

Interviewing within your organization is a double-win strategy because you get knowledge and a chance to forge a valuable alliance. While you're questioning Key Players in your organization, they're noticing you as a player with high team potential. That's the transaction that occurred between Ann Picciuto and her Key Player bosses: she connected with them as people to learn from, they connected with her as someone who would make good use of opportunity.

"Learning your organization" extends beyond knowing official job descriptions and department functions. You have to know the organization culture and personality as well. Who are the real power players? Who are the true leaders? Who talks to whom and why? Who doesn't talk to whom and why not? What are the sacred cows? What are the taboos? What are the team attitudes and traditions? In chapter 2 I described how Cindy Webster got into an all-male fire-fighting team by asking herself, "What's the culture? What are the mores?" She broke the macho barrier, she says, because "I had the determination and the willingness to look at the team and figure it out. That attitude helped."

There's one other reason to know the micro and the

macro of your organization, and that's to avoid costly errors in judgment. If you propose a solution to a problem without realizing that solution has been tried—and failed—in the past, you're going to look foolish. One of my clients made a supposedly bottom-line-conscious decision to get rid of a specific supply of sticky tapes for messages. Since the sticky tapes cost more than ordinary message forms, my client was sure this would save money. It did, but only a few dollars. Because my client didn't know how her whole company worked, she didn't realize that engineers had been using the sticky tapes to track projects. The decision had an adverse effect on the company's research group, and a great deal of productivity was lost as people developed a new tracking system. The "savings" were far outweighed by the cost of lost time in engineers' salaries. The engineers complained about the change, and the loss of the sticky tapes became a major issue in the company—one that could have been avoided if my client, who made the decision, had understood who used the tape, how they used it, and what the consequences of getting rid of it would be.

STEP #6: SHARE WHAT YOU KNOW

Team leaders expect members of their team to share knowledge. Someone who doesn't feed the information flow is seen as holding the whole team back—and the team, not the individual, is where the leader's concerns lie. Look what happened to some high-level players on Mary Haddenham's team when they sat on what they knew:

"The way this office is organized, there are three team leaders who report to me. Each knows different aspects of the technology and they must combine their knowledge to make a solid marketing program. I expected them to share their technologies with each other to produce a complete, high-quality line of products for the customer. They didn't. What I had instead were three individuals marketing to their own set of customers. They didn't share information, they didn't share resources. Two of the players were especially resistant. They refused to give me or their co-workers progress information.''

Sharing information was one of the important rules on Haddenham's team. She didn't allow these players to disregard the rule but, instead, repeatedly insisted that they follow it. So resistant were these employees that they finally chose to quit the team rather than share information. Though Haddenham describes this as ''one of the hardest success stories I can think of,'' she clearly sees it as a success because allowing these two people to hoard information would have hurt the entire team and kept it from achieving its goals.

When you do collect knowledge and share it with your teammates, you're on your way to becoming a Key Player. Knowledge is costly. It takes time to acquire it. When you provide useful information to your teammates, you're saving the whole team time and money. I once counseled a woman who jumped from secretary to Key Player in one move. In talking with her and asking her to list all the tasks she did in the course of a day, I found she made a habit of reading her industry's many trade journals and passing along relevant information. Though this woman's official job was secretary, her real contribution was being able to ''read'' for her team. She had a talent for knowing which articles would be of importance to her teammates and was able to keep them informed. I advised her to begin thinking of herself as the team ''infometrician.'' Eventually she got this task added to her job description and negotiated a substantial raise because of it.

Lynn Williams says her ability to share information has gotten her on several important teams. ''First Interstate Bank requested that I be the point person on their relocation project, which was the largest investment sale ever made in downtown Los Angeles, because they'd worked with me in the past. They requested me because I keep everyone up to speed. I believe the entire team needs to be as well informed as possible. It facilitates the transaction. The client believes that, also.''

Sharing information with your team can also mean keeping information within your team. As secretary to the chairman and the president of her company, Ann Picciuto had to learn how to maintain diplomatic ties without leaking sensitive information. "I had to learn the politics of dealing with people outside," she says. Her use of the word *outside* is telling. It refers to more than the physical logistics of being "inside" or "outside" her bosses' office. It shows how sharply the team dividing lines were in Picciuto's mind: she and her bosses were a team, the people on the inside of the information loop; everyone outside the team was, quite literally, outside the loop. "I was in a high-level position. I had a lot of information. And everybody wanted it. I would walk out of the fishbowl and people would converge on me, trying to extract information. I love to talk, and I had to learn to converse in that situation. I made a game of it, actually. I learned how to let them feel as if they were getting some information without actually telling them anything. That became a fun game, and it worked out well."

How much information can and should be shared outside your immediate team will vary depending on your job and your organization. This is where your knowledge of the micro and macro can guide you. If President Nixon had known the micros and macros of politics, we might never have heard the infamous "What did the president know and when did he know it?"

STEP #7: MANAGE SIDEWAYS

In the late eighties, as business after business looked for ways to trim expenses, middle managers were the big losers. Regardless of the industry, people whose only contribution was managing other people were more and more often being dropped from the team. In the new and tighter formation, people are responsible for managing themselves. That's why we've seen team leaders emphasize the need for players who can "think for themselves" and "fit in with the team." Anytime someone has to be led step by step, anytime the team must call on the leader to resolve conflicts and sort out problems, time and productivity are lost. And the team member who can mediate problems and keep the team running smoothly—who can "manage sideways"—is going to emerge as a Key Player on her team.

Often, what managers think is effective and what the managed know is effective are two different things. The least effective managers see themselves as better than their teams. They foster poor working relationships by creating a sense of hierarchy, by asking team members to do tasks they themselves will not do.

A person who manages effectively—whether she is the official leader or not—never sees herself as better than or separate from her team. She may be confident that her talents are unique, but she is equally confident about her teammates' talents. She creates better working relationships by treating her teammates with respect, sensitivity, and courtesy; she knows when to defer to them and let them lead her, an often overlooked facet of good management; and she works for the success of the entire team rather than for her personal success.

A person who is concerned with personal praise isn't a good manager. For this reason she will never become a Key Player. Barbara Uehling says, "If you have a need for fanfare, you're in trouble. You must be willing not to have accolades." When she looks for players to be on a team, she demands "people whose chief concern is getting the job done; people who feel it's important that we get it done together without worrying too much about who gets the credit."

While working for the City Council of Seattle, Lauraine Brekke discovered that an excellent way to manage sideways is to generate work her team could participate in. Her job in budget analysis entailed producing voluminous reports, many of which failed to receive recognition. "Then I did a report that the council could sink its teeth into," she says. Brekke didn't ask her teammates to promote the report as her work. She let them take it and run with it, confident that whatever contributed to the team's success would ultimately work in her favor. It did. By providing her teammates with a valuable tool—a report they could "sink their teeth into"—she cemented her position as a Key Player. From her position as junior member on a four-person staff, she was soon promoted to staff leader.

Gerry Cunningham promotes team harmony by making her office a "safe haven." She says, "My people can come in the door and start screaming. I tell them to do that. I don't want them to do it out on the floor, and I don't want them to do it to anybody. I want them to come in here and tell me. I tell them to cry, to say whatever they need to say, but just keep it in here. I'll listen, we'll try to work it out."

Cunningham wisely realizes that knowing how to clear up problems and take care of tensions is an important part of management. A team can't work well if misunderstandings and personal grudges get in the way. Key Players don't wait for their leaders to resolve the conflicts. They work to resolve problems on their own and even intercede on behalf of their teammates to solve problems with the team leader. (How to handle troubled players and troubled teams can be found in chapters 10 and 11 of this book.)

STEP #8: EXTEND YOUR REACH
BEYOND YOUR TEAM

Teams don't exist in a vacuum. To be successful, they must connect with other teams and "plug into" the outside world. These connections are forged through personal contact: two people from different teams meet face to face or over the phone to talk business; in the process, each gets a feel for the other's personality—they may even strengthen the alliance by swapping anecdotes from their personal lives. Together they form a human link, a bridge that gives one team access to the other. If either of these people drops out of the picture, there will be a period of transition as a new bridge is built.

Sometimes the new person is not good at forging links, and the connection is never adequately rebuilt. All of us have seen—or suffered from—the fallout of this situation. The supplier you've worked with for years sends a new salesman to your firm, and although the new person is perfectly willing to write up your order, he's more interested in going after new customers than in discussing the needs of your midsize manufacturing firm. It isn't long before you begin hunting another supplier.

People get attached to other people, even in business. Whenever you become the person who forms a link between your team and teams and people on the "outside," you solidify your position as a Key Player.

On her way to becoming an associate publisher of Atlantic Monthly, Cathy Hemming held a variety of other jobs in the book business, including a four-year stint as a traveling sales representative for a major publisher. "I was in different bookstores every day, talking to booksellers. You don't have to be a rocket scientist to get a feeling for what these people are going through. That was probably the best training I had. The smartest people in business have often come out of sales. They have had that kind of day-in, day-out contact with their customers. They know what customers face, and because of that they know how difficult it is to make a sale and get the customer to buy the product.

"Because I previously co-owned a bookstore and because I listened to my customers, I could help them in situations most reps couldn't. Other reps took a one-sided approach. I didn't. I developed close ties with my customers and was an experienced ear they could complain to."

The team you play on may not have the kind of traditional "customers" we usually think of, but it's important to remember that all teams have customers of one sort or another. Whoever is going to use your team's product—whether that product is books or research or placement opportunities—is the customer you're dealing with. If you belong to the marketing research department, for example, your customers are the company's designers and project developers. They must have your product—sound research—to design products of their own. Without your input, success in the marketplace becomes a matter of hit or miss.

Supplying other teams with information or materials they can use to succeed will make your own team successful. Making your team successful by forging important links and facilitating the flow of information will make you a Key Player on your team.

STEP #9: JOIN EXTRA TEAMS

Joining extra teams is networking on a grand scale. It connects you with other groups rather than other individuals; it brings you inside the circle and gives you status and visibility. When you join other teams, you are "net-weaving," not networking; you are making yourself a vital piece of the fabric of the organization.

When players first become aware of teams, they are likely to see one level of teams around them: the team they work on and the teams others work on. With a little practice, as players become more adept at recognizing teams, they begin to see that there are layers of teams and that these layers aren't static; rather, they are in constant motion. In the first chapter of this book, I compared a team to an arch: a structure that could be adapted, disassembled, and reassembled to serve a wide variety of purposes. This is exactly how teams are used in today's "work smarter" industries. Teams are constantly re-forming, combining, and splitting. Special teams come into existence, execute a specific task or project, then dissolve, releasing their players to join other teams. Sub-teams may form within larger teams, or two teams may join forces to gain clout within their department. For business, this fluidity spells efficiency. For individual players, it spells opportunity.

Like many team leaders, Gerry Cunningham makes frequent use of the special teams concept. "When we have a new program, a new technology, or a new approach, we segment the task out to teams. We take people with expertise in different fields—engineering, production, or accounting—and put them on the team to initiate the new project. We also form teams to interact with our sister plant."

For players eager to become Key Players, getting picked for a team like this is a coup. It's an opportunity to get in on the ground floor of something new, a chance to gain experience, and a chance to achieve. Not everybody gets the nod. "When I put together these teams," Cunningham continues, "I look for job knowledge first. These people must be experts in their departments. Then I look for people who can work within a team and enjoy themselves."

Special teams are the elite forces of an organization. Swift, focused, and free of deadwood, they often seem invisible. In fact they are highly visible to the organization's leaders. Players who serve on them gain status as Key Players within the company. Mary Haddenham says joining professional societies is a good way to broaden your team network. "There are two things I did that worked so well for me I now recommend them to almost all women in the lab," she says. "When I first came to the lab, I served as steward to the Federal Union of Scientists and Engineers. Once a week for two hours I got to find out about the organization, to meet everyone, and to ask them questions. There's a danger in not knowing what's going on. As steward, I participated in committees, I helped develop roles for engineers. I negotiated with division directors. All that stuff is real power. I had access to key power linkages. I gained insight into how things worked and how I should conduct myself."

The second thing Haddenham did was become an equal opportunity counselor, a post she filled for eleven years. The knowledge and experience she gained as a counselor, she says, helped her when she filed—and won—a sex discrimination case on her own behalf. "I was able to be objective about my own case," she says. "I knew the ropes."

When it comes to professional organizations, Ann Picciuto advises getting as close to the top as you possibly can. "I got involved with organizations within the company. I was the vice-president of the Management Club and the first woman president. You don't want to be a secretary in these clubs. Go out and be president."

Players are content to belong to one team at a time. Key Players search for—and find—other teams to belong to.

STEP #10: KEEP IMPROVING YOUR JOB

If you know every facet of your job and execute your tasks competently and on time, you're going to be indispensable to your team, right? Wrong. If you know every facet of your job and execute your tasks competently and on time, you can still be replaced.

In graduate school I had a teacher who reminded us before each test, "Absence of error is not the same as excellence." This teacher was notorious for being demanding and exacting. Few people ever earned an "A" from him. Yet semester after semester his classes were jammed. Students knew that taking one of his courses wouldn't help their grade-point averages. They signed up because they wanted to improve their minds.

By refusing to accept absence of error as excellence, the professor was pushing us to go beyond ordinary standards of intelligent thinking and demonstrate an ability to perform at a higher level. We were graduate students, but he insisted that we perform as if we already had Ph.D.'s. This professor taught classical and biblical literature. He spent many hours each day reading dead languages. But he wasn't a foggy academic living in an ivory tower. He knew how real life worked, and by forcing us to perform levels above our actual standing, he gave all of us an important lesson in survival.

In business, if you're just doing your job, you aren't doing well enough. You don't get noticed by failing to make mistakes. Absence of error is not the same as excellence.

"Women have to learn to think big," says Sharon Richardson Jones emphatically. "We have to replace cautious, limited thinking with what I call 'blue sky' thinking—blue sky as in, how blue is the sky, and how high up can we go? We have to step out of our comfort zone. Some people are frozen with fear. They're being held back by themselves. Of course women have stumbling blocks, but we have to remove those stumbling blocks ourselves. We have to decide where we want to go. We have to decide what kind of impact we'd like to make. Then we have to go for it."

Mary Haddenham's philosophy for the workplace is, "Take every opportunity you can take. Grab opportunities when they're offered, and when they're not offered, demand them, because lots of times they won't be offered."

When she and other Key Players urge women to "demand" upward opportunities, they don't mean marching into your team leader's office with a lot of enthusiasm and no track record to back it up. Get the track record first, they advise, then demand the title, the salary, and the status to go with it.

At one point in her career, that's exactly what Haddenham did. "I did a lot of extra work in my department," she says. "I did things I probably shouldn't have done, but I saw it as a chance to get experience I could use when I was sitting in a manager's job of my own."

Haddenham almost got stuck in a trap many of us have encountered: she did so much work for "free" that her male superior didn't want to let her go. "He felt I would go on doing the same things for him," she says. "I was told no, I couldn't transfer, even though they transferred about four males to other positions before me."

A practitioner of blue sky thinking, she applied for a transfer anyway. "I knew he wasn't happy," she says about her boss, "but he survived." Haddenham, who got the transfer, survived, too—as a Key Player.

A WORD ABOUT STEP CLIMBING

Though I've presented these ten steps in numbered order, don't feel you have to take them in order. That isn't always possible. Take whatever steps you can whenever and wherever you can. If a particular move is temporarily blocked to you, make the move that isn't blocked. Remember that whatever you do to add value to your team will increase your value as a Key Player. In the next chapter we'll look at another way to enhance your position—by filling one or more of the roles the team needs to function as a Star Team.

9 ☆

Key Roles for Key Players

Before founding Spectra Communications, Sharon Maeda worked as a producer and general manager for several radio stations in Seattle and was for six years the CEO of the Pacifica Radio Network in Los Angeles. This, she says, is where she learned the value of teamwork:

"I brought people together who had never laid eyes on each other before and got them to travel the whole country together to make a videotape and come out with what we needed—without having any conflicts and without my being there. At Pacifica, I created temporary teams from permanent staff and got them to work together on specific projects for a set period of time. I was very successful at getting things done that way."

Maeda applied the same success formula to her own company. Speaking of herself and her partners at Spectra, she says, "We worked for our clients as a team. We worked well as a team. We covered for each other. Our skills were complementary."

Over the course of three years, however, Maeda's original team fell apart, and she found herself having to build a new one from the ground up. What went wrong with team number one? "Even though we worked well as a team for our clients," Maeda says, "we didn't build a team within our own agency. One partner felt everybody had to know everything about our financial and legal matters and wanted to have lots of meetings about this.

I didn't think this was necessary. I'm comfortable delegating work and had no problem with getting a weekly or monthly report from the partner in charge of finances.'' Maeda also says her team had no established way of responding to a crisis. "When you have to stop work and have meetings to iron out everybody's different ways of attacking a problem, you cut deeply into your billable hours. These were issues we didn't deal with in the planning stage.''

Key Players need the resources, opportunities, and support a Star Team can provide. What Maeda and her partners failed to take into consideration was the flip side of the coin: Star Teams have survival needs of their own. For example, is someone on the team making sure everyone knows what the rules and procedures are? Is someone smoothing out interpersonal conflicts among team members? Is someone steering the team away from potential pitfalls? Is someone helping members stay focused and enthusiastic?

You won't find these roles coded into any job description. They don't go with any one position, but belong to the player who steps into the part. The job of keeping team spirit strong, for example, doesn't necessarily fall to the team's highest-ranking member. I've seen many teams "led" by secretaries and office managers—Key Players who made themselves far more valuable than their job descriptions implied.

TRIBAL POLITICS: TEAM ROLES

As you know from reading chapter 4, "Team Types," there are many different types of teams. Regardless of the type, regardless of the specific work they are engaged in, all have roles that must be filled. Not all teams have exactly the same role needs: certain roles may be unimportant on certain teams; on small teams several roles may be combined. When the necessary roles are filled, the team thrives. When they're neglected, the team follows one of three courses: it continues as a weak team, it disintegrates and must be rebuilt, or it's phased out following a string of defeats. In addition to performing her work, a Key Player nurtures her team and contributes to its success and survival by filling one or more of these roles.

To Function as a Star Team, a Team Needs

- *leaders* to direct the team and coordinate activities of various players. Leaders assign tasks and take primary responsibility for the team's actions. They make sure everyone is on the same page and that everyone knows the rules. On a traditional corporate team, this role often falls to the person with the highest job ranking on the team. On nontraditional teams, the role may be filled by anyone who has the ability to act effectively, and who has the confidence and backing of her team.
- *inspirers*, who are the team's spiritual leaders. Their personal optimism and confidence raises the psychic energy level of the entire team and keeps "team esteem" high.
- *visionaries*, the team's "idea people." They come up with concepts and plans for the team to implement. Depending on the team, visionaries may be concerned with durable goods—products—or with intangibles like services and systems. Visionaries must walk a tight line between imagination and feasibility: they can't ask their team to do the impossible, yet they must provide continual challenge for the Key Players on their teams. Picking safe projects will result in a mediocre product, a ho-hum track record, and a bored team.
- *implementers*, who transform ideas into results. Often implementers work in tandem with visionaries. The visionaries say, "Is this possible?" and the implementers respond with, "We think so, go ahead with the idea."
- *information gatherers* to take responsibility for assembling facts and data vital to the team. The information they provide can cover a wide range of topics: it can

be "hard" data (research, statistics, or technical information) the team needs to complete a project, or it can be the "soft" data that comes through the grapevine and through the complex process of observation and intuition. This second type of data can alert the team to everything from shifts in corporate mood to tips about what the competition's up to.

- *liaisons* to act as the team's "foreign ambassadors." They make strong connections with people and systems outside the team. These connections might link the team to the other teams within the company, the corporate hierarchy, teams in other organizations, outside "free-lancers" on whom the team calls from time to time, or a variety of other "satellites" with whom the team does business.

- *publicists*, who make sure the good work of the team doesn't go unnoticed. These people promote the team's image and help the team maintain high visibility. If the team makes a mistake, publicists head up the damage control effort: they don't try to effect a cover-up that will come back to haunt the team, but they move quickly to put the failure into perspective.

- *reality checkers* to go outside the team to test the waters of the real world. Often, a team becomes too insular: members reinforce each other's wishful thinking, and no one intercepts warning signals and omens coming from the outside. Reality checkers make sure this doesn't happen. Frequently they must be the bearers of bad tidings. If the team is a Star Team, it will accept the information and make use of it.

- *paratroopers*, the people who can be counted on in an emergency. The emergency may be a project gone wrong, an assignment that needs to be done quickly under crisis conditions, picking up after a teammate's error, rescuing a teammate in trouble, or helping to stabilize the team after a loss or setback. Paratroopers don't crumble under pressure. In fact, they usually find the situation stimulating.

- *harmonizers*, the team's psychological support staff.

They keep the peace, smooth ruffled feathers, and promote team esteem by helping members work out conflicts and adjust to each other's personalities. Harmonizers are trustworthy confidants, and a harmonizer's office is often a "safe haven" where team members can let off steam, certain that their words will never be repeated.

- *masters*, the senior players who give the team the benefit of their wisdom. They act as intrateam consultants, sharing their knowledge, and often take charge of one or two rookie-level players. Masters frequently have important forecasting abilities: "If we follow this plan, then this will happen; if we follow that plan, then that will happen." Masters have been down many paths and can tell where many of them come out.

- *legislators* to negotiate on behalf of the team. This means lobbying for power and opportunities. If there is a particular project the team wants to work on, the legislators will try to land it. People who are legislators have goals and ambitions on behalf of the team and serve as the team's steering committee.

- *scouts*, who are in charge of spotting new talent for the team. As in sports, scouts in business must know how to evaluate players: they have to know whether a possibility is really as good as she looks or whether she simply knows how to look good. Scouts also have to know what positions on their teams need to be filled or beefed up. Above all, they must have matchmaking abilities to ensure that new players complement the team's personality and way of doing business. Sometimes scouts recruit the new players themselves, sometimes they pass the task along to someone else on the team.

"IT'S OURS TO LOSE": HOW THE DUKAKIS TEAM FORFEITED THE 1988 ELECTION

To see what happens to a team and its players when no one takes on these roles, let's look at a team that failed in its one and only bid for Star Team status: the Dukakis campaign team of 1988.

I don't belong to the cynical-but-chic chorus that believes an unacceptable candidate can be successfully "packaged" and "sold" to an unsuspecting public. Nor do I believe that slick packaging by one candidate can defeat a candidate with a firm following. But if the public regards the candidate with ambivalence, the candidate's team plays a more important role than it otherwise would, filling up the void the candidate himself has left blank.

In 1988 there was plenty of ambivalence to go around—ambivalence toward Bush, Dukakis, and the dozen or so hopefuls they'd beaten in the long haul of the primaries. It was the best shot the Democrats had had at the Oval Office in years, and given that Dukakis emerged from the Democratic convention with a seventeen-point lead in a national opinion poll, it looked like the "conservative era" might finally be drawing to a close.

What happened to the Dukakis team?

It was more a question of what didn't happen. As a student of team play, I watched in fascination as an almost unbelievable string of foul-ups and blunders flew daily—and sometimes hourly—from the Dukakis campaign machine. Here are just a few of the things that went wrong:

- John Sasso was arguably the most important person on the Dukakis team. He had engineered Dukakis's return to the Massachusetts governor's office after a previous renomination defeat. During the primaries he played an even heftier role, raising impressive amounts of money, recruiting talented people, and building an effective organization. But in the middle of the primary season, Dukakis found himself having to fire the person he'd most counted on to engineer his victory. The reason: Sasso had engaged in "dirty tricks" against another candidate, Delaware Senator Joe Biden. As campaigns go, the trick—a video alluding to Biden's plagiarism—was neither very tricky nor very dirty. But

Dukakis had positioned himself as a political reformer, and the clamor was inevitable: "Hey—don't the rules apply to the guys on your own team?" Although Dukakis at first declined Sasso's resignation, the escalating clamor of the press and of his own aides eventually forced his hand.

The problem: Dukakis, the leader, didn't make sure everybody knew the rules.

- In the midst of an otherwise well run and unified convention, Dukakis badly mishandled Jesse Jackson. Was Jesse on the team or not? Was he a candidate for the vice-presidency or not? At a time when the cry should have been "What does Michael need to win?" the focus instead stayed on "What does Jesse want?" Dukakis never found an effective way of drawing on Jackson's power or appeal. Officially Jackson was taken on board and given an important job: heading up the voter registration effort. But he was also snubbed on the vice-presidency issue and, for the most part, was kept well away from Dukakis and Lloyd Bentsen, his running mate. In failing to make sure Jackson knew of the vice-presidential choice before the press did, Dukakis demonstrated a remarkable lack of understanding of the personalities involved. In their book, *Whose Broad Stripes and Bright Stars*, Jack Germond and Jules Witcover describe the gaffe and its aftermath: "Dukakis advisors should have realized at the moment the decision was made that the first priority was to notify Jackson. Now their failure to do so had created an incident that was clearly more than a distraction."

The role eventually assigned to Jackson—the voter registration drive in the hinterlands—was another miscalculation. Jackson's presence, his gift for public speaking, and his ability to light up a television screen were wasted on a handful of personal appearances. As the campaign wore on, it became clear that Jackson felt as if he'd been exiled. The Dukakis team made the worst-possible deal for itself by turning a potential ally into a disaffected team member and utterly failing to use his strengths. Worse, the Dukakis team offended Jackson's passionately loyal followers, who felt their candidate had once again been offered the back of the bus.

The problem: No reality checkers, no liaisons, no harmonizers, no scouts.

- Dukakis emerged from the nominating convention with an upward bounce, going from neck and neck with Bush to a seventeen-point lead. New to the business of presidential campaigning, Dukakis and his team stepped back to savor the euphoria. No one seemed to realize that the bounce was par for the course—the last three Democratic nominees had received similar boosts on their way to defeat—or that it represented an extremely fickle segment of the electorate.

  The problem: No masters, no information gatherers.

- After winning the nomination, the Dukakis team lost its focus. According to Dukakis himself, it took "about six weeks" for candidate and team to grasp the fact that running a presidential campaign required a completely new and different set of strategies.

  The problem: No visionaries.

- One of the worst problems was the withdrawal of Dukakis himself. Although he'd hired Susan Estrich to replace Sasso, he never connected with her as he had with his former campaign chief. As the campaign wore on, Dukakis felt increasingly ill served and turned against his own team. Many of Estrich's memos and strategies were ignored, and she began to voice recommendations through surrogates or through memos bearing signatures other than her own. According to *Newsweek* staffers who covered the campaign, Estrich would often ask for a meeting with Dukakis, only to have the candidate bluntly inform her, "I can't." The breakdown in team spirit trickled down from Dukakis to Estrich and from Estrich to those under her. Eventually Estrich's deputy, Jack Corrigan, resigned and sent a memo to Dukakis urging him to bring Sasso back to the rapidly disintegrating team.

The problem: Failure of leadership, no inspirers, no paratroopers.

- Dukakis promised to "reach out" to Democrats across the nation—an effort that he himself admitted fizzled sometime in August. According to one official, "People were knocking on the door to get in," but most of them ended up with nothing but bruised knuckles to show for their enthusiasm. Dukakis and campaign manager Susan Estrich retained tight control over the campaign team; Dukakis even went so far as to demand personal interviews with anyone who was hired. The result, according to a Dukakis campaigner in a must-win state, was that "the campaign in Boston came off as a bunch of wise-ass know-it-alls, and they [angered] everyone in the state."

  Instead of benefiting from an influx of new ideas, the team literally starved to death. In their book, *The Quest for the Presidency: The 1988 Campaign*, Peter Goldman and Tom Mathews write, "As the doors swung shut, résumés and strategy memos gathered dust on Estrich's desk . . . unattended and often unanswered. The preferred ideas on Chauncy Street [the campaign's headquarters in Boston] were homegrown, which meant lawyerly, liberal, cerebral and, for the most part, risk-averse."

  The problem: No liaisons, no scouts.

- Throughout the campaign, Dukakis was constantly on the defensive, responding to issues picked and controlled by the opposition. Part of the problem was that the Dukakis team had failed to anticipate the swiftness or intensity with which Bush would launch his attack. They perceived the Republican nominee as a wimp with so many negatives that they scarcely needed to worry about him. But other problems lay within the team: there was no Dukakis agenda and no inspiring vision to offer, and when it was time to publicize the candidate's goals for America, the team came up flat.

The problem: No visionaries, no implementers, no publicists.

- Even when he had a message, Dukakis had a hard time communicating it to the electorate. Reporters couldn't detect any strategy at all in his speeches, advertisements, or media appearances and had to be told, by the Dukakis team, that the candidate was saving his best message for the last. "Why would they put in a message at the end?" asked Kathleen Hall Jamieson, a specialist in political rhetoric at the University of Texas. "That doesn't work." Why indeed? Because, with the departure of advertising executive Sasso, the top echelon of the team was composed almost exclusively of lawyers: Dukakis himself, campaign chairman Paul Brountas, campaign manager Susan Estrich, and "message" adviser Kirk O'Donnell. It seemed logical to them to argue for the presidency as they would have argued a case in court. By the time they reached their closing arguments, the audience had either switched channels, opted for the opponent, or fallen asleep.

The problem: No masters, no scouts.

- To counter criticism that the campaign lacked positions, Dukakis's issue team spent a week perfecting a speech on national defense and relations with the Soviets. The same day the speech was given, Dukakis climbed into a tank and donned an oversize helmet. Given a choice of running a clip from the speech or pictures of Dukakis in the tank, all three networks went for the tank shot, and the careful work of the issues team went down the drain.

The problem: No leaders, no legislators, no publicists.

- Originally Dukakis had a twenty-point lead among women voters. But in the actual election, he "won" the female vote by a narrow six-point margin. While the Dukakis campaign was taking the female vote for granted, the Bush team was targeting it as a priority; while Dukakis was ignoring women, Bush was courting them.

  The problem: No reality checkers, no liaisons.

- In an effort to save a crumbling campaign, Dukakis brought back the exiled Sasso two months before the election. Although Dukakis tried to put a positive spin on the move, citing it as "some kind of turning point in this campaign," the recall was seen largely as a desperation move. One source within the Bush campaign described it as "a sign of drift in the Dukakis campaign" and added that it was "a serious sign that they're having to shift key players, and it's disruptive."

  The problem: No harmonizers, no paratroopers.

- Dukakis didn't officially demote Estrich or outline a chain of command. Instead he created a dubious "balance" in which Sasso was named vice-chairman of the campaign and Estrich put in charge of "day-to-day" management. The result was a destructive internal struggle for control, with Estrich reportedly running meetings parallel to Sasso's and, on one occasion, failing to tell the Sasso people the project they were working on had already been completed by her own staffers. The Sasso coalition finally won control and began to restore order, but by that time, as everyone on the team suspected, the team had forfeited its chance for victory.

  The problem: The team leader, Dukakis, didn't delineate a clear chain of command.

ROLES ON A WINNING TEAM: HELEN GURLEY BROWN AND *COSMOPOLITAN*

In 1990, when Helen Gurley Brown celebrated her silver anniversary at *Cosmopolitan* magazine, her bosses at the Hearst Corporation gave her a lavish party, a chrome typewriter, a silver Mercedes-Benz, and a driver to go with it. Hearst, which owns thirteen money-making newspapers and fourteen equally profitable consumer magazines, knows where its bread is buttered: each month Brown and her team put out a magazine that a *Los Angeles Times* reporter referred to as "the undisputed cash cow of the Hearst magazine group." In 1989, when a sluggish economy resulted in loss of ad revenues for most magazines, *Cosmopolitan* posted a 9.7 percent gain.

Prior to Brown's arrival in 1965, *Cosmopolitan* was a stodgy publication aimed at well-heeled women. Its circulation was in a downward spiral, and the magazine was headed for extinction. Enter Brown, with her fingers on the pulse of a new, young, as yet untapped audience. Brown did a total revamp of the magazine, aiming at a reader who was young, single, adventurous, and self-supporting. *Cosmopolitan* pulled out of its tailspin, and sales started to climb.

A quarter of a century later the sales are still there and *Cosmopolitan*'s shrewdly formulaic article mix—spicy sex, juicy self-help, glitz, and fashion—has weathered a generation of economic, demographic, and cultural shifts. Even feminists who once deplored the magazine are more and more often praising its business acumen. Betty Friedan, who once described the magazine as "quite horrible," today describes Brown as "a very smart and gutsy lady."

To build a successful team, says David Brown, Professor Emeritus of Management at George Washington University and no relation to Helen Gurley Brown, managers should emulate orchestra leaders. The true business maestro doesn't command but, like a conductor, leads by "injecting others with his or her own moods, feelings, and values."

The *Cosmopolitan* crew is an excellent example of this type of team. Helen Gurley Brown is the official team leader (a term she resists); she is also the team's visionary, inspirer, and chief publicist. Her unique ability to transmit her vision to her team lies at the heart of *Cosmopolitan*'s success.

"I don't know of any team," says Brown, "whether it's a baseball team, a corps de ballet, or an office team, that functions without one person being in charge and having the blueprint in his or her head. The challenge is to get everybody to go along with what you decide to do, and the team will only work if the person in charge is somewhat enlightened about getting people to cooperate with each other.

"Good teams don't fall into place because each member is an outstanding person. That may be true, but unless you have somebody coordinating everything, you won't get from the place you are to the place you want to be. A team can have the same members on it and be good or ineffective depending on who's in charge."

According to Brown, one of the primary obligations of a team leader is to act as visionary—"telling them what's needed"—and inspirer—"encouraging them to go about it."

This frees team members to work with a high degree of confidence. "Once you know what she [Brown] wants," says Danya Darrington, an associate editor in food and decorating, "it makes your job a lot easier."

Says Susan Karones, a former senior editor at the magazine, "Mrs. Brown is smart. She has a clear and consistent vision of what this magazine should be, and 99 percent of the time she's dead right." Like most team members, Karones gradually absorbed Brown's vision. "It was a process," she says. "I always felt that I was doing good work. But after a certain point, I knew I was doing good work that was also right for the magazine."

Brown's ability to transmit her vision has an even bigger payoff. Once team members share her perspective, they can become true Key Players, capable of effectively filling a wide variety of roles and leading their part of the action.

At *Cosmopolitan* everyone becomes an information gatherer and a reality checker. Brown uses her entire team to keep in touch with the reader. Says Darrington, "Mrs. Brown gets a lot of input from us and will often ask us to give our opinion of the '*Cosmo* Girl'—how the *Cosmo* Girl feels about money, about her career, her life, and her children." This wouldn't work if team members had a faulty perception of the magazine; Brown would receive a plethora of unusable data.

Brown's ability to transmit her ideals and ambitions also means that editors can become visionaries themselves. Senior editors supply a steady stream of article ideas that Brown approves, rejects, or revises. Approved ideas are transformed into results by editors who now step into the role of implementers, making assignments, setting deadlines, and submitting finished results. In the course of doing this, editors also act as liaisons and scouts, interacting with free-lance writers and photographers and bringing new talent on board.

Magazines can be—and often are—high-pressure environments where turf wars are the norm. Perhaps the most striking thing about *Cosmopolitan* is that harmony does prevail. "The nice thing here," says editor Susan Karones, "is that there's a minimum of politics."

"In any office there is politics," says Brown, "and it can either throttle all of you or it can be kept to an absolute minimum. Politics derives from people being human beings and being petty and jealous sometimes, compassionate and forgiving at other times. Cooperation in an office comes from the top. As a team leader, you want to bring out the best qualities in people and not let them get away with pettiness."

Brown learned this, she says, long before she became a team leader. "I had lots of jobs before I got to *Cosmo*," she says. "I was in seventeen secretarial jobs before I got to write advertising copy. And in advertising, I had five or six different copy chiefs, so I knew all about situations that didn't work well. If the person in charge only feels comfortable when people are at each other's throats, then you can't have good teamwork. I've worked for people like that, people who simply enjoy discomfort in other people. It doesn't appeal to me.

"As a leader, your role is to help people get along with each other. Things are quite harmonious at *Cosmo*, usually. People here know they're appreciated. They know their jobs are not in jeopardy. We don't pit one person against another."

Easy to say when times are good and ad revenues are up, but what happens when the team experiences a setback? In 1981, when the magazine suffered an uncharacteristic dip in circulation, no finger pointing was done and no editors found pink slips in their message boxes. Instead Brown commissioned a national survey, polled her readers, and put her team to work fine-tuning the product. The message: We're all paratroopers on this team.

By adopting a strong, persuasive style of leadership, Brown has created an environment where talented professionals work in concert with each other, sharing roles and promoting team success while performing to the peak of their individual abilities.

WHY ROLES COUNT

What's at stake here? A lot. When the Dukakis team lost, the bright and talented players on it lost opportunities for advancement. When a team like Helen Gurley Brown's *Cosmopolitan* crew wins, everyone advances.

In the course of team play, roles are often combined, divided, added, and subtracted. Who fills what role at any given moment isn't important. What matters is that all the roles are filled and that you fill your share of them as they are needed. As you analyze the teams around you, you'll notice that many people never go beyond their job descriptions. They never contribute to the needs of the team; they never even suspect that the team has needs; they never fill one of the important team roles. One other "never" about these people: they never become Key Players.

Your value as a player rises in direct proportion to your contribution to the team. When you fill one or more of the important roles, you help your team thrive. If enough team members do the same things, together you will transform your ordinary team into a Star Team. But even if you have the misfortune of being stranded on a weak team, you will emerge as a Key Player because of your efforts.

10 ☆

Problems with Players

What benefit do you get out of dealing with a difficult team member or resolving a situation you'd rather dump in the leader's lap? First of all, you get a better team to play on, a team that functions as opposed to a dysfunctional team. Second, you strengthen your own position on the team by acting as liaison and demonstrating your ability to ''manage sideways.''

Effective leaders notice—and appreciate—players who take responsibility for resolving problems. Wendy Reid Crisp says that when she was the editor and team leader at *Savvy* magazine, ''there were people I would have let go, but their teammates saved them by pointing out the special hidden talents these 'problem players' had or by helping them do their work more effectively.'' This precluded losing good people, avoided disruptive hirings and firings, and left Crisp free to act as leader rather than disciplinarian; the Star Team remained a Star Team, and this benefited the career of everyone on the team. Whenever you deal with a problem player, you're doing three things: protecting your own position as a Key Player, helping your team maintain or improve its performance, and gaining leadership experience that will entitle you to lead an ever bigger part of the action in the future.

FOUR BASIC PERSONALITY TYPES:
HOW THEY RUN AMOK,
WHAT YOU CAN DO TO KEEP THEM ON TRACK

When we encounter a problem player, we often believe the challenge facing us is unique: no one, we reason, has ever had to cope with someone quite as difficult as the person we've been saddled with. Because we're human, we get wrapped up in the details—the "who did what to whom"—and this blinds us to what's really going on. Over the years, as I've helped hundreds of business teams overcome all sorts of player-to-player conflicts, I've learned that problem players aren't unique. If a person on your team is causing trouble, he or she is probably an example of one of the following four types.

Problem Player Type #1: Don't Think, Just Do

The Type: It's important to produce results, but when results-oriented people go over the edge and become only results-oriented, problems arise. These are persons who put product before all else and who are willing to pay any price to come up with results. They are highly assertive and not responsive to the suggestions and desires of fellow teammates. Because these people have lost their perspective on the game, they're likely to make excessive demands on teammates' time and patience; they may throw caution and ethics to the wind and become mavericks, straying from the team, which they perceive as a hindrance. Ironically, the results these players sacrifice everything for are often flawed: these persons become so obsessed with doing they usually forget to ask themselves if what they're doing is worth the effort.

Behavior Tip-offs: How can you recognize this type of player? The Don't Think, Just Do player frequently

- acts dictatorial and makes excessive demands on teammates.

- is restless and impatient.
- is insensitive, abrupt, or sarcastic.
- believes in winning through intimidation.
- is critical and fault-finding.
- sulks when not in the spotlight.
- overrides the needs and decisions of others.
- is inattentive to details.
- is bored by "routine" work.
- resists cooperating with the team.
- bends—or breaks—the rules of ethics.
- is prone to straying from the team and acting on impulse.
- spends too much time doing and not enough time thinking and planning.

Infamous Examples: Just about any business outlaw you care to name, including the Wall Street players whose indictments signaled an official end to the eighties: Milken, Boesky, and the guys who sank E. F. Hutton. Failed military efforts, as well, are good places to look for this type of player. Lord Cardigan, who led the suicidal charge of the Light Brigade during the Crimean War, and George Armstrong Custer at the Little Big Horn would have benefited from less action and more team input and planning. In literature, Captain Ahab of Herman Melville's *Moby Dick* was a Don't Think, Just Do team leader who was willing to lose his ship, his crew, and his own life in pursuit of the great white whale.

The Treatment: Often, the damage this player can do can be limited by the team leader and the rest of the team. For this to happen, the whole team must act in concert, giving the Don't Think, Just Do player no opportunity to split the team and form a clique.

The most effective way to keep Don't Think, Just Do players from going off the deep end is to force them to play aboveboard and in the open: no covert operations here. A good way to do this is to put everything in writing: goals and results as well as specific guidelines for accomplishing them. This way everyone on the team has access to the plan and can question its validity. Whenever you talk with this person, it's important to be clear, concise, and unemotional: stick to business, give simple and direct answers to questions, and stress logic. If you talk about your feelings, beliefs, or aspirations, this player will tune you out. Another good tactic is to ask lots of questions that begin with "what"—as in "What are we doing here?"—rather than "how"—as in "How are we going to do this?"

Of the four types of problem players, this one is most likely to have made it to leader position. Following this person can land you in trouble, particularly if the leader has persuaded you to break the rules. If you're stuck with a leader who puts results above all else, you and your teammates may retain control by acting in concert. Remember, however, that you're dealing with someone who is not responsive to others and is willing to abuse authority: punitive actions may be severe. (More on problematic team leaders can be found on page 241 of this chapter.)

Problem Player Type #2: Do You Really, *Really* Like Me?

The Type: Being responsive to teammates is important. Being too responsive is something else again. Problem players type #2 focus on feelings rather than facts. Above all, they want to be liked. This yearning takes precedence over all else. The Do You Really, *Really* Like Me? players are often chameleons, unconsciously absorbing and mirroring the goals and beliefs of those they are with at the moment. In the headlong rush to like and be liked, critical judgment often goes by the boards. The Do You Really, *Really* Like Me? players are putty in just about anyone's hands; they are sitting ducks for the Don't Think, Just Do player and can easily be persuaded to join in dubious covert activities. Because these players are relationship- rather than goal-oriented, they lose focus easily; sticking to business and achieving goals aren't necessarily the order of the day. Since it's impossible to please everyone, these players often end up in a paralyzed position, fearful of saying anything that will incur dissent; these players rob the team by squelching their own opinions and failing to make a unique contribution.

Behavior Tip-offs: How can you recognize this type of player? The Do You Really, *Really* Like Me? player frequently

- is more concerned with getting recognition than with getting results.
- avoids all conflicts and confrontations, even healthy ones.
- oversells himself or herself to others.
- is unrealistic in evaluating others and is likely to overestimate their abilities.
- trusts others indiscriminately.
- acts impulsively, feeling it's more important to go with "gut reaction" than reasoned response.
- overlooks details.
- is a poor researcher.
- makes decisions based on surface data only.
- manages time poorly.
- fails to realize the importance of deadlines and often misses them.

Infamous Examples: Many people in the arts fall into this category. Acting, painting, writing, composing—these careers are often so fraught with sacrifice and difficulty that only a compelling need of mass approval spurs the person onward.

The Treatment: Of all the types of problem players, the Do You Really, *Really* Like Me? player is the easiest to manage. When brought under control and directed appropriately, this player's flaw becomes an advantage—the ability to focus on collaboration and teamwork. What this player needs, initially, is supervision and support. Supervision includes such strategies as setting time limits, putting expectations in writing, breaking large tasks into smaller steps, and spelling out exactly what the player is responsible for. Do You Really, *Really* Like Me? players function best in a supportive environment—one that provides recognition, rewards, and a certain degree of friendly and stimulating conversation. Encouraging these players to verbalize is extremely important: it helps them feel acknowledged and at the same time provides a forum for rational, rather than impulsive, decision making. Because these players *are* adaptive and responsive, they will absorb the confidence, optimism, and enthusiasm you show. Handled correctly, these players are extremely productive and can wield power without abusing their authority.

Problem Player Type #3: Cog in the Wheel

The Type: These folks make up the great bulk of the work force. They see themselves as cogs in the great machinery of business: essentially powerless and, therefore, not very important—a position they believe releases them from responsibility. Cog in the Wheel players can drive teammates to distraction with their lethargy, their lack of initiative, and their willingness to follow the same old mediocre formulas. In extreme cases, Cog in the Wheel players see themselves as hapless victims of "the system." This attitude fosters an us-against-them mentality that undermines team spirit and productivity. Because Cog in the Wheel players believe the bosses are callous and unappreciative, they are vigilant about protecting their personal dignity: they are likely to be sensitive to criticism and to engage in petty feuds. At best, Cog in the Wheel players perform their duty—no more, no less—and are the nine-to-five persons who never play on extra teams. At worst, Cog in the Wheel players are chronic underachievers whose habitual goofing off is a way of "getting even" with the system.

Behavior Tip-offs: How can you recognize this type of player? The Cog in the Wheel player frequently

- strives to maintain the status quo.
- is less creative than other members of the team.
- has a hard time conceptualizing and grasping new ideas.
- is too relaxed about meeting goals and expectations.
- delays initiating action.
- is slow to adjust to new procedures.
- feels threatened by change.
- takes criticism personally and is easily hurt.
- holds grudges and resists open confrontation.
- functions poorly in crisis mode and other stressful situations.
- is reluctant to offer input.
- has difficulty with authority.

Infamous Examples: Detroit lost control of the automobile business by having too many Cog in the Wheel players: people who believed it was their right to go on doing things the way they'd always been done. This attitude infected the entire industry, from rank-and-file workers to designers and CEOs, all of whom were catastrophically slow to perceive the urgent need for change. In the end, what was good for America—small-size, fuel-efficient imports—wasn't good for GM, Ford, or Chrysler.

The Treatment: Time and patience are the keys to getting the most out of Cog in the Wheel players. If you are initiating changes in procedures or training them to be part of a new team, present things clearly, in detail, and in writing: flow charts and step-by-step procedures will help these people see where they fit in. Emphasize that their role is important by pointing out that the team cannot achieve its goals unless they lead their part of the action. Encourage risk taking by providing reassurance and rewards. Remember that most Cog in the Wheel players got to be the way they are by being mistreated by management. You'll have to show that you, at least, value them as Key Players. If you are asking these players to change their way of working, show them how participating in the change will benefit them: talking about payoffs will offset anxiety. If you suspect that a Cog in the Wheel player is nursing a grudge, act as a referee to get the problem out into the open. Don't expect a Cog in the Wheel player to respond at once—this is a person who needs time to think, absorb, and adjust to information. Give the Cog in the Wheel player a chance to do this and you'll be rewarded with a capable, highly organized worker.

Problem Player Type #4: By the Book

The Type: The By the Book player puts rules above all else. If it isn't written down, if it isn't somewhere in the company handbook, the By the Book player doesn't want to know about it. This player lets the rules become boss, investing them with ultimate power, authority, and responsibility. In the process, goals, results, and the exercise of simple common sense often go by the boards. All of us have encountered these players, either on our teams at work or in the course of day-to-day living, and all of us have been frustrated by their rigidity, their loyalty to even the most arcane procedures, their self-righteousness, and the apparent joy they take in reporting on co-workers who break the rules. If anything goes wrong—if your team fails to meet the goal or if an emergency arises—don't look to the By the Book player for help. This player will assure you he or she was "just doing the job" and pass the buck to the nearest boss or team leader.

Behavior Tip-offs: How can you recognize this type of player? The By the Book player frequently

- is overdependent on leaders.
- hesitates to act unless instructed to do so.
- is bound by rules, procedures, and rituals.

- inappropriately enforces rules with co-workers.
- resists leadership roles.
- blames someone—or something—else if there is a problem.
- is paralyzed by a fear of making mistakes.
- resists necessary changes.
- is unusually defensive and responds to criticism poorly.
- yields in a conflict but holds grudges.

Infamous Examples: In the movie *Five Easy Pieces*, there's a now famous scene in which Jack Nicholson goes to great lengths to get a side-order of toast from a waitress who insists it isn't possible. Nicholson does get what he wants, but only after a wild series of verbal maneuvers. The scene became an instant classic because everyone identified with it: the By the Book waitress and her counterparts are everywhere in our society. The grocery store clerk who won't help you find detergent because it's "not his job" and the teammate who won't stay past five to help you finish a report are classic By the Book players.

The Treatment: Instead of trying to wean By the Book players away from rules completely, capitalize on their penchant for a written agenda: be exact about what you expect, put your expectations in writing, and you'll have workers who live up to the standard. Remember that these players will be as good—or as bad—as the written agenda they are provided with. When assigning a task, put every step in writing, and be detailed. If you want them to do something differently or if you are dissatisfied with their work, you must be equally specific and detailed. These persons are slow but logical thinkers and will go along with you if you show the rationale behind your decisions. Providing them with lots of data is also a good strategy, since they will be sure to read it. You can encourage independence by presenting these players with both sides of an issue and giving them responsibility for making the decision. Remember that these players shun responsibility because they are afraid of being penalized for making the wrong decision. You can turn this attitude around if you are patient and persistent. You must provide By the Book players with leeway to make mistakes and rewards for taking responsibility.

TROUBLESHOOTING: STICKY SITUATIONS, STAR SOLUTIONS

The section above is designed to give you the big picture: a broad understanding of problem players and approaches for dealing with them. You may not always need a comprehensive approach. Below are ten problem behaviors and tips for coping with them.

What to Do About the Player Who Blames

Players who blame are courting failure, for themselves and for the entire team. The player who blames avoids responsibility. He or she sees outside forces as reasons for failure, a point of view that makes the player a victim, without power and without accountability.

Cheryl Stern says, "I find the biggest flaw of small-business people is to place the blame for not succeeding on someone else—the landlord, the mall, the new store that opened across the street, whatever. I give this very short shrift, with myself and with my store managers. These are excuses, not reasons."

When Stern hears one of her managers laying blame, she listens carefully. "I will say to a manager, 'Why are sales down at your location?' and he or she will say, 'Such-and-such has happened.' Perhaps a competitor has opened a store across the street. I can't ignore this as a factor, but I can't let it be the reason for lost revenues, either. I tell the manager, 'No, that's an excuse. What are we doing that's allowing this competitor to gain an edge?' That's when I hear reasons for the decline: everybody isn't on their toes, or the store is having a change of staff, or more staffing or better pricing is needed."

Once Stern has moved a player away from the blame

position, she asks the player to formulate a battle plan. "After a manager has identified the internal problems, I ask, 'What are you going to do about it? How are you going to make the shift from problems to solutions?' "

Stern's strategy—putting outside factors back in perspective, then identifying factors that can be controlled—frees the player from the passive position he or she has adopted. When asked to come up with an action plan, most players meet the challenge with enthusiasm and renewed confidence.

What to Do About the Player Who Wants to Do It All

The player who wants to "do it all" takes on more than he or she can handle and becomes overwhelmed in the process. This player hurts the team by producing mediocre work and failing to meet many deadlines. This player is also detrimental to team spirit because his or her attitude conveys lack of trust: "I must do it all myself because my teammates aren't competent."

Most people try to help this player by telling him or her not to try so hard or do so much. The player who wants to do it all won't see what you're talking about. To deal with this player you must, as with the Do You Really, *Really* Like Me? player, be specific: set guidelines and limits that will help this person get his or her priorities straight. Identify the work for which this player is responsible and set realistic deadlines for completion. Describe, as precisely as possible, what the finished product must include—having a standard to live up to will help keep this player focused.

To get this player back on track, you will have to get him or her to surrender some tasks. Don't make this a power struggle. Instead, be positive and encouraging and keep the tone casual. Make sure the player knows that "letting go" isn't a sign of failure. Try an approach like "We really need your expertise on this marketing study—Joe is going to do the focus groups so you'll have more free time to spend on it." This assures the player that all bases will be covered and encourages him or her to focus on a specific task.

What to Do About the Indecisive Player

This player spends a lot of time thinking but little time actually doing. This is the player whose desk is laden because he or she can't decide what to attend to first, who delays writing a crucial memo because there are so many different approaches to take, who can't decide whom to hire or which word-processing program to buy.

The key to handling this problem player is to set limits on the available options. Giving this player a large, unstructured task is a mistake: he or she will spend far too much time looking at all the possible ways to get the job done. Instead, provide structure for this player by breaking the task down into small steps that include just a few decisions. For example, suppose your team wants this person to develop a list of potential clients. If you state the assignment in just this way, the player will waste time trying to decide what factors identify a "potential" client. By breaking the task down, however, you get the results your team needs: "We need a list of people who have purchased products similar to ours in the past," "We need a list of people who would use our product in their business," "We need a list of people who fall within a certain demographic pattern," and so on. This will help the player get on with the work.

Another way of helping this player is to provide him or her with a list of criteria. Asking someone like this to choose a word-processing program for the office might lead to endless research—and procrastination—unless you present some guidelines. Emphasize, for example, that you need a word-processing program that has desktop publishing capabilities, is easy to learn, and includes both a spell checker and a thesaurus. Specific guidelines will help this player make clear decisions.

Setting time limits can also help this player. If he or

she is responsible for work that requires preliminary research, develop a schedule that limits the research phase and calls for "real" work to begin on a certain day. Ask to see results from time to time and check in for progress reports to force this player to produce.

What to Do About the Player Who Overlooks Details

The player who overlooks details is in many ways the opposite of the two previous players. Instead of trying to do it all, instead of getting caught up in the minutiae of making each move correctly, this person opts for the fast-and-dirty solution. He or she likes to act quickly, make the big hit, and move on. Like that of the indecisive player, this person's desk may also be loaded with files and correspondence—not because he or she can't decide what to do with them, but because taking care of them seems boring, trivial, and not worth the effort.

On a team, this attitude can be lethal. All work involves a certain amount of attention to detail. It isn't exciting or glitzy, but it's a necessary part of achievement. If one person foists this responsibility onto the rest of the team, there's bound to be resentment. The answer is to give everyone on the team equal parts of the action and to emphasize that follow-through is a crucial part of the process. Danya Darrington, at *Cosmopolitan*, says that everyone on her team is highly detail conscious. When it's time to photograph a creative, carefully styled layout, she says, "we take lots of Polaroids and study them. Hopefully, you'll catch the flaws that way—a lighting cord running through the picture or a shadow in the wrong place. But not always. So we all spend a lot of time looking through the camera. Everybody's got to keep their eyes open."

Another way to encourage players to take responsibility for detail work is to present them with start-to-finish instructions for getting the job done. If this player sees, in writing, that updating names and addresses is step #8 of the project and getting three cost estimates for a projected mailing list is step #9, he or she will complete the work. If you don't specify these steps as part of the overall execution, however, they'll be overlooked or inappropriately delegated to someone else.

In some cases you may have a team player whose time *is* truly wasted on details. Highly creative people or people who put together big deals may contribute more to the team if their energies are directed only toward what they do best. If this is the case, others on the team must agree to take on the detail work themselves.

What to Do About the Disorganized Player

Although this player puts time and energy into the job, he or she has a hard time coming up with results. This player works hard but somehow that work never jells into a finished product. Because this player needs constant supervision to be effective, he or she slows down the entire team.

The good news is that a player like this often has the makings of a Key Player: he or she has commitment and is willing to put time and energy into the job. To become a Key Player, however, this person must learn how to self-manage.

As a teammate, you can help by showing the player how to set priorities. Disorganized players put the cart before the horse, hop randomly from task to task, or become preoccupied with tasks that have nothing to do with the finished product. What seems clear to you—a logical ordering of steps and priorities—isn't at all clear to this player.

Providing the disorganized player with written guidelines is one way of tackling the problem. A better way is to ask the player to come up with a written plan of his or her own. This will help the player learn to establish goals and priorities. The first outline the disorganized player produces is likely to need editing and revision. By being patient, by pointing out what tasks are irrelevant and which steps need to be reordered, you'll help this player learn to manage his or her time efficiently. If you're not the team leader, you can't require this player to develop a written plan. You can still help by saying, ''Let's see how this project is going to get done.'' Come up with a written plan together. Help your teammate put tasks in the right order and share your own organizational abilities—you will have a positive effect on the player and improve the quality of the work he or she does for the team.

What to Do About the Player Who Procrastinates

Procrastinators are deadline junkies: they like the thrill of performing under pressure. Sometimes they manage to come in under the wire, but not always. Poor managers of time, they often miss deadlines completely.

How the procrastinating player got this way is a subject for psychotherapy, beyond your control to decipher or change. If you try to wean the procrastinator away from his or her obsession with deadlines, you'll fail. This player uses deadlines as motivational tools. He or she works best against the clock and knows it. The praise, incentives, and rewards you offer as an inducement for change will never equal the self-satisfaction this player derives from cliff-hanging performances.

Instead of trying to change this player, participate in the deadline-setting process to whatever extent you can. Make sure the player knows that a deadline is firm. If the project is a large one, break it into stages and set a deadline for each stage—this will keep the player from leaving too much for the last minute and give the player satisfaction as he or she meets successive deadlines along the way. It's also important to let this player know that doing the work on time is important for the team. Emphasize that if he or she misses the deadline, the whole team will be stalled. Procrastinators usually take pride in their work and enjoy seeing themselves as Key Players—knowing that the team is counting on them will provide tremendous incentive to stay on schedule.

What to Do About the Change-Resistant Player

It isn't unusual to find one or more players on a team who are seemingly change-proof. No matter what the new agenda is, they're against it. In ways both subtle and overt, they dig in their heels and stand firm, slowing the progress of the team and even, in extreme cases, fomenting rebellion by converting others to their point of view.

Change-resistant players seldom know why they're against modification. If you ask them, you'll get vague answers like "I just don't think it will work" or "This is a bad policy." However, there is always an underlying cause for their resistance. Finding out what that cause is and addressing it is the key to turning this player around. Here are some reasons people resist, along with approaches to take:

People resist change when

- *the purpose is not clear.* Discuss what specific problem the change will correct and explain the anticipated positive effects. List the consequences of continuing to do business as usual.
- *they feel left out of the decision-making process.* Before change is implemented, consult and inform team members who will be affected.
- *they receive inadequate or incorrect information about the new procedure.* Provide written—not just verbal—explanations and give team members time to read and digest. Allow them to ask questions. To make sure there is full understanding, ask players to verbalize changes to you.
- *they fear failure or embarrassment.* Reassure players that you do not expect 100 percent error-free performance: change involves learning, and some mistakes are to be expected.

- *excessive pressure is placed on them to comply.* Help people see how the proposed changes will benefit them personally.
- *the "cost" is too high to offset the reward.* Realistically assess demands made in terms of time, effort, job security, and mental energy. Bring incentives in line by increasing rewards or reducing demands.
- *there is a lack of trust in the leader.* The leader can build trust by asking for input and listening to players' concerns. If the leader isn't responsive, the team must take the lead. Team members meet with the resistant player, emphasize the importance of the change, and ask for the player's trust and cooperation.
- *habits are ingrained.* Teach new techniques, provide opportunities for practice, keep expectations clear, and use praise to reinforce new behaviors. Explain the consequences of failing to make the transition.
- *vested interests are involved.* Explain how relinquishing turf, power, or other perceived prerogatives will bring greater payoffs than struggling to defend them.
- *they feel change is being imposed by "outsiders."* Make sure new personnel are incorporated into the team and accepted as members before change is implemented.

What to Do About the Player Who Ignores Your Input

If a teammate (or teammates) habitually ignores what you have to say, your best tactic is to add your input formally, at a team meeting. Even this tactic isn't foolproof: women frequently tell me they have a hard time effectively presenting their ideas and agendas in meetings.

What you don't want to do is become angry and accusing: you may get "air time," but you won't achieve the results you want because your words will fall on deaf ears. To make yourself heard, lay the groundwork by letting the meeting chairperson or team leader know ahead of time what you need to contribute and why. Prebrief the leader on your subject and negotiate an agreement that if time runs out, you'll become first on the agenda at the next meeting.

When Marcia Coleman, a laboratory director with Du Pont, found her input ignored at meetings, she approached a male teammate, Vice-President Anthony Cardinal. "Did you notice what happened in the meeting whenever a woman offered a thought?" she asked. When Cardinal replied that he hadn't noticed anything unusual, Coleman challenged him to watch at the next meeting. She didn't impose her view on him but trusted him to make his own observations.

The strategy worked. Cardinal noticed that when women made suggestions, their ideas were discounted. The conversation went on without pause or interruption. When men offered suggestions, much more consideration was given, with a greater amount of time devoted to discussing their ideas. "I never appreciated the problem before," Cardinal told a *Business Week* interviewer. "I started to get an inkling of what women go through every day." Today, Du Pont is one of the many American corporations working to identify and change behaviors that subconsciously exclude women.

What to Do About the Sexually Harassing Player

It isn't fair, but this is one of those battles women still must choose very, very carefully. It may be coincidence or it may be indicative of a trend that, although I did interview Key Players who filed sex discrimination suits when their careers were blocked, none of the Key Players interviewed for this book went public with sexual harassment complaints. The reason may be that this is one battle that's all but impossible to win: even if the woman wins her suit, her progress within the company often comes to a crashing halt. The way to handle an unwelcome advance is to confront the player immediately, openly, and positively: state that you value the working relationship you have and are not going to jeopardize it in any way.

What to Do About the Angry, Jealous, or Resentful Player

Teammates become angry, jealous, and resentful when they perceive you as someone who threatens their own position. Their behavior is emotion-driven. Don't worsen the situation by making a similarly emotion-driven response.

If the issue they're making war over is work-related, stick to the issues. Suppose a colleague accuses you of going behind his or her back on a project to curry favor with the team leader. Many people make the mistake of addressing the wrong point of the accusation: whether there was or wasn't an attempt to curry favor. Set this accusation aside and look at the facts. Did you leave this person out of the information loop? Should you have included him or her? If so, acknowledge your mistake and explain that next time you will provide them with data. If the accusation is groundless, explain why you did what you did. Ask the person what contribution he or she would have made to the project. Maybe this person does have something valuable to offer you, in which case you can effectively use his or her support. If the person has no input, you've demonstrated why your initial decision was correct.

Emotion-driven players need "fuel" to keep their anger burning. Whenever you fail to supply this fuel, you've taken a step toward defusing them. Barbara Uehling says, "I was surprised to find out that some women, for whatever reasons, felt threatened by me. They acted jealous and angry. I've had people walk up to me and say in a hostile tone, 'I'm certainly glad I don't have your kind of marriage.'" Uehling's marriage, a long-distance one, is successful and long-lasting. Instead of defending her marriage, Uehling reports, "I would agree, 'I'm glad you don't have my type of marriage, either, if those are your feelings.' ''

Some Key Players do more than refuse to play into the hands of angry and jealous colleagues: they actively win them over. One of my clients told me that while she was working for a large insurance company, she was stuck on a technical assistance team with an extremely hostile male colleague. This man harbored resentment toward women in the workplace and complained bitterly about women "bumping off" men in pursuit of advancement. (He'd competed with a woman for team leader position and lost.) Instead of cooperating with my client, this teammate was rude and unresponsive; he refused to share information with her and told her he was marking time until his retirement. The team's assignment was to build bridges and mend fences with satellite offices of the company. Whenever my client would succeed in making a start toward this goal, her colleague would undo the work she had done.

My client did not wage war with her colleague, and she did not go to the team leader with her justifiable complaints. Instead she opted to wage an aggressive campaign to win him over. She discovered what his favorite restaurant was and took him to lunch there. During the course of the meal, my client leveled with her angry teammate. She cited specific examples of his effort to undermine her work. She emphasized that both she and the team needed his skills and talents, which were considerable. She assured him that although the company hadn't promoted him, she admired his unique expertise and hoped that he would begin teaching her these needed skills.

In this polite and open way, my client won over her hostile teammate. Her straightforwardness caught him off guard. Her awareness and appreciation of his talents soothed his hurt feelings. Her humor, her lack of pettiness, and her direct request for assistance made it impossible for him to maintain his angry stance. This man rejoined the team and became one of its most valuable members.

WHEN THE PROBLEM PLAYER IS
THE TEAM LEADER

All of us have known—and worked for—team leaders who are undeserving of the title. Some are inept, some are lazy, some are caught up in personal difficulties, and some exploit team members unlucky enough to work for them.

Bad leaders come in all shapes and sizes. They can resemble any of the troubled players already described in this chapter, and the same strategies can be employed against them. Or they can be unique, because their position is unique and affords them greater opportunity to inflict damage. Below, a look at a few more types of loutish leaders and recommended coping strategies:

Napoleons

These leaders have a penchant for the ill-advised campaign. They pick goals that are unattainable or fail to establish goals that contribute to the company.

Suggested Strategy: If your team feels the goal is truly unattainable, you'd better be able to demonstrate why. Napoleons don't take "no" for an answer unless you convince them with facts and figures. If the goal is attainable but unimportant to the company, use research to argue your case. Find precedents of other teams that failed to meet company goals and demonstrate what happened to them. Most of all, demonstrate what happened to their leaders.

Marie Antoinettes

Rose-colored glasses are the favored props of these leaders, who never know what's going on outside their own snug corner of the world. As a result, the team loses touch with the corporation; it fails to meet corporate goals or respond to corporate expectations because it doesn't have a realistic view of these goals and expectations.

Suggested Strategy: This team needs competent information gatherers who will collect data and feed it to the team leader. Often this leader ignores information because he or she feels overwhelmed by it. In this case the team can help by preparing—in advance—a list of possible responses. In other words, the team tells the team leader, ''Here's what's going on in the corporation,'' then, ''And here are some things we can do about it.''

Henry VIIIs

These leaders have a constantly shifting roster of players. Instead of working to develop the team, Henry VIII–style leaders dismiss players at the first sign of imperfection. Not surprisingly, this leader is prone to blame individual players for setbacks and failures.

Suggested Strategy: Whenever an assignment is made, ask the leader to put his or her expectations in writing. What will you be responsible for? What time limit is involved? What must the finished work include? Do you need support, materials, or training to complete the project? If so, make a list of needs and discuss these with the leader. Unless you are clear about not being able to ''do it all'' on your own, you may find yourself held responsible at a later date. Since Henry VIII doesn't see teamwork as a two-way street, it's up to you to lead the way. Decide what assistance you expect from your leader and let your expectations be known. A good approach: ''How can we accomplish this together?'' This is a person who easily forgets that he or she is part of the team.

Lucretia Borgias

No one disputes this leader's competence, brilliance, or persuasive charm. The problem is, you're never quite sure whether you can believe what you're hearing. Does this person really have team interests at heart? Will players receive rewards and recognition for their work, as promised, or will they be cast aside after the work is done? If you saw the movie *Working Girl*, you saw a stereotypical Lucretia Borgia in action. In the film, Sigourney Weaver portrayed a team leader who said all the right things but surreptitiously appropriated her employee's winning idea for her own aggrandizement.

Suggested Strategy: The best way to cope with this leader is to get everything in writing. Don't be led astray by flattery, promises, and assurances that you'll be protected in case of trouble. With Lucretia Borgias, this isn't always the case. Asking this team leader to clarify expectations and commit to promises in writing will help keep him or her in check. And, in case you do find you've been set up, you have a portfolio of evidence to fall back on.

Jesse Jameses

Jesse James seems to be part of the organization, but this is only a ruse. In reality this leader regards the company as the enemy. Sometimes there's an explanation for the grudge—a personal slight, loss of a promotion, and the like—but just as often there isn't. Jesse Jameses often believe that success is only achieved by looking out for number one; they act as if everyone in the corporation is gunning for them and adopt a hostile, embattled position. Although Jesse Jameses think of themselves as clever, cunning, and subtle, they rarely are. It isn't long before they're found out. The danger for you, as a player, is being considered part of the outlaw gang and getting caught in the cross fire.

Suggested Strategy: If your team is led by a Jesse James, you're in an extremely difficult position. You and your teammates can try to bring this leader on board the company bandwagon, but don't expect to be successful: Jesse Jameses are extremely defensive and resist change tenaciously. To safeguard your own place in the organization, resist becoming embroiled in turf wars and begin looking for another team to play on. In the meantime, don't let yourself be coaxed into denigrating the organization, its key personnel, or its goals—your words and actions will almost certainly come back to haunt you. Unfair as it seems, Jesse Jameses will often keep their job while their teams get the ax.

Queens of Hearts

In *Alice in Wonderland*, the Queen of Hearts was mad— but that didn't keep everyone in the kingdom from going along with her. When she wanted the roses painted red, players mobilized to paint the roses; when she insisted down was up and up was down, everyone scrambled to follow suit. In real life, Queens of Hearts are seldom this humorous. Their personal compulsion may be workaholism, alcoholism, or some other form of aberrant behavior, which they seek to sustain by getting the team's cooperation. The problem: as long as the team goal is protecting the leader's dysfunctional point of view, the team itself will not function effectively.

Suggested Strategy: This is one time when helping your leader look good is a mistake. There's nothing to be gained by covering up dysfunctional behavior—not for you, not for your team, and not for your team leader. If your team leader is self-destructive and addicted, he or she needs help—help that you and your teammates may or may not be able to suggest. Many people deny their problems until the consequences are extreme; covering up and making excuses will only permit the behavior to continue. If your leader is a Queen of Hearts, keep your focus on producing results for the team. If the behavior interferes with team performance, you need to alert the human resources department of your company. Don't act alone—the whole team must go to the human resources department together.

WHAT CAN YOU REALLY DO?

Trying to deal with a problematic team leader is always risky. If the leader is vindictive, your actions may be punished: demotions, bad reports, and finding yourself out of the information loop are typical forms of revenge. Therefore, before deciding to take action, weigh the risks against the possibilities of success. You may decide the odds are too much against you. Your decision may be to sit tight until the odds improve or to leave the team.

If you do decide to take action, here are seven important steps to take:

1. *Build a coalition.* It's difficult, if not impossible, to take on a team leader by yourself. Before you act, enlist the support of as many of your teammates as you can.
2. *Keep the problem simple.* Exercise discipline and limit your complaints. This isn't the time or the place to air a long list of grievances. Be sure to keep the focus on actions and behavior, not personality.
3. *Propose solutions.* For every problem behavior, have a solution in mind and decide how you and your teammates can act to bring the change about.
4. *If you confront the leader, don't make threats.* Be calm and keep your attitude conciliatory. Emphasize that you're not challenging the leader for control but are trying to help him or her be more effective.
5. *Reinforce improvements, however small.* Change is difficult. If your team leader shows even small signs of improvement, reinforce the behavior by maintaining high spirits and supporting the leader even more than usual.
6. *Keep written records.* Make sure you write down events as they happen: what actions your leader took that adversely affected the team and the company, how

you tried to improve the situation, and how your team leader did or didn't respond to requests for change.

7. *Build bridges*. Forge alliances with other people in the company and play on extra teams. That way, if you have to leave the team, you'll have a place to escape to.

11 ☆

Crisis Time: Facing Team Troubles

Crises, pressures, and challenges are an expected part of the business game. A team that does not take on new projects and prepare to meet the demands of the future will stagnate and die. Key Players are often able to help their teams survive by taking action in troubled times. Not always, however. There are some team troubles that individual players are powerless to correct or control. This chapter examines some common team problems, gives you guidelines for coping, and when all else fails, shows you how to leave a team without losing status as a Key Player.

TROUBLED TEAMS

Below are seven portraits of teams in distress and ideas about what Key Players can—and can't—do to help.

Troubled Team #1: The Five-Hundred-Pound Gorilla

The Problem in a Nutshell: The team is so large and powerful that it's almost impossible to control; like a five-hundred-pound gorilla, it sits wherever it wants to.

EXAMPLE:

The National Aeronautics and Space Agency, once innovative and results driven, has become a top-heavy bureaucracy, a five-hundred-pound gorilla that's short on results, long on excuses, and unresponsive to new ways of managing chaos and change.

In a critical look at NASA that appeared in the *Los Angeles Times* in 1990, writer Gregg Easterbrook quoted one recently retired NASA official as saying, ''We simply cannot get anything done anymore. We've stopped thinking and stopped innovating. All NASA energy now goes to endlessly rejustifying the budgets for bad ideas from the past. We haven't had a winner new idea since Skylab.'' Skylab was launched almost twenty years ago, in 1973.

The problem isn't a shortage of Key Players—NASA has plenty of them, including the Morton Thiokol engineers who warned against launching the *Challenger*, designers who've repeatedly argued for safer, more affordable booster rockets, and planners who favor replacing the expensive and problem-ridden shuttle with a smaller and safer—if less flashy—space plane.

These people have been ignored and even, in the case of the Morton Thiokol engineers, deliberately hushed up. This is the typical response to dissent on a five-hundred-pound gorilla team: it sits on anyone who gets in its way, even if that ''anyone'' is a team member with a crucial contribution to make.

''The way you get ahead inside NASA,'' said the retired official, ''is by denying there are problems and being the loudest one to attach the blame to critics for anything that goes wrong.''

SOLUTIONS:
Are there answers to NASA's string of costly and tragic mistakes? Yes, but they aren't the ones NASA keeps coming up with. The agency not only needs to recover from the *Challenger* disaster, as it often insists, but to recover from the decision-making process that made the *Challenger* disaster occur. It needs a checks-and-balances

system to restore accountability and protect the careers of Key Players who oppose business as usual.

What can you do if you play on a five-hundred-pound gorilla team that routinely ignores your input?

First of all, make sure the decision reached without your input really does represent a problem. This is the time to pick your battles carefully. If you are convinced the decision you oppose will have detrimental results, put your "dissenting opinion" in writing. If possible, get teammates who share your opinion to participate in this with you by formulating a clear, thorough, and fact-based report that supports your concerns. In presenting this information to the team leader, remember your Key Player skills: stay flexible, let the other guy save face, and don't insist on personal glory. Help them see your point of view.

Troubled Team #2: Civil War

The Problem in a Nutshell: The team cannot resolve deep conflicts and fractures into factions.

EXAMPLE:

- One of the team's co-leaders is upset because her protégé—her husband, in fact—isn't being shown "respect" by the rest of the team.
- Newcomers to the team quickly discover they must align themselves with one of two—and sometimes three—warring factions.
- Since work so often disappears into the void of team conflict, players are sometimes told not to bother to do their jobs.
- When work *is* done, one side will often deep-six projects completed by the other side, refusing to pass them along to the team's leaders.
- When one coalition makes a successful presentation, the other coalition pouts.

No, this isn't the Hatfields and the McCoys. It's the production staff of "Roseanne," as seen through the eyes of Barbara Klaus, a free-lance writer who worked for the show in late 1989 and early 1990. During Klaus's stint, Roseanne Barr, star of the ABC sitcom, married Tom Arnold and promoted him onto the writing staff, a move that caused considerable friction between Barr and then-executive producer Jeff Harris. The production staff fell into two camps, with some members supporting Barr and some rallying to support Harris. According to Klaus, when Barr hired two writers without consulting Harris, "other writers immediately branded [the new writers] as enemies and discussed nothing in front of them." Not surprisingly, one of these writers later pulled Klaus aside and asked, "Is it really as crazy as it seems here?"

Team civil war is crazy: destructive, counterproductive, stressful, and at odds with the very concept of teamwork. Ironically, while the "Roseanne" team has been in a constant state of feud since the show's debut in 1988, despite behind-the-scenes chaos, revolving-door personnel changes, rumors, and bad publicity, the show has consistently ranked in the weekly top ten and produced the hundred episodes needed to guarantee syndication.

Is team civil war a problem if the team manages to meet its goals anyway? Yes. No matter how successful the product is, divided teams are inefficient: time, energy, financial resources, and player talent are consumed in massive quantities. The multimillion-dollar promise of syndication gave "Roseanne" a bigger budget for error than most teams enjoy. Even so, chaos became so costly that the show verged on cancellation a number of times.

SOLUTIONS:

What can you do if you play on a team at war with itself? Unless you're the team leader or play for a leader who is peace-minded, not a lot. Peace, in this case, begins at the top. A leader who's part of the war is often resistant to waging peace. He or she often has an "I'm the leader, I don't have to negotiate" attitude; this person may feel that even listening to the "other side" represents defeat. If this is the case, work to soften the leader's position: show how strife is hurting the team by wasting resources and interfering with results. Point out that everyone's reputation (including his or hers) is being damaged, but that this damage can still be repaired if the team manages to heal its wounds.

Once the team leader is willing to call a cease-fire, negotiations can begin in earnest. A good first step is to get everyone on both sides to agree that a truce is necessary. A positive second step is to convince both sides to stop blaming each other for foul-ups, failures, and intrigues.

After both sides have left the trenches and adopted a neutral position, planning for the future can begin. During this phase, it's important to allow both sides to state their points of view; if one side feels it hasn't been listened to, civil war will break out again. It's also important not to let these negotiations go on forever or deteriorate into an airing of petty grievances. This can be avoided by staging a summit conference rather than a rowdy town meeting: have each faction send representatives to the table and make it clear that the goal is to hammer out an agreement both sides can live with.

Once an agreement is reached, make sure everyone on the team knows what the score is: emphasize what the new expectations are and provide opportunities and incentives to practice new procedures.

Troubled Team #3: Saboteurs in the Midst

The Problem in a Nutshell: One or more people on a team wage a secret war against one or more other members of the team or against the team itself.

EXAMPLE:

A woman I'll call Liza was a bright young scientist with a large manufacturer. One of her responsibilities was to handle the disposal of chemical materials. After examining a number of alternatives, she was about to choose one when some of her colleagues gave her a bit of advice. It was an unwritten team rule, they explained, to get rid of materials in the cheapest-possible way. Since this was against company policy, the team leader couldn't go on record advising her to do so, but that was nevertheless the case. Liza, new to the team, was pleased that her colleagues had shared this unwritten rule with her. Eager to become a Key Player on the team, she acted on their advice and disposed of the toxic materials in a cheap—albeit "unapproved"—way. Her action saved quite a bit of money, and the whole team profited from having a bigger budget to play with.

Months later Liza had to face a furious team leader. Contrary to what she'd been told, this leader did not support unethical disposal of waste materials. Too late she realized she'd been set up by her advice-giving teammates. When her team leader discovered she'd disposed of toxic materials incorrectly, she was written up. Just as her sabotaging teammates had hoped, Liza lost her credibility on the team. Now she would have to spend months—perhaps years—rebuilding her reputation. A memo in her file blocked her next promotion.

Compared to team sabotage, team civil war is civilized warfare. When team civil war breaks out, the battle lines are clearly drawn. You know who's on whose side at all times. Opposing camps fly their banners and champion their causes openly. And although some do try to elbow you out of the way, you can see the body blocks coming.

Team sabotage is another matter. Whether the sabotaging element is one person or a coalition, it won't make its intentions—or its actions—known. The aim of the accomplished saboteur is to escape suspicion as well as detection. Not only does the victim not have time to rally a defense, he or she often fails to spot the attack.

SOLUTIONS:
There are two steps you can take to protect yourself and your team from sabotage. The first is to be vigi-

lant enough to spot the sabotage. The second is to defuse it.

How can you uncover a saboteur in your midst? Here
are some questions to ask yourself.

TEN WAYS TO SPOT A SABOTAGE

1. *Is someone on my team being too helpful?* This is
   the clue Liza failed to spot. New to the team and
   hired at a senior level, she was given an initial cold
   shoulder by some of her colleagues. When these
   same teammates suddenly shared inside advice with
   her, she should have been suspicious.

2. *Is someone playing Mephistopheles?* In the Faust
   story, Mephistopheles is a cunning devil who offers
   mortals too-good-to-be-true propositions. Beware
   teammates who offer the same kinds of deals.

3. *Is there an information gap?* A favorite ploy of saboteurs is to isolate victims by interrupting the flow
   of vital information and creating information mo-
   nopolies for themselves.

4. *Has part of the team been given a suicidal mission?*
   Often, saboteurs will maneuver their enemies into
   taking on an impossible assignment.

5. *Who stands to profit by someone else's difficulties?*
   Here's another clue Liza should have been alert to.
   By convincing her to do something illegal, her jealous colleagues profited in two ways: they benefited
   from the increased budget, and they eliminated her
   as a threat to their own careers.

6. *Who's feeding the gossip mill?* Be suspicious of the
   person who feels "duty-bound" to pass along a
   damaging story about his or her teammates. Saboteurs often pose as messengers when, in fact, they're
   the source of the rumors.

7. *Who's keeping a tally sheet on mistakes?* People on
   teams make mistakes, and Key Players pull together
   to correct them. Saboteurs frequently highlight the

mistakes of others and blow small errors out of proportion.

8. *Are strange alliances forming?* If teammates who've never been especially close are suddenly thick as thieves, find out why.

9. *Does someone feel his or her job is in jeopardy?* Fear and anxiety can cause formerly stable people to act in unstable ways.

10. *Are some people on the team "jumping" the chain of command?* When players bypass the team leader and report directly to someone higher up, they may be framing the entire team. Saboteurs pass on selected information and make themselves look good at the team's expense

Once you spot saboteurs in your midst, you must decide how to deal with them. Exposure and confrontation are good alternatives if you can back up your accusations and have team support. Saboteurs usually take care to cover their tracks and seldom commit anything to paper. Make sure you don't get trapped into making claims you can't prove.

Another way to stop sabotage is to defuse the saboteurs' motivation. If part of the team feels they are "losing ground" or that their jobs are in jeopardy, giving them special recognition or an especially juicy project will bring them back to the team. This is a hard strategy for many of us to implement because our impulse is to punish, not reward, people who undermine us. If you are sophisticated enough to focus on the long-term goal, however, this is one of the most effective strategies to mount.

A third way to deal with saboteurs is to string the game out. Once you're aware of what's going on, you can avoid stepping into the trap while giving saboteurs enough rope to hang themselves. Remember that sabotage consumes time and energy. While saboteurs are trying to undermine you, they aren't getting their own work done. The longer the game goes on, the worse things become for saboteurs: their lack of productivity comes to light, and the risk of discovery increases dramatically.

Troubled Team #4: Rose-Colored Glasses

The Problem in a Nutshell: The team refuses to face problems and challenges.

EXAMPLE:

Sally Geis, today an administrator at the Iliff School of Theology in Denver, has weathered one of the most difficult of all career transitions: her whole team went out of business. Geis chaired the Sociology Department of the Colorado Women's College, an all-women's school that closed in the mid-1980s.

Geis says, "One of our strengths became one of our weaknesses. Faculty people are able to theorize and conceptualize very well, and that makes them less interested, and perhaps less skilled, in pragmatic concerns. We had many discussions that revolved around interesting ways to teach or interesting ways to develop students' minds. We should have been having discussions about what would attract lots of students so we could stay open."

As an example, Geis cites a family studies curriculum that failed to receive faculty support, even though this curriculum was popular with students and their parents. "I didn't want to be perceived as interested in motherhood and the family. It seemed too traditional. I wanted to be part of social change in women's roles and I wanted my students to be that way. So we threw the baby out with the bathwater," she says.

In Geis's view, the core of the problem was the school's inability to face the problem. "We had always had a protected, Ivy League life. We were somewhat like Marie Antoinette—we couldn't grasp the idea that the revolution was really coming."

This is the essence of a team that wears rose-colored glasses. It focuses on pleasing methods rather than finding a way to achieve desired results. Everyone holds hands, enjoys the ride, and goes down together. By the time people do realize the urgency of the situation, it's often too late to save the team from extinction.

SOLUTIONS:

The only way to turn this team around is to take off the rose-colored glasses and tell it like it is. If you're the player who takes on this role, however, don't expect to be thanked. Many times you won't even be successful.

At Colorado Women's College, Geis says there were people who pointed to declining enrollment and argued for swift action. These people, she says, "were perceived as scolds. There was an attitude of 'kill the messenger' and an idea that concern over enrollment statistics was somehow beneath us. These people were voices crying in the wilderness."

Eventually Geis became one of the messengers. "There was a time when we could have merged with the University of Denver and maintained our tenured status," she says. "I supported the idea because, while I felt it ought to be possible to support a private women's college in that area, pragmatically I didn't see where the support was going to come from." The merger was rejected. No one believed the team was facing extinction. The college closed once and was revived before it was sold to the University of Denver.

Once you, like Geis, see the handwriting on the wall, you must try to convince your team to face reality. If you can't get the team to do this, don't face extinction with them. A team in its death throes is a dangerous team to play on: team members begin blaming each other, turf wars break out, and loyalties crumble. All of this takes its toll on the players, who begin to feel like helpless victims. Though the faculty and administration at Colorado Women's College was composed of well-balanced, intelligent, academically well-credentialed people, Geis says, "Anybody who stayed to the end was exploited and used. The faculty suffered breakups of marriages, alcoholism, heart attacks—all kinds of serious problems. It would have been helpful if we could have had a formal end, a ritual of some sort. There were too many people who didn't want to let go.''

Geis herself let go in time. She got out of the victim position and started circulating her résumé.

Troubled Team #5: Challenged to Change

The Problem in a Nutshell: The team is asked to meet new goals and/or change its methods of operation.

EXAMPLE:

In the early 1980s Ron Boehm took over his family's business: ABC Clio Publishers, a privately held company specializing in reference books and professional publishing. At the time, the company had a traditional departmental structure with the president of the company sitting at the top of the pyramid. The company wasn't in trouble or even close to it, but Boehm felt that, to stay competitive in the future, a change was called for. He wanted to replace the traditional structure with one that encouraged creativity and intrapreneurship at all levels. Boehm also wanted a different role for himself. Rather than occupying the top of the pyramid all alone, he wanted a shared leadership system that would free up some of his time for research and development.

As a consultant, I was hired by Boehm to help his company meet the challenge. I worked with him to develop a nontraditional, highly innovative structure that included a matrix team called the O-Team. The O-Team was to be a decision-making body made up of team leaders throughout the organization. This team's mission was to provide leadership and transform traditional departmental structures into teamwork systems. Not surprisingly, these concepts were alien to the old guard. In the process of trying to figure out how they were supposed to operate, the O-Team frequently circled and stumbled.

SOLUTIONS:

In a situation like this, it's important to see stumbling and circling as learning, not failing. Boehm gave his company plenty of room for experimentation. He didn't expect the O-Team to fall instantly and effortlessly into the leadership role. They were always allowed to go back to the drawing board and try again. Finally one of the experimental strategies worked. Ann Hartman, the most focused and confident member of the O-Team, was "allowed" (by the rest of the team) to experiment with the role of executive leader. She would be permitted to develop and implement strategies on a trial basis. If she was not successful, her provisional leadership would be rescinded and a new strategy would be tried.

With support and guidance from Kerry Andrade, the company's human resources manager, Hartman redefined and retrained the team in order to get it to function as a core management team. The strategy was dual-pronged: while Hartman worked top across, teaching members of the O-Team team-oriented leadership techniques, Andrade worked from the bottom up, identifying employee concerns and creating incentive programs. Once members of the O-Team were given rewards to offer their team members, they became more confident about being able to implement the new system. Gradually they became more responsive, excited, and involved; without realizing it, they began to make suggestions of their own.

Today Hartman, Andrade, and the other members of the new core management team enjoy a unique partnership with Boehm, the company's president, and employees at all levels benefit from such team-minded policies as child care, flextime, and opportunities to suggest, develop, and create new products.

Troubled Team #6: The Shooting Star

The Problem in a Nutshell: In an effort to avoid bureaucracy and stagnation, the team begins moving too fast and veers out of control.

EXAMPLE:

At Wavefront Technologies, a software graphics think tank and developer, rules are of necessity kept to a minimum. In a turn-on-a-dime high-tech industry, teams must be able to move fast to remain on the cutting edge. When a team begins moving too fast, however, there are frequent midair collisions. Wavefront was beginning to experience these problems. Team members didn't know who was doing what and frequently took off in different directions. Though the company had worked hard to hire the best players available, these players weren't jelling as a team. Instead of collaborating and benefiting from the team's talent-rich roster, players frequently felt other players were in their way.

President Larry Borels and CEO Bud Enright faced a tough problem: how to encourage teamwork without discouraging creativity and independence among team members or burdening the company with bureaucratic procedures and controls.

SOLUTIONS:

In its desire to travel light, Wavefront overlooked a key ingredient of team play: maintenance. Unless there's a system to keep players moving in the same direction, they will quickly fall into their own orbits and collide. This is especially true when the team is made up of action-loving self-starters. To correct the problem, I worked with Borels and Enright to establish a consistent management approach. This involved training managers throughout the company to slow down long enough to clarify results, rules, procedures, and roles with their team members. Another part of the solution was to open lines of communication. This remedied the problem of players getting in each other's way, fostered a feeling of team spirit, and allowed teammates to build on each other's achievements. Since many of the company's managers are located in remote sites, meetings are time-consuming. The team made better use of time by improving the use of electronic communications systems.

Another hazard of the Shooting Star Team is Key Player burnout. Though Wavefront hadn't experienced this problem yet, it was eager to avoid future problems. I worked with human resources manager Janice Witmer Howell on this aspect of team maintenance. A strong incentive system and personal support programs for employees and their families have kept Wavefront's bright young team focused and enthusiastic.

Troubled Team #7: The Rookies

The Problem in a Nutshell: The team suffers from a lack of experienced players.

EXAMPLE:
I once worked with a government team that, through attrition, had lost almost all of its experienced Key Players. The problem isn't unique. In fact, mass turnovers occur frequently in both the public and the private sectors: a particular field or industry will get "hot," and lots of new players will come on board; years later they will mature and leave at the same time, taking their expertise with them. The U.S. Forest Service, for example, aggressively recruited new players in the 1960s. Now, over the next few years, attrition will rise as high as 75 percent in some teams as these onetime recruits retire.

When experienced players leave en masse, remaining team members often feel abandoned. They lack confidence and don't feel optimistic about the future. If they haven't been prepared for the transition, they resist moving into senior roles rather than seeing this as an opportunity for advancement. They may view new recruits as burdens and resent being made responsible for them. Even if remaining team members have a positive, upbeat attitude, a period of adjustment is to be expected as old players adapt to new roles and new players familiarize themselves with the rules and procedures for team play.

SOLUTIONS:

A team facing a loss of experienced Key Players can minimize the damage by looking ahead. If you play on a team like this, form a data collection task force to gather wisdom and information from players who are about to leave. Perhaps management will support you by encouraging a staff retreat—an excellent strategy because a friendly, no-pressure environment encourages the departing experts to transfer important trade secrets to the protégées they will leave behind.

Whenever I'm called in to help a team in this situation, I implement practice sessions. Teaching and training aren't enough. No matter how enthusiastic, talented, or informed players are, they need time to practice playing together. By simulating situations, experimenting with roles and procedures, and getting a feel for each member's strengths and talents, the new team creates the rituals and rules that will enable it to function as a Star Team. If you're a player on a team like this, it's extremely important to remain flexible and open-minded. Don't expect your new team to be exactly like your old team or function in precisely the same way. Instead realize that such a high mix of newcomers will result in a different, and possibly better, way of operating.

WHAT YOU CAN DO ABOUT TEAM TROUBLES: A SEVENTEEN-POINT PLAN

Above, I offered suggestions for dealing with specific team problems. Below is an all-purpose, step-by-step guide for dealing with team problems of all sorts. Before you decide to take on the formidable task of turning your team around, pay special attention to Phase II below. Can you get most of your team to support you? Are a significant number of players willing to take action with you? If you are to succeed, it's crucial that you have support.

Star Steps: Resolving Team Troubles

Phase I: On Your Own

Step #1: Play out today's scenario. What will happen if the team continues to function as it's functioning today? This step will help you uncover "problems" before they become obvious.

Step #2: Identify trouble. Write down incidents that represent problems, conflicts, or missed opportunities your team has had over the past year.

Step #3: Check the roster. Are some members of the team consistently part of the problem? These people may need special attention and support from the rest of the team. Are there other players you haven't acknowledged? Get them on the roster.

Step #4: See the pattern. Look at the list of incidents you made. Do the same kinds of problems happen over and over again? Is there a particular point at which things seem to go haywire? Although the specifics of problems and the players involved are often different, it's rare to have a team suffer from recurrent unrelated problems. Almost always there is a common thread to be seen.

Step #5: Evaluate. If you can detect the pattern, you may well be able to see why the pattern is occurring. Are team members role driven rather than results driven? Is there poor communication? Do the rules need to be revamped? If you can get to this point, you've done the work of a true Key Player.

Step #6: Be able to state the problem concisely. You're almost ready to bring your team into the picture. To ask for their help, you must know how to state your case clearly and succinctly. If your presentation becomes too long, you'll lose support: your teammates will feel confused and overwhelmed.

Step #7: Propose solutions. You may not be able to formulate a recovery program by yourself. However, if you can suggest solutions to your teammates, you'll find them more receptive to you because they won't feel you're dumping a mess into their laps and saying, "Fix it."

Step #8: Scout the horizon. Make a mental list of teammates who are likely to become part of the solution.

Phase II: With Your Team

Step #9: Poll your teammates. Find out how many members of your team believe, as you do, that there's a problem.

Step #10: Get a formal consensus. Your next—and most crucial—step is to get others on your team to agree that there's a problem and that action must be taken. If you cannot get anyone on your team to see it your way, re-think your position. Proceeding alone is very dangerous because your team may turn against you. If you can't get your team's cooperation, give serious thought to switching teams. If your team agrees that there's a problem to correct, proceed with Step #11.

Step #11: Create a task force. Form a "special team" that will go to work on the problem and report back.

Step #12: Decide—as a group—what the problem is. You've already defined the problem on your own. Now let your teammates add their points of view. You'll get more accurate results and better cooperation if you lead them through the steps you went through on your own, rather than forcing your conclusions on them.

Step #13: Determine whether outside help is needed. A team cannot always solve—or even identify—its own problems. If your task force gets "log-jammed" and can't agree on what the source of the trouble is or how to remedy it, you may need outside help. Often this help can come from within the company. In other cases a business consultant is an asset to the team.

Step #14: Strategize. Develop plans for overcoming the problem. Stay flexible and creative and don't dismiss "unconventional" solutions. Make sure there are several plans to try and be ready to improvise as you go along.

Step #15: Get a "green light" from the team. Make

sure that everyone on the team understands the new plan (rules, rituals, roles) and is committed to giving it a fair try.

Step #16: Set the timer. Put a time limit on the plan you decide to implement. This will keep you from committing too much time and energy to an idea that may not work. It will also foster teamwork: even people who doubt an idea's feasibility will be more inclined to cooperate if they know there's a provision for change.

Step #17: Review. As the plan nears its expiration date, evaluate the effect it's had on the team. Has the problem been corrected? Ameliorated? Should the plan be renewed or modified? Should another plan be tried instead? Keep going until you find a solution that works.

DOUBLE TROUBLE: CAUGHT IN A TAKEOVER

There was nothing wrong with Marilyn Weixel's team or with her job when she worked at a California-based pension software developer in the 1980s. The organization was a small, employee-friendly company, and Weixel found herself lucky to be in the right place at the right time. "Very quickly," she says, "my job evolved from personnel manager to human resources manager to director of human resources to vice-president of human resources."

After two rounds of personnel cutbacks, Weixel found herself a high-ranking Key Player on a lean, efficient team. Then, in 1988, the owner of the company began to talk about selling to a Florida-based firm. Weixel was concerned, but not alarmed. The owner of her company, she says, was very assuring. "He told us, 'None of you has to worry because the company I'm selling to is a logical extension for us.' And from a marketing viewpoint, this made sense. The company that bought us produced planned documents for pensions. We produced software for pension plans. So it seemed like a natural merger."

Despite the promising look of things, the "merger"

never happened. The acquiring company swallowed Weixel's company whole. Virtually every Key Player was forced out, including Weixel.

Reading the Writing on the Wall

Not all takeovers end this badly. Some mergers are truly mergers, and some takeovers work to the advantage of the acquired team, providing players with fresh resources and opportunities. Whenever you're involved in a team takeover, the important thing is to find out which way the wind is blowing—fast. Here are some signs that, for Weixel, became the handwriting on the wall.

- *Different management styles.* The acquiring company took a command-and-control approach, which they quickly imposed on Weixel's collaborative-style team.
- *A different corporate structure.* ''The acquiring company,'' says Weixel, ''had a very big cadre of entry-level people, few people in the middle, and a large number at the top. We were the opposite. We had no secretaries and few people at the top.'' This difference, Weixel believes, illustrated the companies' conflicting attitudes toward employees. ''The new company's feeling was, you hire people to do a job, make them do their job—and that's that.''
- *Unrealistic promises.* Weixel reports that the president of the acquiring company assured employees that ''nothing would change.'' Given the different styles and structures of the company, the assurance lacked credibility. ''If they had said, 'Obviously, we'll need to merge our two styles. Maybe there is duplication that we'll have to eliminate. We'll do our best to ensure that jobs are not eliminated capriciously, but we can't make guarantees'—if they had said that, our reaction would have been better. All of us knew it was unrealistic to say nothing would change.''
- *Overlapping titles, different duties.* Weixel discovered that the acquiring company already had someone with

a job title similar to her own. "On paper," she says, "it sounded like she did the same job I did. In reality, her position was a less powerful one."

- *Skimming off the cream.* "Very quickly," Weixel says, the acquiring company began "picking off the executive team. They made it extremely clear that they didn't want us to run the company, they wanted us to be puppets."

- *Imposing cumbersome procedures.* A simple process like hiring an assistant for the controller became a frustrating and drawn-out process. According to Weixel, "It would have been easier to get a Supreme Court justice confirmed. First, the salary and the job description had to be negotiated and approved by managers of the parent company in Florida. They not only wanted me to interview the person and the controller to interview the person, they sent someone out from the home office to interview the person. Then the controller in Florida had to interview the person, the accounting firm had to interview the person, the candidate had to meet with the presidents of both companies. There were eight or nine people to go through, and some significant discrepancies in terms of what people were looking for."

- *Lack of communication.* Teams in the acquired company were frequently left out of the decision-making process and informed of changes that affected them after the fact.

- *Indifference.* One of the worst signs, to Weixel, was her new team's unwillingness to listen. "They were egocentric," she says. "They were the only ones who knew how to do anything right."

- *Insensitivity.* "One thing that still irritates me to this day," says Weixel, "is what they did with the company name. It had always been spelled in capitals because it was an acronym. When we were taken over, the new company put it in upper and lower case."

Stay or Go?

Weixel saw the handwriting on the wall—but put off the decision to leave. "I was loyal to my team," she says. "In the five years I had been there, I had hired over 80 percent of the people. I felt I had made an impact on the company. We had a lot of good people and many of them were on the edge, waiting to see what would happen. I felt I had a responsibility to stay. I thought that if anyone could counter the situation, I was the one who had a reasonable chance." Eventually she did leave the company and is today director of human resources at AGIA, Association Group Insurance Administrators.

What to Do When You Lose Your Team

Marilyn Weixel is a Key Player who played on a Star Team, lost her team, and made her way to Key Player position on another Star Team. She experienced setbacks, but she didn't let those setbacks damage her career.

If you're a Key Player, you must know how to ride out experiences like this. As a business consultant, Sharon Maeda devotes much of her time helping players adjust to the loss of a team. She says the situation isn't nearly as important as the attitude of the person who's caught in it. "What's clear," she says, "is that people respond differently to the same situation. There are different levels of anxiety and a wide variety of solutions that people come up with."

Maeda's right: people do respond to situations in different ways. Some have little trouble making an adjustment, others have a difficult time coping with the situation. On page 268 are twelve steps that will help anyone make the best of a difficult situation.

TWELVE STEPS TO TAKE
WHEN YOU LOSE YOUR TEAM

1. VIEW CHANGE AS PART OF LIFE. People who expect change have an easier time adapting to it when it occurs.

2. BE REALISTIC ABOUT YOUR ROLE. If you have no role in the decision-making process, accept the fact. Coming to terms with the fact that things are out of your hands isn't easy, but it will reduce the pressure and anxiety you feel.

3. ADJUST TO A PERIOD OF UNCERTAINTY. People who expect instant resolutions are fooling themselves and creating needless tension. If you accept the fact that things will take time to settle down, you'll be able to proceed more calmly.

4. REFUSE TO SEE YOURSELF AS A VICTIM. Sharon Maeda says, "I'm very hard-nosed about not letting people play 'poor me.' I tell them, 'You're a victim only if you allow yourself to be.' "

5. REALIZE THAT BUSINESS AS USUAL CAN— AND SHOULD—PROCEED. No matter what's happening with your team, remind yourself that you were hired to do a specific job. Get on with it.

6. FIND AN AVENUE OUTSIDE YOUR JOB TO VENT YOUR FEELINGS. Don't try to ignore the frustration you feel. Instead, find an outlet. Physical activities provide opportunities to "work the kinks out."

7. DEVELOP AN ALTERNATIVE SOURCE OF SATISFACTION. People whose whole world is work are in big trouble when their teams collapse. Make sure you have alternative resources to fall back on. Friends, family, hobbies, volunteer work—all can help you keep things in perspective.

8. REMIND YOURSELF THAT YOU HAVE AT LEAST ONE OPTION. Whenever you begin to feel helpless, remind yourself that you always have at least one option—to stay or go. No one says you have to stay to the bitter end.

9. CREATE BACKUP PLANS. Don't jump into a frenzy of job hunting before you explore the different alternatives. To consider: sitting tight, changing teams within the company, going back to school, getting career counseling, looking for another job in your field, exploring a new path entirely.

10. DON'T MAKE SNAP DECISIONS. Give yourself time to explore all the options before you choose one.

11. TEST THE WATER BEFORE YOU JUMP SHIP. Never quit before you see what's actually going on in your job market.

12. LEAVE THE SMART WAY. If you do decide to leave, do it the smart way. Practice your interviewing skills and hone your résumé by going to your least promising contacts first. By the time you work your way up to your best leads, you'll be able to make the kind of polished presentation that will get you on the team.

One final word: Remember that Key Players thrive on challenge and, in the course of the game, learn to improvise. Team trouble is your chance to strut your stuff.

EXERCISES: ☆

Working It Out

EXERCISE #1

Learning to Use the Four R's

The four R process (see page 105) refers to results, rules, rituals, and roles. Keeping these four steps in mind, a team can use this process to reconcile differences, accomplish tasks, and become a Star Team.

It is critical to the success of a team that the four R process be followed in order: results, rules, rituals, and roles.

In this exercise, we will analyze a case history to see how the four R process works.

A local weekly newspaper is thinking about adopting desktop publishing rather than continuing to pay high costs for outside typesetting. The publisher assembles a team of people to study the possibilities and recommend what action, if any, should follow.

What Type of Team Is This?

The team players are

> The owner/publisher
> The chief financial officer
> The production manager

The art director
The editor-in-chief

Each team player initially has different goals (desired results) and fears regarding the possible outcome of having desktop publishing. The publisher's desired result is to have a high-quality paper at less cost. The chief financial officer is only concerned with staying inside the projected budget. The production manager supports the idea because she sees herself getting more people in-house to manage and possibly gaining control over the art department. The art director believes the quality of the paper will suffer, and he fears having to go through the production manager to design the paper. The editor-in-chief is not interested in changing her methods of editing to include new technology, she does not want to be responsible for correcting her own errors, and she doesn't want to spend extra time learning new systems.

You are the publisher—the team leader. How do you conduct your first meeting of this team? How do you encourage each team player to express his or her fears about the project (undesired results), and how do you bring about team consensus on the desired result?

At this point, it is important to recognize the characteristics of each team player:

You, the publisher, are results-oriented.

Who is rules-oriented? Who cares more about the processes and procedures (rituals)? Which team players are most concerned about their roles and the roles of other players?

Following each step in the four R process will address the concerns of each player and bring the team into play as a strong, coordinated unit.

Once the team has agreed to the desired result—a high-quality paper at less cost—it is important to determine what rules the team will play by.

What are the time limits involved in the study? What are the constraints of the budget? How much work on this project will the schedules and the available time of each player allow?

When these questions and other rules issues have been determined and accepted by the team, it is the moment to begin the rituals. Rituals refers to the process by which the result is achieved—it is often the step most in need of creative input.

As the publisher in our case history, you must lead your team in the rituals. What tasks need to be done to research the available equipment? What studies need to be undertaken to assess the quality of the typesetting and design? What procedures should be evaluated to inform and, later, train the staff?

The final R is roles: who will do what by when. For roles, do a timeline and a coordinating chart with the players' names. As the publisher, to what team players or groups of team players would you assign specific tasks? Keep in mind the undesired results of the individual players and the different characteristics of each player.

The four R process eliminates many predictable conflicts and crises that may occur if you mix up or eliminate one of the steps. For example, discussing roles first is premature: you haven't agreed on the results and the rules. Rituals are the wrong place to start, too, because deciding on the processes before the results are stated and the rules are determined is a waste of time. Many teams may want to use tired old methods to achieve new results.

EXERCISE #2

Honing Your Team's Skills

Does Your Team Think and Decide Like a Star Team?

Before taking action, do a final check on your plan by asking the team the questions below. If you visualize skipping one of them, you can quickly see what can happen. For example, what if some members are not trained to do expected tasks, or your customer's viewpoint has been ignored? Most teams' problems come from skipping one or more final checkpoints when rushing becomes more important.

1. Do we agree on the definition of expected results, and do we support the mission and outcomes?
2. Have we identified all aspects of our expected outcomes, and do we agree on the criteria, features, or factors that are important?
3. Is the available or critical information known and understood by all team members? (Note: You'll never have all the information you need, and timeliness is always a factor in success.)
4. Have we solicited the points of view of nonteam members and viewpoints from customers, suppliers, or the competition to refine our thinking?
5. Have we looked at the long-term consequences of our action plan to debug it?
6. Have we chosen the simplest, least costly alternative to action with the fewest negative consequences for others?
7. Does everyone know what his or her specific assignments are and the scheduling?
8. Are all team players trained and ready?
9. Have we identified potential obstacles in our path, and do we have a strategy or backup plan and a second string to deal with them?
10. Do we really want to do this?

EXERCISE #3

Predictable Traps for Teams and Quick Solutions

Does Your Team Have These Problems?

1. *Information Exchange*
   a) Some members of the team are left out of discussions or are not consulted on important matters that affect them.

b) Electronic messages are either long-winded or too brief.
c) The team is getting inaccurate data.

STRATEGIES:
- Make a list of desired information and routing procedures.
- Use telephone and face-to-face contact rather than electronic messages when clearer contact will lead to better results.

2. *Coordination of Roles*
   a) Players forget to share information or to notify other players of changes.
   b) Players forget to coordinate timing and resources.

STRATEGIES:
- Invest time to clarify who is consulted or informed at each step.
- Define limits of decision-making authority.

3. *Mutual Respect and Acceptance of Different Styles*
   a) Players become judgmental and intolerant of different values and methods.
   b) Problems are not kept confidential within the team and lead to gossip.

STRATEGIES:
- Schedule meetings to clear the air, level with each other, and resolve conflicts.
- Make rules on courtesy, appropriate humor, consideration of others, and confidentiality about personal team matters.
- Use the techniques discussed for dealing with different personality types (beginning on page 222).

4. *Overcommitment*
   a) Players fail to estimate how long tasks will take to complete.
   b) Players commit to too many tasks that dilute focus.

STRATEGIES:
- Spend time estimating how long tasks will take before committing to deadlines.
- Periodically check on your progress using the four R process described in chapter 5 (pages 105–121).

5. *Toxic Team Members*
   a) Players ignore or avoid problem players.
   b) Problem players dominate meetings and refuse to cooperate.

STRATEGIES:
- Resolve problems by giving the troubled players team feedback and expect them to alter their behavior.
- Have ground rules about the conduct of meetings and hold people accountable.

6. *Accountability*
   a) Players fail to follow through on assignments.
   b) Players don't improve after they agree to.
   c) Player pays poor attention to ground rules of the team.

STRATEGIES:
- Insist on compliance with the rules.
- Ask them not to play on the team.

7. *Professionalism*
   a) Players are dishonest, unethical, or disloyal to the team.
   b) Players make deals without consulting team members.

STRATEGIES:
- Develop a code of ethics for the project or task.
- Create procedures that train people how to communicate and negotiate with outsiders when they are playing roles.

PART IV ☆

12 ☆

Star Tracks: Career Paths for Key Players

As I began working on this book, I looked forward to discovering how Key Players set and achieved their goals. One of the most surprising discoveries I made was that, contrary to conventional wisdom, Key Players at the top didn't start out at age twenty-four with an MBA in one hand and a detailed plan in the other. Key Players don't impose agendas on themselves. As we saw in chapter 2, they succeed by getting into the game, creatively exploring their interests, developing their talents and strengths, and recognizing the opportunities that come their way.

If you ask a "traditional" player to describe her career path, she is likely to describe a mountain with a pinnacle to be scaled or a racetrack with a ribbon gleaming at the finish line. Both define success in only one way: getting to the top of the mountain, crossing the finish line of the race. If you get tired of climbing or running, you fail.

Key Players have broader definitions of success. When you ask them about their careers, they are likely to describe a path with many enticing detours, many possible destinations, and many ways of winning. Improvisation and exploration—not plotting and plodding—are the strategic bywords of the true Key Player.

Few Key Players I interviewed were in careers they had prepared for academically. Many had changed industries at least once in their working lives. Some had lost their teams, and some had reached a dead end. None of the Key Players I interviewed saw these switches as negative. Instead they viewed their previous experiences—successful and unsuccessful—as foundations on which to build. This is the number one career strategy of the Key Player: the willingness to remain open and to make use of the past by parlaying.

THE FINE ART OF PARLAYING

Yue-Sai Kan is one of the most "watched" women on television. She may also be the first globally famous broadcaster. Dan Rather wasn't recognized in China when he covered the Tiananmen Square uprising in 1989, but Kan certainly would have been. "One World," her series on Western life, has been seen by an estimated 400 million Chinese. The series, which debuted in 1987, is a ground breaker on several fronts. It was the first program produced by a foreigner (Kan is American) for China's government-controlled network; it contains commercials from American sponsors like Procter & Gamble, Gillette, and General Foods; and it is broadcast uncensored.

In America, Kan is better known for two series on Eastern life: "Looking East" and "Doing Business in Asia," both popular offerings on public television.

How did Kan become a Key Player on the global gameboard? Profile pieces that describe her simply as an "entrepreneur" miss the boat. Kan is an entrepreneur, but an entrepreneur in the new, team-oriented sense of the word. A look at Kan's track record reveals a pattern that goes like this: join a team, parlay, join a team, parlay—a neat two-step that has led her straight to the top.

Kan was born in China, raised in Hong Kong, and came to America to study music. In the mid-1970s she decided to put her knowledge of Asian markets to work by launching an import-export business. Kan didn't try to go it alone but teamed up with her sister, Vickie. The partnership meant both sisters could spend less time on paperwork and more time interfacing with customers. This was crucial to the company's success. According to Kan, "maintaining a personal touch on a face-to-face level is very important because [Asians] need to feel that they can trust you. The more you get to know someone, the better the business prospects." Kan's partnership provided her with time, which she used to cultivate clients. Her company flourished and became a multimillion-dollar business.

While Kan was importing Asian-made typewriter ribbons and exporting American-made goods, she was also laying the groundwork for her next career move. Kan's interest in television had been whetted in 1972, when she worked as an anchor on a New York cable television station. Her import-export experience had taken her all over the Far East and had made her an expert on Asia. She thought her two interests might be a good match. In 1980 she sold her share of the business and invested in a television production company. The company's series on Asian culture, "Looking East," debuted on public television in 1981 and is now in syndication.

Linking her production team with the PBS team provided Kan with another chance to parlay. In 1984 PBS had arranged to carry a live broadcast from Beijing commemorating the thirty-fifth anniversary of the Maoist revolution. Two days before the broadcast, PBS learned that the two-hour satellite feed would carry no English translations or subtitles. They needed to find someone who could translate the ceremony and articulately discuss the nuances of Chinese history and culture. As someone already attached to the PBS team, Kan was the natural choice.

Americans weren't the only ones who saw Kan's work on the broadcast. Chinese officials were so impressed they asked her to do a series, to be aired in China, on Western life and culture. In the course of producing "One World," Kan kept parlaying her experience and creating opportunities for the future by forming alliances with Key Players on other teams.

"From my television production [experiences]," she says, "I learned that you need to get in touch with high-level people [in Asia] to get things done. It's important to find someone reputable to introduce you, because this person becomes your guarantor."

The *guanxi*—connections—Kan forged while producing "One World" opened more doors. She got government approval to film inside China, permission that resulted in a number of television projects. One of these projects, "China: Walls and Bridges," an ABC network special, won Kan an Emmy. When Kan wanted to do a second PBS series on Asia, she had little trouble finding a team to play on. Seattle's KCTS, a leading producer of programs on Asian life, decided Kan's business contacts in Asia, her reputation as a producer, and her experience as an on-air interviewer made her a hot property.

The new team's product, a four-part series called "Doing Business in Asia," began airing in 1990. Kan used her knowledge of Asia to increase her access to television, then used the success of her television production team to open more doors in Asia. Her highly developed ability to parlay isn't unique. If you were to examine the career paths of every woman in this book, you would have many similar examples.

Key Players never plateau; they build on their talents and their accrued knowledge and experience to move their careers forward, always continuing to develop as Key Players. For some this strategy is fulfilled within a large corporation; for others it involves a series of mini-careers in one industry or a variety of industries or professions. Any of these scenarios can lead the Key Player to a position of team leadership at any time in her career.

When a Key Player becomes a team leader, she doesn't

need to acquire a new and different set of skills. The skills she needs to lead are already in place: they're the same skills she's been developing as a Key Player for her team. Instead of using these skills only to manage her own career, she now uses them to manage the success of her team. Because she has developed a constellation of successful team skills and because she knows how to parlay, the Key Player is free to make the transition to player-coach at any point in her career.

PLAYING AT THE TOP: THE PLAYER-COACH

A *player-coach* is a Key Player who has graduated from the ranks to head a team of her own. She can be inside the corporation or outside of it. She has leadership responsibilities, but she doesn't see herself as "the boss" in the traditional sense of the word. In fact, the Key Player leader sees her role and her relationship to the team in such an untraditional light that coming up with exactly the right term was a bit of a problem. Helen Gurley Brown resists the term *leader*. Instead she sees herself as "the person with the blueprint in her head" whose chief challenge is to "get people to cooperate with each other."

What motivates the player-coach? Cindy Webster sees her move from fire fighter to fire captain as a natural progression. She says: "You go from overidentification [with the team] and loss of self . . . to a stage beyond that. In the fire service, I saw women start to say, 'How can I benefit the team by bringing what's uniquely mine to this team?' At first the female fire fighter might have stood back and been cool and unemotional because that was the way to be. Over time she might have snuck in some nurturing to the grieving family. Finally you say to yourself, 'Not only will I give my unique talents to the grieving family member, but I will teach the men these skills.' "

In the course of interviewing women for this book, I had the opportunity to talk to many player-coaches.

Whether in banking, publishing, or industry, they shared a strikingly similar point of view. Like Helen Gurley Brown and Cindy Webster, they eschewed "power" words. No one saw herself as "the person on top," and no one referred to her team as "the people who work for (or under) me." Instead I heard words like "collaborate," "listen," "encourage," and "participate." Just as a constellation of shared traits emerged among Key Players, so these new-style leaders—player-coaches—shared a handful of revolutionary attitudes and attributes.

This is a far cry from the sometimes popular notion that in the process of making it to the top, women become more like the "old boys" than the old boys themselves. In fact, as you read about each of these traits in detail, you'll see how unlike their predecessors these women really are.

Player-Coach Star Trait #1: The Willingness to Listen and Learn

In 1990 Judith Rosener of the University of California at Irvine's Graduate School of Management surveyed 456 male and female executives to determine if men and women have different leadership styles. The study, commissioned by the International Women's Forum, concluded that the sexes have "dramatically different" approaches. Whereas men tend to "give an order, explain the reward for a job well done, and pretty much keep their power and their knowledge to themselves," women "inspire good work by interacting with others [and] by encouraging employee participation."

Key Players believe that consensus is strength; they know how to gather and synthesize important information, to help their team score by sharing what they know. When a Key Player becomes a player-coach, these traits don't vanish. Player-coaches go on sharing, informing, and keeping the team "up to speed" on what's happening. Most of all, they continue to listen and to learn. The information flow is bidirectional: from the player-coach to members of the team and from members of the team to the player-coach.

THE THREE STAR QUALITIES OF THE PLAYER-COACH

1. *The willingness to listen and learn*
2. *The courage to foster independence in others*
3. *The belief that to lead is also to serve*

Anne Adams says that gaining a consensus has always been part of her management style. "I've found that people are more interested and involved if they feel they'll be able to contribute and be part of the decision-making process."

When a team member blunders, says Cheryl Stern, "I'll let them have it between the eyes. But I always temper it with, 'What else is going on here?' " Since Stern's company involves more than a dozen stores coast to coast, this kind of information is especially vital. Once she learns the hows and whys of what went wrong, she says, she can help team members make corrections. This has cut down on employee turnover. "I have good longevity with the people who have been working for me," Stern says. "Two of the corporate staff have been with me for eleven years."

Candice Dunn is a lighting director for the ABC television network in New York. Her regular tour of duty is "Loving," aired five days a week, but she also fills in on news shows like "Good Morning America" and "World News Tonight." One of just a handful of women in a predominantly male field, Dunn is younger than 50 percent of her team. She describes herself as a "flexible" leader who's "open to technical suggestions."

"I'm always willing to listen to lighting ideas," she says. "I incorporate whatever's appropriate into the lighting plan. If I can't use an idea, I explain that, too. I've found this helps keep crew morale high. People are willing to work hard, but they need to know their work and expertise are appreciated."

On the opposite coast and in a dramatically different field, banking, Lois Rice practices the same philosophy.

"I'm in tune with what's happening out there because I ask questions," says Rice. "It's amazing what you learn if you take the time to talk to someone for a couple of hours."

The information Rice gathers helps her identify possible trouble spots and design better team procedures. It also helps her maintain esprit de corps.

"The first step to creating team camaraderie," says Rice, "is listening. We don't listen enough, we at senior management. We don't listen because we don't want to hear. Once you get feedback, you have to do something about it, and this takes an enormous amount of energy. If I don't ever go out to the branches and communicate with the managers, a lot of them end up feeling bad for the wrong reasons. This happens because they don't feel informed. They haven't been asked about a proposed change, they've been told. They don't feel like they're part of the team."

Rice concludes, "You can't buy loyalty. It's got to be real. People have to feel good about Wells Fargo, and I can't make them feel good only by managing. Today, we're spending more time bringing employees into the picture, and it's working. There is a big loyalty to this company."

Player-Coach Star Trait #2: The Courage to Foster Independence in Others

The command-and-control-style manager sits at the top of the pyramid, a necessary position for the leader who wants to see what everyone on the team is doing every minute of the day. You won't find player-coaches sitting on their pyramids. In fact, the whole concept of command-and-control, pyramid-style management is anathema to the true player-coach.

In *The Female Advantage*, author Sally Helgesen quotes Frances Hesselbein, national executive director of the Girl Scouts of the U.S.A., as saying, "I never adjudicate with senior staff. I expect them to work problems out among themselves. If I get involved, then every time a dispute arises, people will feel as if they have to know what I think. They won't take responsibility among themselves."

Getting players to "take responsibility among themselves" is a recurrent theme among player-coaches, not just where conflicts arise, but in every aspect of the game.

"If you're the captain or the coach on the team," says Deborah Slaner Anderson, "you're only as good as your weakest player. You have to be able to motivate and to teach, and you have to provide skills to everyone on the team."

Ann Hartman, vice-president/publisher of ABC Clio Publishers, says her first task is to get her team to buy into the mission. "Then," she says, "you have to give them the tools and the support they need."

Sergeant Karen Krizan believes in keeping out of her crew's way. "If you have a team that's really good," she says, "you watch what they're doing but give them a great amount of space to run their own investigations."

Sometimes standing back isn't enough; occasionally player-coaches must actually push their players to independence. In the mid-1980s The Prudential Insurance

Corporation decided to change the structure of its West Coast operation. They wanted to increase communication and cooperation among departments, eliminate divisional lines, and create a system of interconnected teams. To accomplish this, Laura Felberg was brought in and made director of human resources in the West Coast office; her mission was to convince department heads to use the human resources department to meet the company's new goals.

Felberg could have gone to each department head herself. A persuasive saleswoman with a background in marketing, she would have had little trouble getting people to listen to her. It would have been easy for her to make the important connections, set things up, and let her team take care of the follow-through. This strategy, straight from the command-and-control rule book, is what many members of Felberg's team expected and preferred. They weren't used to taking the initiative; many were intimidated at the prospect of interacting with high-level staff. Yet that is what Felberg pushed them to do. She wanted her team members to gain credibility by building their own one-on-one relationships with the department heads. She backed them with support and encouragement, but she didn't succumb to the temptation to set things up for them; nor did anyone on her team get points for bad-mouthing the impenetrability of the status quo.

An approach like this requires not only trust and patience, but a fair amount of courage as well: courage to let team members make—and learn from—their own mistakes, courage to succeed as a leader without making the team dependent on oneself.

What motivates a player-coach to this unique style of leadership? The answer came to me in two separate interviews, one with Craig Kardon, Martina Navratilova's coach, the other with Cheryl Stern.

Craig Kardon is, literally, a player and a coach in the game of tennis. His team is the exact inverse of the traditional one: instead of a unit composed of one coach and many players, Kardon is one of several coaches who works with a single player, Martina Navratilova. In describing the mission of the coaching staff, he says, "What Billie Jean [King] and I have tried to get Martina to do is to think on her own. To develop a framework for her to correct things on her own and be able to change things during the course of a match. We've tried to get Martina to hear her own voice, to educate her in her own game."

Cheryl Stern puts it even more succinctly: "I am a firm believer in giving people the authority they need to do the job. That makes them Key Players. If you don't give people the authority and the ability to make mistakes and to succeed, they will never become Key Players and you will never have a Star Team."

The player-coach's mission isn't to "command and control," it's to cultivate and develop Key Players. Her investment of time, patience, and trust has a practical goal: the transformation of her ordinary team into a Star Team—something that can come about only if players are encouraged to "lead their part of the action."

Player-Coach Star Trait #3: The Belief That to Lead Is Also to Serve

Peri Levin, ESL instructor and partner in Language Express, a company that provides on-site English as a second language instruction to businesses, offered this portrait of her favorite player-coach:

"To be in her presence was an incredible experience for me. She took time to care about you. If you needed a book and couldn't find it, you could call her. If you needed something and couldn't find it, you could call her. If you were having a problem, you could call her. Here she was, this high-muck-a-muck, and it didn't matter to her."

The player-coach in question is Sadae Iwataki. You've already met her daughter, Miya Iwataki, whose teamwork helped win reparations for Japanese-Americans detained in camps during World War II. Sadae Iwataki was one of these camp survivors. After her release she resumed her education, got a master's degree, and became a Key Player in the adult education movement. She authored a textbook that helped thousands of Asians learn English. She was indeed a ''high-muck-a-muck,'' head of the Los Angeles Unified ESL network, and the higher she moved, the more responsibility she felt toward each player on her team.

Sadae Iwataki is an inspiration—but she isn't an exception. Over and over again I heard player-coaches express their belief that leadership meant responsibility to—rather than power over—members of the team.

With this revelation goes what is perhaps the last and most treasured myth about women as leaders: that we're too soft, too emotional, and too ''maternal'' to be effective leaders; ''caring'' is irrelevant at best, paralyzing at worst. Conclusion: A woman who can't lead like the boys had better get off the playing field.

Sadae Iwataki didn't get off the playing field, nor did she redesign herself. Instead she became an effective team leader. So did Lois Rice, Cathy Hemming, Helen Gurley Brown, Victoria Jackson, Nancy Peterson, Barbara Uehling, and a number of other women who unabashedly expressed the idea that the leader is the servant of her team, not vice versa. Those still caught in the command-and-control school of thought should take note: these women aren't leaders in no-paying and low-paying fields; they're leaders in banking, publishing, industry, and higher education.

In the tightly woven world of publishing, Cathy Hemming has an asset that doesn't appear on her formal résumé: her reputation as a team builder and leader is well known. She feels an intense loyalty to her team. When asked to describe her management style, she says:

''I'd like to think I get the best out of people. I stay on good terms with everybody who's worked for me. When I was moving up and watching people in business, I saw many who were better behaved with their bosses than they were with their employees. I told myself I was never going to be like that, that I would be at least as vigilant at caring about the people who worked for me as I was toward the people I worked for.''

Hemming takes her responsibility to her team seriously. Speaking of one of the few times she ever had to fire someone, she says, ''The guy I fired is still one of my closest friends. He says it's one of the best things that ever happened to him, but it was one of the worst things that ever happened to me. He was a great guy, but he wasn't ready for the job I had given him. It was ultimately my fault, because I was the one who hired him for the job.''

Hemming's propensity for caring about her team as much as she cares about her bosses hasn't stood in her way. Just the opposite. Her reputation for effectiveness as a team leader has helped her advance to her current position as associate publisher and general manager at Atlantic Monthly Press.

Like Cathy Hemming, Barbara Uehling sees herself as more responsible than powerful. ''I build teams to work with me,'' she says, ''but I don't expect anyone on the team to take the brunt of what I'm taking. As a team leader, you're responsible: the buck stops here.''

Some player-coaches say their sense of responsibility was the catalyst that helped them succeed as leaders. In 1979 Nancy Peterson's husband died, leaving her in charge of Peterson Tool Company of Nashville. The combined shock of losing her husband and finding herself in charge was substantial. Peterson says, ''I was standing at the funeral, and I looked over at all the employees and I thought, Oh, God. . . . These employees and their families were relying on me. There were a lot of mouths to feed. Everybody was looking to me.'' Peterson returned to work a week after her husband died and took charge. In the dozen years she's run the company, Peterson Tool has grown from ninety employees to three times that, relocated to a larger building, and quadrupled its revenues.

When Nancy Peterson took over, she at least had the benefit of having worked in the family business. Victoria Jackson was twenty-two, two days away from her college graduation, and planning a career in fashion modeling when her father died. His business partner had died just two weeks earlier. Other than willing their respective halves of the business to their survivors, neither partner had made provisions for such an event.

"I had inherited responsibility for the lives of seventy people," Jackson explained to *Savvy* magazine in 1985. "I knew the anguish they were going through, and how much depended on the decisions I made."

Spurred by her sense of responsibility, Jackson secured a bank loan, bought out the partner's share, and became sole owner of Diesel Sales and Service of Nashville. To compensate for her lack of business experience, she went back to school and earned her MBA. She also let her team lead her, decentralizing the power structure and giving managers more leeway. The result in Jackson's own words: "People blossomed. They had new confidence in their work."

Jackson blossomed, too. Dissatisfied with the quality of engine parts available through suppliers, she established a division to manufacture her own; by the mid-1980s the new division, Pro-Diesel, was selling $10 million worth of parts a year. Motivated by the conviction that she'd "inherited responsibility for the lives of seventy people," Jackson became a creative, respected, effective team leader in an astonishingly brief period of time.

Player-coaches are willing to take the weight when things go wrong. When things go right, they step back and let their team have the glory. Not only do player-coaches "let" this happen, they enjoy seeing it happen just this way.

"I do everything I can to make people successful," says Lois Rice. "It's much more fun to see somebody who's waning make the turn than it is to get them off the team."

TO BRING YOUR TEAM TO STAR STATUS:

- *Be easily accessible to the team members.*
- *Listen carefully and patiently to each team member's point of view and don't jump to conclusions.*
- *Level with a player and tell her honestly how you feel she can improve—"I expect improvement for the team's sake."*
- *Judge people by their desire to keep learning, their ability to focus, and their reliability rather than solely by their past experience with the tasks at hand or by academic degrees.*
- *Monitor the stress levels of the team closely so players don't burn each other or themselves out. Keep an appropriate sense of humor on call to tame frustrating moments.*
- *Monitor the team for conflicts so they are effectively resolved; expect players to forgive and move on.*
- *Allow players to build their own reputations by giving them opportunities to develop visibility with executives or other Key Players.*
- *Never throw players to the wolves, overestimating their skills and their abilities. Coach them first.*
- *Expect professionalism and appropriate conduct since every player represents the whole team, its values, and past efforts to build a positive reputation.*
- *Believe your role is to support individuals and the team and to get them the information and the resources they need to get the mission accomplished, even if it means challenging and renegotiating with your boss.*

- *Refuse to play favorites or gossip with other players about their teammates—this breeds mistrust and competition.*
- *Keep looking for new talent, and provide opportunities for "spectators" to become Key Players by creating "Star Team tryouts" (as backups) or special internships with existing teams.*
- *Refuse to tolerate excuses. Encourage a "let's fix it" attitude.*
- *Emphasize the importance of continuous improvement even though the team is a Star Team.*
- *Give the credit for great performances to the team, realizing that you get your recognition through its success.*

Now that Lauraine Brekke is a team leader, she has little desire for personal fanfare. She gets more satisfaction, she says, from promoting her subordinates and letting them shine. " 'Cause I know how much fun it was for me," she adds.

Helen Gurley Brown says that when you're the team leader, "you don't need credit from anybody. You've already got the top job. You don't have to say, 'That was my idea.' You can give all the credit to the people who work with you. Usually they're the ones who come up with the ideas anyway."

The high-level player-coach serves the team by taking responsibility and facilitating each team member's success. When a Key Player succeeds, the player-coach succeeds, too.

I began researching and interviewing women for this book because I believed the American work force was on the brink of a revolution. All around me I saw a new kind of player entering—and succeeding in—the workplace. I saw the workplace itself began to change as it responded both to the demands of an ever-more-global economy and to the presence of this new style of player. As I went from interview to interview, talking with women about their work lives in a way few of us ever have the chance to, I came to the conclusion that this "new wave" had swept farther and faster than even I had imagined. The voices of these women, and particularly the words of the player-coaches in this chapter, made one thing absolutely clear: The revolution is already off the drawing boards; it is well under way. In ever-increasing numbers, women who are Key Players are fashioning a new way of achieving: a way uniquely suited to our talents and our times. It only remains for the rest of us to follow their lead.

Bibliography

"Aide Who Quit Under Fire Returns to Dukakis." *San Jose Mercury News*, 2 September 1988.

Baker, Bob. "Bringing Teamwork to America." *Los Angeles Times*, 16 June 1990.

Battiata, Mary. "Susan Estrich and the Marathon Call." *Washington Post*, 16 October 1987.

Bolick, Nancy. "Staging a Comeback." *Savvy*, April 1985, 48.

Brady, James. "In Step with Connie Chung." *Parade* Magazine, 21 October 1990, 23.

Broder, David. "The Dangers of Being Lawyerly." *Washington Post*, 11 September 1988.

Brooks, Nancy Rivera. "Hyatt Touch Leaves Labor Touchy." *Los Angeles Times*, 27 September 1990.

Brumas, Michael. "Margaret Tutwiler Speaks for Nation." *Birmingham News*, 30 March 1989.

Carmody, Dierdre. "Beating Time Warner at Its Own Game." *New York Times*, 8 April 1990.

Carter, Bill. "Forecast for 'Today': Cloudy." *New York Times Magazine*, 10 June 1990.

Collin, Dorothy, and Timothy McNulty. "Newest Issue: The Candidates' 'Handlers,' " *Chicago Tribune*, 7 October 1988.

Cooper, Kenneth, and David Willman. "Dukakis Ran as Lawyer, Not Politician." *San Jose Mercury News*, 10 November 1988.

Cose, Ellis. "Breaking News Ground: How Allen Neuharth Put a Risky Idea into General Circulation." *Chicago Tribune*, 28 April 1989.

Daria, Irene. *The Fashion Cycle*. New York: Simon & Schuster, 1990.

Deutsch, Claudia. "Less Is Becoming More at A.T.&T." *New York Times*, 3 June 1990.

Deutsch, R. Eden. "Tomorrow's Work Force." In *Careers To-*

morrow, edited by Edward Cornish. Bethesda, Md.: The World Future Society, 1988.

Deutschman, Alan. "What 25-Year-Olds Want." *Fortune*, 27 August 1990.

Dowd, Maureen. "Spokeswoman on Foreign Affairs: A Behind-the-Scenes Player Is Up Front." *New York Times*, 20 September 1989.

Drew, Elizabeth. *Election Journal*. New York: William Morrow, 1989.

Easterbrook, Gregg. "What Goes Up: A Can-Do Agency Becomes a Can't-Do Bureaucracy." *Los Angeles Times*, 22 July 1990.

Eichel, Larry. "Dukakis' Next Move May be Crucial." *San Jose Mercury News*, 5 September 1988.

Fierman, Jaclyn. "Why Women Still Don't Hit the Top." *Fortune*, 30 July 1990.

Finke, Nikki. "The Times Are Changing, But Not at *Cosmo*." *Los Angeles Times*, 20 April 1990.

Germond, Jack, and Jules Witcover. *Whose Broad Stripes and Bright Stars*. New York: Warner Books, 1989.

Goldman, Peter, and Tom Mathews. *The Quest for the Presidency: The 1988 Campaign*. New York: Simon & Schuster, 1989.

Hall, Jane. "TV News, Women, and Deborah Norville." *Los Angeles Times*, 26 November 1989.

Helgesen, Sally. *The Female Advantage*. New York: Doubleday, 1990.

Hendrix, Kathleen. "What Gender Gap?" *Los Angeles Times*, 16 January 1989.

Hoban, Phoebe. "The Loved One." *New York*, 25 July 1990.

"Jackson Calls for Campaign 'Partnership.' " *San Jose Mercury News*, 16 July 1988.

Konrad, Walecia. "The Best Companies For Women." *Business Week*, 6 August 1990.

Klaus, Barbara. "The War of the Roseanne." *New York*, 22 October 1990.

Krensavage, Mike. "3 Business Women on Path to Success." *Los Angeles Times*, 23 July 1990.

Lauter, David. "Resigned Advisor Sasso Rejoins Dukakis Staff." *Los Angeles Times*, 3 September 1988.

Lentz, Philip. "Dukakis Taking a Tougher Line." *Chicago Tribune*, 6 October 1988.

Levine, Bettijane. "Top Women and Their Distinct Style." *Los Angeles Times*, 23 October 1990.

Naisbitt, John, and Patricia Aburdene. *Megatrends 2000.* New York: William Morrow, 1990.

Nelson, Jack, and David Lauter. "Dukakis Loan Program Effort to Seize Offensive." *Los Angeles Times*, 8 September 1988.

Ostrow, Ronald. "First 9 Japanese WWII Internees Get Reparations." *Los Angeles Times*, 10 October 1990.

Pichter, Paul. "Hearst Corp. Has Gained Vigor by Changing Focus." *Los Angeles Times*, 2 November 1989.

Romano, Lois. "Chris Edley, Issues and Images." *Washington Post*, 21 September 1988.

Rosenberg, Howard, "Anchors Away: From L.A. to Pacific Grove." *Los Angeles Times*, 13 May 1990.

Samon, Katherine Anne. "To Coax or Clobber." *Savvy*, March 1986.

Sautter, Carl. "How to Spot a Sabotage." *Savvy*, December 1984.

Schlosstein, Steven. "U.S. Is the Leader in Decentralization." *New York Times*, 3 June 1990.

Shales, Tom. "Much Ado at 'Today.' " *Washington Post*, 4 October 1989.

———. "Pauley to Leave 'Today.' "*Washington Post*, 11 October 1989.

———. "Jane Pauley's Sad Send-Off." *Washington Post*, 28 October 1989.

Sharbutt, Jay. "The Gumbel Rumble." *Los Angeles Times*, 1 March 1989.

Singer, Mitchell. "Realty Lawyer Gets in on the Ground Floor." *Los Angeles Daily Journal*, 16 December 1988.

Smith, Dinita. "Murder, She Said." *New York*, 13 August 1990.

Solomon, John. "In Managementspeak, Patton Is Passe." *Los Angeles Times*, 18 October 1990.

Spencer, Stuart. "Jackson: A Team-Player or a Trouble-Maker?" *Los Angeles Times*, 31 July 1988.

Stacey, Michelle. "There's No Business Like Show Business." *Savvy*, December 1984.

Stead, Deborah. "Secrets of a Cosmic Cosmetician." *New York Times*, 23 September 1990.

Swoboda, Frank. "The Workplace: A Coming Shift in the Power Balance." *Washington Post*, 8 October 1989.

Tannen, Deborah. *You Just Don't Understand: Men and Women in Conversation.* New York: William Morrow, 1990.

Taylor, Paul. "Dukakis' Campaign in Doldrums." *San Jose Mercury News*, 29 August 1988.

Tumulty, Karen. "The Dead-End Kids." *Los Angeles Times Magazine*, 28 October 1990.

Vittolino, Sal. "The Biggest Boss in America." *Human Resource Executive*, June 1988.

Walsh, Edward. "Dukakis Camp Regroups." *Washington Post*, 9 October 1988.

Watanabe, Teresa. "Tactics Are Varied, But Aim Is the Same." *Los Angeles Times*, 10 June 1990.

Weiss, Elaine. "Big Deals." *Savvy*, May 1985.

White, Diane. "So Very . . . Cosmo." *Boston Globe*, 28 April 1990.

White, George. "Ex-Entrepreneur Parlays Expertise on Asian Business Into a TV Series." *Los Angeles Times*, 1 October 1990.

"Why More Execs Are Temps." *San Jose Mercury News*, 26 February 1990.

Wolfe, Tom. *The Right Stuff*. New York: Bantam, 1980.

Index

301

Taking
Care
of
Business...